The *Bereavement Ministry Program*

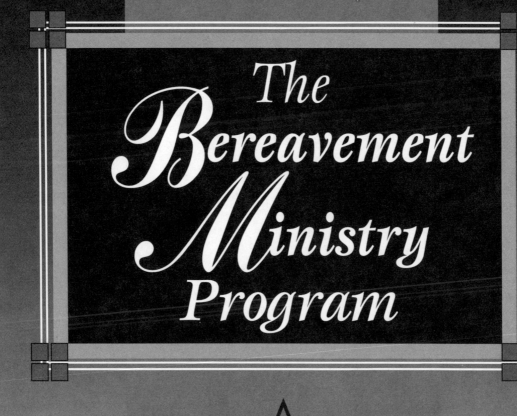

The Bereavement Ministry Program

A Comprehensive Guide for Churches

Jan Nelson   David Aaker

AVE MARIA PRESS
Notre Dame, Indiana 46556

Dedicated to the memory of

Arthur and Hermione Aaker

and Gordon Nelson

and in gratitude to

Jane Nelson

International Standard Book Number: 0-87793-645-5

Cover design by Katherine Robinson Coleman.

Printed and bound in the United States of America.

Library of Congress Cataloging-in-Publication Data

Aaker, David A., 1946-

Comfort and console : a comprehensive resource for bereavement ministry / David A. Aaker, Jan C. Nelson.
        p.   cm.
    Includes bibliographical references and index.
    ISBN 0-87793-645-5

    1. Church work with the bereaved. 2. Grief--Religious aspects--Christianity. 3. Loss (Psychology)--Religious aspects--Christianity. 4. Consolation.   I. Nelson, Jan C., 1958-   II. Title.

BV4330.A19 1998

259'.6--dc21   97-35308
                                                                                        CIP

We wish to express our appreciation to the following people:

Elim Lutheran Church for allowing us the time and resources to write and publish this book and **Hallie Anderson**, Elim's former church secretary, for her support and encouragement.

Hospice of the Red River Valley for the use of their library and their services and **Sonja McManus**, past bereavement coordinator of the hospice, for her ideas in serving those who are grieving.

Hotline, a program of Community Resources, Inc., and **Mark Bourdon** for their invaluable list of community resources and expertise in setting up support groups and crisis intervention.

Sharon Dardis and **Mona Barz** for their inspirational work with children who are grieving.

Friends who helped inspire us and offered their individual expertise: **Penny Andrist, Gail Benson, Steven Geske, Charlene Lucken,** and **Gene Olson**.

Maryanne Kaul, R.N., for her enthusiastic willingness to share her experience and information as former bereavement coordinator at Olivet Lutheran Church in Fargo.

For all those who have experienced grief in their life and were willing to share their insights for this book: **Wilma Werth, Mary Schlecht, Gwen Pitsenbarger, Rev. Matt Valan, Haakon Hanson, Coralee Fix, Rev. Brian Erickson, Rev. Carol Solovitz, Linda Rogers, Mitch and Sheila Branden, Kristen and Shannon Uecker,** and **Jule' Laney**.

Hanson-Runsvold Funeral Home for their invaluable resource library and **Marlys Shafer**, former receptionist, for her support and encouragement.

Jule' Laney for her enthusiasm, insights, and her willingness to allow us to include "Reflections for Journaling," which she authored.

MeritCare Reproductive Endocrinology Fertility Center and staff for answering our questions and providing feedback on our infertility section.

My husband **Stan** and our children, **Jonah** and **Hannah**, for understanding my need to give back to the world what the world has taught me.

My wife **Faye** and our children for their support in allowing me the time to work on this book.

Our editor **Holly Taylor Coolman** for her enthusiasm for our work, her concern and flexibility during the flood, and the continued positive reinforcement that has surrounded us from the beginning.

Contents

The entire text of The Bereavement Ministry Program is available as a text file enabling the user to tailor the handouts and forms to a particular context. To obtain the file, send an e-mail to bereavement@avemariapress.com. The file will be returned to you as an attachment.

Foreword

What do we live for if it is not to make life less difficult for each other?

GEORGE ELIOT

When my father died, I was 27 years old, single, and a professional woman. I was a capable and confident adult. Yet I had a gnawing question whether I was grieving "right." How could I break down in tears—with strangers no less—when after a year I saw a man with Parkinson's disease shuffling out the door just like my father had done? I had other questions too, like "Where did our friends go?" and "Where's the so-called 'Christian community?'" I was angry. During the two years of his convalescence and the year following his death, we received only two visits from members of the church—and they were the pastors.

Later, I went to graduate school, where I ended up focusing my studies on death, dying, grief, wellness techniques, and ministry of health/parish nursing. My study answered a lot of my questions about the process of grieving and allowed me to experience a multitude of bereavement situations and examine the importance of follow-up care.

I learned that the lack of bereavement support and understanding, especially after a critical death such as a suicide, murder, death of a child, etc., can trigger dysfunctional coping mechanisms such as alcoholism, drug abuse, suicide, divorce, premature marriage, hypochondria, sleep disturbances, chronic sickness, bitterness, isolation, and psychiatric problems.

I also learned that our society's increasing phobia of death and the de-ritualizing of funerals will only increase the need for bereavement care in the future.

With my specialization in health ministry, I was hired at Elim Lutheran Church and soon started visitations with those who were chronically ill or grieving. After working for a few months, I came to understand more about the lack of support I had experienced. I had already recognized that one factor was simple fear of the unknown; many were simply afraid to venture into the shadowy world of death and dying. But I came to recognize two other factors as well. First, there were scheduling constraints. After I saw the multi-faceted ministry of congregational pastors, I could see why they ran out of time. Second, there was a lack of awareness; churches weren't aware of the importance of a bereavement program, nor knowledgeable about how to start one.

The bereavement program contained in this book aims to overcome these obstacles by providing the information that churches need to effectively meet the growing need for grief ministry. Its flexible format allows for as much lay involvement as your particular congregation can provide.

This program has evolved and grown over time. Rev. David Aaker, the pastor at Elim Lutheran Church, and I had worked together previously through Hospice and other bereavement care, so it was natural that we collaborate on this project also. This program was initially intended for our congregation, but it has been so effective among our parishioners that we felt it was important to share it with other churches.

In recent days, the importance of bereavement ministry hit us as never before as we battled a devastating flood in our own town of Fargo, North Dakota, and then saw the devastation of friends and family in Grand Forks, North Dakota, and East Grand Forks, Minnesota, only 70 miles north of us (we were filling sand bags and trying to write the natural disaster section of this book—talk about stress!).

The response of the church has been marvelous in sending disaster teams to Fargo and Grand Forks to help the clergy deal with their own grief and the grieving of their parishioners. We will never forget Pastor Foster McCurley and Rabbi Alan Weitzman, who flew from Pennsylvania to provide workshop training for clergy. To know that someone in Pennsylvania cared for us and was praying for us. . . . To know that we were not alone. . . . What a blessing to feel that support. This book is about that. It is about support, encouragement, and empowerment. It says to those we minister to, "You are not alone."

Our prayer is that this book will help you in your ministry of encouragement.

With hope and encouragement,

Jan Nelson

Therefore encourage one another and build one another up.

1 THESSALONIANS 5:11

Part I

GETTING
STARTED

Approaches to Bereavement Ministry

There a number of ways to approach bereavement ministry. Some churches have clergy people who are able to spend considerable amounts of time in face-to-face or phone contact with those who are grieving. Others rely on a combination of clergy and lay resources; some of these, in fact, have bereavement ministries carried out almost entirely by lay people. In other churches, the amount of personal visitation is much less. In some cases, a bereavement support group is set up to supplement personal visitation and comes, in fact, to play a crucial role in bereavement ministry.

The program described in this book is meant to be very flexible and can be used by anyone from a single clergy person to a large team of clergy and lay people. It can replace or supplement the bereavement ministry which already exists in your church.

No matter how you choose to use the resources in this book, we suggest that you always include three main elements as you minister to each grieving person: (1) an initial visit, when bereavement ministers bring an "Initial Packet" of materials appropriate for the situation; (2) a program of regular letter-writing over at least the first year of bereavement; and (3) an accompanying schedule of personal visitation.

Many churches have found that a bereavement support group can be very helpful to grieving people. We have included guidelines for creating such a group so that you can include it in your bereavement ministry if you would like to do so.

What This Book Contains

Basic Resources

The heart of this program is the material included in the "Basic Resources" section. These materials have been created with the assumption that those who suffer a deep loss become involved in an ongoing process of grief—a process which creates different needs at different points in the process. The Basic Resources, then, have two primary components:

- An "Initial Packet," which contains materials to be given to the grieving person immediately after the loss occurs. These materials address the person's needs during the initial phase of grief.

- "Monthly Messages" for the second week, the first month, and so on, through the first year of the grief experience. These materials are intended to address the issues which arise as people work their way through the grief process.

These Basic Resources come in three sets—one for adults, one for children, and one for teenagers. There is some overlap (the Initial Packet page entitled "Prayer," for example, is used in the section for children as well as the section for teenagers; the Monthly Message entitled "Working With Your Grieving" is included in the section for teenagers as well as the section for adults), but, in general, the three sets have been tailored to meet the needs of these respective age groups.

Supplemental Resources

The section entitled "Resources for Holidays and Special Days" offers supplemental materials which bereavement ministers may send on special occasions. The first Christmas or the birthday of the deceased, for example, is often a painful time.

The section entitled "Resources for Special Circumstances" includes materials helpful in various specific experiences of grief. Circumstances addressed include:

- death of a spouse
- infertility
- death of a child (of any age)
- death of a parent
- suicide
- murder
- natural disasters
- rape or other assault
- death of a pet

Materials included for these special circumstances give directions for assembling an individualized Initial Packet and, in most cases, also give directions for sending ongoing Monthly Messages.

A final section includes a number of miscellaneous resources for bereavement ministers. Included here are forms helpful in organizing your bereavement program as well as detailed instructions for setting up an ongoing bereavement support group.

We encourage you to familiarize yourself with both the Basic Resources and the Supplemental Resources so that you can make full use of them.

About the Electronic Text File

The text file that is available with this book contains data files for the entire book. (Page numbers are coordinated with those in the book.) It is our hope that these files will make this book even more useful to you.

If you wish to use them, these data files will help you in at least two ways.

First, you will easily be able to convert the information found in the "Basic Resources" into letter format. Having these letters in this format will allow you to modify and personalize them and then to print them out—on church stationery if you prefer.

Second, you will be easily able to reproduce any of the information included in the book—for your bereavement team or for those you are serving.

How to Use This File

The file you will recieve is saved as text file (txt), a sort of "generic" format. In order to use the file, you must have a computer and word processing software which allow you to access it. Either a Macintosh or Macintosh-compatible computer, or an IBM or IBM-compatible computer using a Windows operating system will be able to open the files. Send an e-mail to bereavement@avemariapress.com and the file will be returned to you as an attachment.

Organizing Your Bereavement Program

Bear one another's burdens and so fulfill the law of Christ.

GALATIANS 6:2

Gathering a Team

If it is at all possible, try to gather several members of your congregation who can work together as a bereavement ministry team. This group might include a parish nurse, the clergy, "Stephen Ministers,"[1] "BeFrienders,"[2] or other interested lay people.

Call an initial meeting in order to familiarize the team with the bereavement ministry program and to divide responsibilities among the various members of the team. After that, meetings will probably be needed at least once a month in order to evaluate the program's effectiveness and coordinate ongoing care.

Education

This book assumes that those doing bereavement care already have basic training in this area; members of your team who do not have such training will need it. You may find it helpful to have all team members—experienced and inexperienced—go through a training program together. Two especially helpful tools for study are *Grief Counseling and Grief Therapy: A Handbook for the Mental Health Practitioner* by J. William Worden (Springer Publishing Co., 1991) and *Grief, Dying, and Death* by Therese A. Rando (Research Press Co., 1984).

You may also contact any of the following to get information on bereavement training in your area:

- the office of your bishop, your diocesan office, your denomination's regional office, or your local ministers' organization
- your local hospice
- the chaplain(s) at your local hospital
- your local diocesan Family Life office
    (For more information: National Association of Catholic Family Life Ministries, University of Dayton, 300 College Park Avenue, Dayton, OH 45469. (937) 229-3900.)
- National Catholic Ministry to the Bereaved
    606 Middle Avenue, Elyria, OH 44035. (440) 323-6262
- Stephen Ministries
    2045 Innerbelt Business Center Dr., St. Louis, MO 63117-1448.
    (314) 428-2600
- BeFrienders
    Coordinator of BeFrienders Ministry, The St. Paul Seminary School of Divinity of the College of St. Thomas, 2260 Summit Ave., St. Paul, MN 55105. (612) 647-5095.

---

1 Stephen Ministries is a system of training, organizing, and supervising lay people for caring ministry in their congregations. For further information, contact Stephen Ministries at the address or phone number listed above.

2 BeFrienders ministry is a lay pastoral care program to train people to enter into caring relationships with others at times of special need. For more information, contact the coordinator of BeFriender Ministry at the address or phone number listed on page 17.

As your new bereavement ministers are trained, those who already have expertise can serve as mentors; for example, a less-experienced person and a more-experienced person may make pastoral visits together.

Ongoing training is also important. You may want to take time out of each meeting of your bereavement ministry team to study grief issues. Focus on the material in this book as well as the books listed in "Suggested Reading for Bereavement Ministers" in Part IV (pages 294-298).

Gathering Information

You will need to do some legwork in order to complete some of the materials contained in the Basic Resources section; the "Monthly Messages" for the sixth month and for the eleventh month of bereavement require information which is specific to your local area.

The material for the sixth month deals with support groups. Begin with the list on pages 291-293 and add groups available in your local area. Contact various local hotlines, the United Way, your Chamber of Commerce, the public library, other churches, hospices, hospitals, as well as school counselors, psychologists, and other mental health professionals to help you identify support groups and other resources in your area. When dealing with one of the specific situations that this books addresses, such as the loss of a child or suicide, be sure to refer to the list of support groups provided for this situation. If you live in a small town and the closest support group seems far away, please add it to your list anyway. We've found people who have traveled 150-200 miles for one meeting! You may also want to start your own bereavement support group. (See guidelines for starting a support group in Appendix B, pages 307-316.)

The material for the eleventh month is entitled "Getting Involved Again." Use the resources described above to identify recreational, social, educational, and employment opportunities (especially those for people aged 60 and over) in your area. Don't forget to consult your local YMCA and the office overseeing parks and recreation. You may also want to include updated information on Elderhostel, a program offering travel and education for older adults (75 Federal Street, Boston, MA 02110).

Finally, you may want to begin collecting other resources that you find helpful in bereavement care. Poetry on grieving, for example, could be gathered in a specially designated notebook. If you plan to reproduce copyrighted material, you will need to get permission from the party holding the rights to that material.

Coordinating Other Resources

Practical, everyday assistance is a big part of bereavement ministry. After all, what are our words without actions? You may want to canvass your parish or congregation to find additional volunteers who would be willing to assist in meeting these needs. (See p. 301 for a form which will make it easy for you to recruit volunteers within your church body.) Some of the most common needs are as follows.

For an older widow/widower:

- help with finances
- homemaking and house maintenance tasks such as laundry, yard work, making meals, grocery shopping, etc.
- help with personal care
- transportation to and from appointments

For a young widow/widower:

- child care
- help with finances
- help in learning job hunting skills and locating a job
- help with housekeeping

For anyone in the early stages of grief:

- meal preparation
- grocery shopping
- child care
- those willing to come and simply sit with the bereaved

You will no doubt become aware of other such needs in the course of bereavement care.

Implementing Your Bereavement Program

Determining Which Section in This Book to Use

Each section in this book outlines bereavement care for a particular situation. At some points, however, you may be unsure as to which section to use. In general, you should look for the *most specific* description of the grief being faced. For example, if a woman loses her husband, you should follow the program of bereavement care outlined under "Death of a Spouse" (in Part III) rather than simply the "Grieving Adults" section (in Part II).

You may occasionally find a situation in which two factors are at work in a grief situation; you may, for example, minister to a man who has just lost his wife after a long battle with cancer. In that case, the materials under "Death of a Spouse" and "Death After Long-term and Debilitating Illness" would both be appropriate. Or you may find a child who has lost a close relative to suicide. In that case, the materials under "Grieving Children" and "Suicide" would both be appropriate. In cases such as these, we suggest that you make use of both sections, combining materials as appropriate.

The Initial Visit

Clergy will often be involved very early in the grieving process, often before the loved one actually dies. This bereavement program, however, assumes an "initial visit" shortly after the loss actually occurs.

At the initial visit, the bereavement minister should bring the appropriate "Initial Packet" materials. In preparation for unexpected initial visits, you should make copies of the Initial Packet materials needed for various circumstances and place each set in an attractive folder (preferably one with pockets). You may choose to label this folder with the words "Grieving Workbook" or with another appropriate title.

At the initial visit, read through the folder with the grieving person. Remind him or her that the folder is his or hers to keep and explain that you will also be sending monthly mailings that may be placed in the folder. You may want to find a place together where the folder will always be kept.

Be sure to give the bereaved person an opportunity at this meeting to discuss the recent events surrounding his or her loss. You may want to begin with a question such as "What were the last few days before Florence died like?" or "Arlene, could you tell me more about how Bill died?" This is a very important part of pastoral visitation; it gives bereaved people a chance to tell their story. Remember to end the visit on an encouraging note and point out the positive aspects of how the bereaved person is handling the grieving process. The gift of hope and humor, when appropriate, can be very helpful.

Ongoing Bereavement Care

Letters

In addition to "Initial Packet" materials, you will find a series of "Monthly Messages." Of course, pastoral visits must be a part of any effective bereavement ministry, but we have found regular letter-writing to be a helpful way to supplement this personal visitation. We recommend that you send out most of these Monthly Messages in the form of personalized letters. Look carefully for ways you can individualize letters by including names, making pronouns the appropriate gender, adding details, referring to specific kinds of grief, etc.

Here is a sample letter, incorporating the final Monthly Message, "The Journey Continues:"

Dear Joan,

It's hard to believe that it has been a year since Mike's death. Please know that we are thinking about you on this difficult anniversary. The following quote offers an interesting insight:

"Most of the more intense reactions of grief subside within 6 to 12 months. However, the saying 'once bereaved, always bereaved' still remains true. There are some parts of the loss that will continue to be with the griever until she or he dies." —Therese Rando

Even as you get stronger and go on, there is no doubt that Mike will always be a part of you.

Now, however, your journey continues. We hope that these letters and contacts have been helpful during this past year. This year has been a time of many changes for you. Some may have been very painful. Some may have been good. Our prayer is that this year has been a healing journey for you.

In early Christianity, the day on which an individual died was celebrated as his *dies natalis,* the "day of birth" into the divine world. You may not feel like celebrating the experience of Mike's death, but perhaps you can also see ways in which this has been a new birth. Now is a time to reflect on the gifts God has given you, including the love of God reflected through your loved one, blessings of friends, and hope and faith in life everlasting.

At this point, our letter ministry will end, but our contacts with you on special days will continue throughout this coming year.

Please let us know of ways that we can continue to support you. Thank you for the privilege of being able to come into your home through visits and letters. God bless you as the journey of life and love continues.

Sincerely,

Ann Henderson
& the bereavement team at St. Mary's

We suggest that you also send greetings by mail on holidays and other important days. You may incorporate the materials on pages 122-124 into letters or cards. (One source for cards with a religious theme is The Printery House, 1-800-889-0105.) If cards with a pre-printed message are used, a brief message written by hand should also be included.

One additional resource you may want mail out is the "Bereavement Surveys" found on pages 303-304. These sheets allow grieving people to make the church aware of their needs. The Bereavement Surveys may be especially appropriate in larger churches or for those who are less closely connected with the church.

Visitation

Personal visitation is an essential part of any bereavement ministry. There are two ways to incorporate the "Monthly Messages" into visitation: (1) The most recent letters you have sent could serve as discussion material for the visit. (2) You could occasionally print out the material contained in the Monthly Message and bring it in person rather than mailing it. Personal visits are also a good time to deliver the miscellaneous handouts included in the third section of Part III.

Be sure to continue to encourage those who are grieving to tell the story of their loss and their grief. Others may grow tired of hearing their story; it will be your job to provide an outlet as they try to come to terms with what they have experienced.

A Plan for Long-term Care

During the first year of bereavement care, combined letter-writing and visitation should allow you to contact the bereaved person as many as two dozen times, including approximately twelve "Monthly Messages," two to four additional letters or cards on special days, and four to six personal visits.

In the second year, you will probably want to simply mark holidays and special days with a card. If those grieving are having an especially difficult time coping, you may want to place them on a visitation schedule for the second year of bereavement.

During the third year of bereavement care, you may want to remember only the anniversary of death or other especially important days. After the third year, we suggest that you save the file, but it can usually be marked "inactive."

Two Examples of Scheduled Bereavement Care

Your program of letter-writing and visitation will depend on your own resources and limitations. Here are the schedules that two churches followed:

Elim Lutheran Church has 600 members and two bereavement ministers: the pastor and the minister of health. The "Monthly Messages" were sent out in letter form at the appropriate times, and the following personal visits were also made:

Pastor	Initial visit
Pastor and Minister of Health	4 weeks
Minister of Health	2 months
Minister of Health	3 months
Pastor	6 months
Minister of Health	9 months
Pastor and Minister of Health	One year

Olivet Lutheran Church has 3,300 members and eight bereavement ministers: four pastors, one Stephen Minister coordinator, one volunteer coordinator, one parish nurse, and one bereavement coordinator. The "Monthly Messages" were sent out in letter form at the appropriate times, and the following contacts were also made:

Stephen Minister	Initial visit (brought home-baked bread)
Parish Nurse	1-3 weeks
Pastor visit	4 weeks
By mail: Survey Sheet (see p. 303)	6 weeks
Pastor phone call	2 months
Parish Nurse visit	3 months
By mail: Survey Sheet (see p. 304)	4 months
Pastor visit	6 months
Parish Nurse visit	9 months
Pastor visit	One year

(For those receiving additional personal visits)

Stephen Minister and/or Parish Nurse	15 months
By mail: Survey Sheet (see p. 304)	18 months
Pastor visit	24 months

Your own schedule of visitation will vary, of course, depending on your resources and the needs of the individuals to whom you are ministering.

Record-Keeping

There are two basic ways in which you will need to keep records.

First, you will need to create an ongoing file for each bereaved person. At the initial visit, you should get the information needed to fill out the "Basic Information" form found on page 302. A file should then be established containing this form and a "Record of Contacts" such as the one found on page 305. This file will help you to keep track of bereavement care; each phone call, visit, or letter/card should be recorded on the appropriate Record of Contacts form, along with any other helpful information. This form should be reviewed before each contact.

The second form of record-keeping is a "master calendar." After an initial visit with a grieving person, you can enter a number of important dates into your calendar:

- the date of death (or other loss)
- the (two-week and) monthly anniversaries of the death (or other loss) over the coming year
- the anniversary of the birthday of the deceased (if applicable)
- the birthday(s) of the survivor(s)
- the wedding anniversary (if applicable)

Keeping this master calendar will allow you to plan future bereavement care in a timely way.

Of course, if you have access to a computer, your record-keeping can be made easier. The individual file on each person could be created using a word-processing program. (Don't forget to make backup copies, both on disk and on paper!) Your master calendar could be set up using a calendar program such as "Calendar Creator Plus."

Establishing an Initial List of Those Who Are Grieving

In order to create an initial list of those who are bereaved, go through the official church record book (or ask those involved in past bereavement care) and note deaths or other important losses within the last two years. Add these parishioners to your calendar. In your next contact with these people, you will probably want to let them know about the new bereavement care program.

As your bereavement care program becomes known in the community, you may find that people are also referred to you through funeral homes, outside resources, or personal contacts with a pastor or congregation member.

Part II

BASIC RESOURCES

Grieving Adults

Setting Up a Program of Bereavement Care for Grieving Adults

There are many kinds of loss which can create an experience of grief, including the death of a family member or friend. The following materials will be appropriate for many different situations.

Initial Contact

As suggested on page 19, you should make an initial visit to the grieving person as soon as possible. The following materials are designed to be given to the grieving person at your initial visit:

Physical Symptoms of Grieving	(page 29)
Exercise and Nutrition	(page 30)
Getting to Sleep	(page 32)
Suggested Reading After a Major Loss	(page 34)

Monthly Messages

In addition, the following Monthly Messages should be used during the first year of bereavement (see pages 19-21 for instructions on incorporating these messages into personalized letters or otherwise including them in bereavement care):

The Grieving Process	(page 38)	2 weeks after loss
Common Myths About Grief	(page 39)	1 month after loss

Also add "Special Day Messages" on pages 122-124 and Bereavement Surveys on pages 303-304 as appropriate.

Ongoing Visitation

See suggestions for visitation on page 21.

Physical Symptoms of Grieving

Grieving is work. The exhaustion from grieving is similar to a heavy physical workout. These "symptoms" of grieving are sometimes mistakenly diagnosed as strictly physical problems.

Common complaints are as follows:

> chest pains or heart problems
> dizziness
> dry mouth
> empty feeling in the stomach
> fatigue
> feeling of "something stuck in the throat"
> headache
> inability to sleep
> loss of sexual desire or having an overly active sexual desire
> loss of weight
> nausea and vomiting
> oversensitivity to noise
> pain
> purposeless activity
> shortness of breath
> trembling
> uncontrollable sighing and sobbing
> weakness in the muscles
> various gastrointestinal symptoms: constipation, diarrhea, or excessive gas

(This information taken from books and research by Lieberman and Jacobs, Worden, Olders, and Rando.)

Any of these symptoms can be a normal part of the grieving process, but if they persist or become very uncomfortable, please make an appointment with your physician and tell her/him that you have experienced a recent major loss.

If you are on medication from your physician, do your best to continue to take it without fail. If necessary, use (according to directions) pain relievers like aspirin, acetaminophen, and ibuprofen for headaches and aches and pains. Avoid over-the-counter sleeping medications, if possible. They may only further interfere with your sleep and your overall recovery.

Meditation and relaxation techniques are very useful tools in coping with these physical symptoms of grief. Ask your bereavement minister about relaxation tapes to try, as well as a list of books and other materials that can help with meditation and relaxation.

> *Come to me, all you that are weary and are carrying heavy burdens,*
> *and I will give you rest.*

MATTHEW 11:28

Exercise and Nutrition

Grieving often affects physical well-being. You may not be sleeping well at night, or you may be rerunning events over in your mind and feeling especially tired. Allow yourself the freedom to relax. You have suffered a great shock to your mind, body, and spirit. Physical injury requires rest as an important part of recovery, and emotional injury does too. Your energy will come back in time; now you must take care of yourself.

If several months go by and you still find yourself wanting only to sleep, you should let your pastor, bereavement minister, or physician know.

Exercise

You may find that even though you have been used to an active routine, just getting out of bed in the morning seems like a heroic act. Do whatever you can. If you haven't been active, don't push yourself into a vigorous exercise program. Consider simply going out for a regular walk, or if you are unable to walk easily, simply move your arms and legs while seated. Exercise, besides being great for your physical body, is also a wonderful release for your emotional self. It can allow for the release of emotions such as anger, guilt, anxiety, or restlessness. It will give you more energy. Researchers have proved that exercise can temporarily relieve mild depression and improve mood.

Nutrition

Eating right may seem like a hard thing to do. You may have lost your appetite and even your interest in preparing food. These few suggestions may help:

1. Take people up on their offer to go out to eat.

2. Take a multi-vitamin daily. It can't replace a well-rounded diet, but it can fill in some of the gaps temporarily.

3. Eat with the TV or radio on, if it offers company to you. Set a pretty table, and make your meal as colorful and appealing as you can.

4. Eat extra foods high in protein—your body is in a state of repair.

    a. You can increase your protein by adding one additional glass of milk a day or one extra serving of three to four ounces of meat, cheese, or peanut butter a day.

    b. Most microwavable entrees include three to four ounces of meat. If you need to watch your fat, Healthy Choice, Lean Cuisine, and Weight Watchers are good choices.

    c. Cold snacks such as peanut butter or cheese on crackers or bread can substitute for one ounce of meat.

    d. Add 1/4 cup nonfat powdered milk to soups, casseroles, etc., to increase protein.

5. Follow the USDA food pyramid for daily healthy eating:

    6-11 servings of carbohydrates (bread, pasta, rice, and cereal)

    2-4 servings of the fruit group

    3-5 servings of the vegetable group

    2-3 servings of the dairy group

    3-4 servings of the protein group (meat, poultry, fish, nuts, dry beans, eggs)

Suggestions #4a-#4d courtesy of Linda Aamold, LRD (Licensed Clinical Dietitian) at MeritCare Hospital in Fargo, North Dakota.

Getting to Sleep

Everyone knows how important a good night's sleep is. Sleep restores and prepares our bodies for daytime alertness and better health. The experience of grief often makes it difficult to sleep well, but the following suggestions may help:

1. Exercise daily to promote good sleep. This releases energy and mental tension. Exercise early, though; late-evening exercise disturbs peaceful sleep.

2. Maintain regular sleep habits. Get up at the same time each day, no matter how well you have slept. This maintains your internal clock and will result in establishing a fairly regular bedtime.

3. Slow down and unwind before bedtime. Try pleasure reading, a warm glass of milk, or a relaxing soak in the tub.

4. Your bedroom should be a comfortable resort for sleeping: dark, cool, quiet.

5. Breathe deeply to induce drowsiness. Take a series of three very slow, deep breaths, exhaling fully each time. This helps break tension.

6. Accept occasional nights of less sleep. They're part of life. Although uncomfortable, all of us experience a few nights when sleep is more difficult. Read Psalm 77: even the psalmist experienced sleepless nights!

7. If you have a friend or loved one who can offer reassurance, you may be able to get help on the most difficult evenings by making a short bedtime phone call to her or him.

8. Use relaxation tapes, read a book about progressive relaxation, and, if all else fails, contact your physician.

Here are some suggestions on what to avoid:

1. Don't try to force yourself to sleep. If you can't fall asleep within 15-30 minutes, go into another room and do something relaxing until you feel sleepy, then return to bed. If you still can't sleep after 15-30 minutes, get up once more, and repeat this pattern until you become sleepy.

2. Do not nap during the day. Although naps feel refreshing, they tend to decrease the amount of sleep at night. Stay up no matter how tired you may feel.

3. Don't do strenuous mental or physical activity during the evening. The mind and body need to relax before sleeping.

4. Avoid caffeine in the evening. All coffee (even decaffeinated), most teas, colas, and chocolate contain caffeine. (Did you know that it takes three hours for one cup of coffee to leave your system?)

5. Avoid smoking before bedtime. Nicotine is a stimulant, and smoker's cough may disrupt sleep.

6. Avoid alcohol in the late evening. The sedation tends to wear off in two to three hours and causes disturbed sleep in the latter half of the night.

7. Avoid long-term use of sleeping medications. These may cause dependency and can eventually reduce quality of sleep.

8. Avoid going to bed on an empty stomach, especially if you are dieting. Eat something low in calories to keep your stomach satisfied.

9. Try not to take your problems to bed. Try relaxing yourself into sleep with soothing music or pleasant imagery (like walking on the beach or in the woods). Counting sheep is the oldest trick in the book for a simple reason—it works! According to research, this technique distracts both sides of the brain with soothing and repetitive activity—you literally bore yourself to sleep!

Suggestions adapted from material from the Alabama Society for Sleep Disorders, by Maryann Kaul, R.N., copyright © 1967. Used by permission of the author.

Suggested Reading After a Major Loss

There are several resources you can use in locating these titles: your local library (and inter-library loan system), your church library, bookstores, your bereavement minister's personal library, local support groups' lending libraries, hospices, and funeral homes.

Remember, if a book doesn't seem to make sense right now, try reading it again later.

About Mourning: Support and Guidance for the Bereaved. S. Weizman and P. Kamm. Human Sciences Press, 1984.

Affliction. E. Schaeffer. Raven's Ridge Books, 1993.

Along Your Desert Journey. R. Hamma. Paulist Press, 1997.

Are You Listening God? (I Need You). Joan Bel Geddes. Ave Maria Press, 1994.

Befriend the Darkness, Welcome the Light. J. Rupp. Ave Maria Press, 1995. (cassette tape)

Beyond Grief: A Guide for Recovering from the Death of a Loved One. C. Staudacher. New Harbinger, 1987.

Blessed Grieving: Reflections on Life's Losses. J. Guntzelman. St. Mary's Press, 1994.

Christians Grieve, Too. D. Howard. Banner of Truth, 1980.

Christ's Comfort for Those Who Sorrow. A. Coniaris. Light & Life, 1978.

Companion Through Darkness: Inner Dialogues on Grief. S. Ericcson. HarperCollins, 1993.

Cries of the Heart: Praying Our Losses. W. Simsic. St. Mary's Press, 1994.

A Deeper Shade of Grace. B. Keaggy. Bethany House, 1996.

Don't Take My Grief Away: What to Do When You Lose a Loved One. D. Manning. Harper San Francisco, 1984.

Everyday Comfort: Reading for the First Month of Grief. R. Becton. Baker Books, 1993.

The Eyes are Sunlight: A Journey Through Grief. S. Koers. Ave Maria Press, 1986.

Facing Death, Finding Love: The Healing Power of Grief and Loss in One Family's Life. D. Church. Aslan, 1994.

The Fall of a Sparrow: Of Death, and Dreams, and Healing. K. Koppelman. Baywood, 1994.

The First Year of Bereavement. I. O. Glick et al. John Wiley and Sons, Inc., 1974.

For Those Who Hurt. C. Swindoll. Mutnomah Press, 1977.

Forever in His Presence. E. Milligan. Milligan, 1995.

From Grief to Grace: Images for Overcoming Sadness and Loss. H. Lambin. ACTA, 1997.

Good Grief. G. Westberg. Fortress, 1962.

Good-bye to Guilt. G. Jampolsky. Bantam, 1985.

Grace Disguised: How the Soul Grows Through Loss. G. Sittser. Zondervan, 1996.

Grief: Climb Toward Understanding: Self-Help When You Are Struggling. P. Davis. Sunnybank, 1992.

Grief for a Season. M. Tengbom. Bethany House, 1989.

A Grief Observed. C. S. Lewis. Bantam, 1983.

Grieving: A Love Story. R. Coughlin. Random House, 1993.

Grieving the Death of a Friend. H. Smith. Augsburg Fortress, 1996.

Grieving: The Pain and the Promise. D. Edwards. Covenant Communications, Inc., 1990.

Growing Strong at Broken Places. P. Ripple. Ave Maria Press, 1986.

Healing Our Losses: A Journal for Working Through Your Grief. J. Miller. Resource Publications, 1993.

Healing the Greatest Hurt: Healing Grief & the Family Tree. D. Linn et al. Paulist Press, 1985.

Hearts in Motion, Minds at Rest: Living through the Loss of a Loved One. M. Brite. Barbour & Co., 1993.

Hello Mr. D: A Journey Through Grief: "There Is a Light at the End of the Tunnel but You Must Go Through the Tunnel to See the Light." C. Weddington. JM Publications, 1993.

How to Go on Living When Someone You Love Dies. T. A. Rando. Bantam, 1988.

How to Survive the Loss of a Love. M. Colgrove. Prelude Press, 1991.

Hurts of the Heart: Friend or Foe? P. Ripple. Ave Maria Press, 1996. (cassette tape)

I Never Know What to Say: How to Help Your Family and Friends Cope with Tragedy. N. Donnelly and Herrman. Ballantine, 1990.

I Tell You A Mystery: Life, Death, and Resurrection. J. C. Arnold. Plough, 1996.

Illusions. R. Bach. Dell, 1989.

In Memoriam. H. Nouwen. Ave Maria Press, 1980.

In Sickness and In Health. E. Grollman.

In the Midst of Winter: Selections from the Literature of Mourning. M. Moppat, ed. Random, 1992.

In This Very Hour: Devotions in Your Time of Need: Loss of a Loved One. R. Monroe. Broodman, 1994.

Into the Light: For Women Experiencing the Transformative Nature of Grief. S. Olson. Seasons, 1993.

Letters I Never Wrote, Conversations I Never Had. C. Bissell. Macmillan, 1983.

Life After Loss: A Personal Guide to Dealing with Death, Divorce, Job Change and Relocation. B. Deits. Fisher Books, 1992.

Life After Loss: The Lessons of Grief. V. Volkan and E. Zintl. Macmillan, 1994.

Listening to God's Silent Language. D. Osgood. Bethany House, 1995.

Living Beyond Your Losses: The Healing Journey Through Grief. N. P. Murray. Morehouse, 1997.

Living the Promise of God: 365 Readings for Recovery from Grief or Loss. P. Keller. Augsburg Fortress, 1988.

Living Through Grief. H. Bauman. Lion USA, 1989.

Living Through Mourning: Finding Comfort and Hope When a Loved One Has Died. H. S. Schiff. Viking Penguin, 1986.

Living Through Personal Crisis. A. Stearns. Thomas More Press, 1984.

Living—When a Loved One Has Died. E. Grollman. Beacon Press, 1977.

Lord: If I Ever Needed You, It's Now! C. Davis. Baker, 1981.

Love is Letting Go of Fear. G. Jampolsky. Celestial Arts, 1988.

Loved and Lost: The Journey Through Dying, Death, and Bereavement. J. Quinlan. Liturgical Press, 1997.

Meeting God in Our Transition Times. Joyce Rupp. Ave Maria Press, 1993. (cassette tape set)

Men and Grief. C. Staudacher. New Harbinger, 1991.

Mourning Handbook. H. Fitsgerald. Simon & Schuster, 1944.

Mourning into Dancing. W. Wangerin. Zondervan, 1996.

Mourning Sickness: Poems, Paintings, Stories, & Dreams. K. Smith. Rainbow Press, 1993.

Mourning: The Prelude to Laughter. B. Bruno. Zondervan, 1993.

My Companion Through Grief: Comfort for Your Darkest Hours. G. Kinnaman. Servant, 1996.

Necessary Losses. J. Viorst. Fawcett Gold Medal, 1986.

A New Leaping: A Journey from Grief. D. Gandy. Celilo Publishers, 1985.

Not Just Another Day: Families, Grief, & Special Days. M. Lowery. Centering Corporation, 1992.

On Being Alone. J. Peterson. AARP, 1982.

One to One: Self-Understanding Through Journal Writing. C. Baldwin. M. Evans and Company, 1977.

Our Greatest Gift: A Meditation on Dying and Caring. H. Nouwen. Ave Maria Press, 1994.

Overcoming Life's Hurts. P. Ripple. Ave Maria Press, 1993. (cassette tape)

Painful Times, Graceful Moments. W. Breault. Ave Maria Press, 1996. (cassette tape)

Praying Our Goodbyes. J. Rupp. Ave Maria Press, 1988.

A Rumor of Angels: Quotations for Living, Dying, & Letting Go. G. Perry and J. Perry. Ballantine, 1989.

Safe Passage: Words to Help the Grieving Hold Fast and Let Go. M. Fumia. Boro Publishing, 1992.

Seven Choices. E. H. Neeld. Clarkson N. Potter, 1990.

The Silent Passage. G. Sheehy. Random House, 1992.

Solitude of Loneliness. J. Woodward. 1988.

Spirituality of Grief: Exploring Faith-Grief Dynamics. M. A. Stamm. Cloverdale, 1991.

Such is the Way of the World: A Journey Through Grief. B. Brisson. Paulist, 1997.

Surviving Grief—And Learning To Live Again. C. Sanders. Wiley, 1992.

Teach Only Love: The Seven Principles of Attitudinal Healing. G. Jampolsky. Bantam, 1984.

A Time to Grieve: Help & Hope from the Bible. C. Lynn. Barbour, 1995.

A Time to Mourn. J. Spiro. Bloch, 1985.

To Live Again. G. D. Ginsburg. Bantam, 1989.

An Untimely Loss: A Passage to the Gentle Side of Grief. L. Zelenka. Paulist, 1996.

When Bad Things Happen to Good People. H. Kushner. Schocken, 1981.

When Death Touches Your Life. M. Thompson. Prince of Peace, 1986.

When Going to Pieces Holds You Together. W. A. Miller. Augsburg, 1976.

When Mourning Comes: A Book of Comfort for the Grieving. W. Silverman and K. Cinnamon. Aronson, 1994.

When Someone Dies. E. N. Jackson. Fortress, 1971.

Where Do I Go from Here? A Musical Dialogue in the Journey of Loss and Grief. K. Medema and J. Nadeau. Color Song Productions, 1993.

Where is God When I'm Hurting? S. Barret. Ave Maria Press, 1987. (cassette tape)

The Will of God. L. D. Weatherhead. Abingdon, 1944.

Woman's Book of Grieving. N. Rapoport. Morrow, 1994.

Women in Mourning: Stories of Grieving Women. J. Clayton. Centering Corporation, 1996.

Kahlil Gibran writes on loss and life in general:

The Prophet. Knopf, 1952.

Tears and Laughter. Philosophical Library, 1949.

The Voice of the Master. Citadel Press, 1958.

Unfortunately, a time of grieving can leave one more vulnerable to fraud or theft. Four pamphlets from the American Association of Retired Persons (AARP) (Write: Criminal Justice Services, AARP, 1909 K Street, NW, Washington, D.C. 20049):

"How to conduct a security survey"

"How to protect you and your car"

"How to protect your home"

"How to spot a con artist"

Monthly Messages

The Grieving Process

God can see into your broken heart, my friend.
He hears the groaning from the depths of your grief.
He can understand what you are experiencing and thinking and feeling.
He knows what you want to say or need to say, but find it impossible to say.
He accepts that helpless feeling as your prayer.

DR. OSWALD HOFFMANN

I can't imagine all the thoughts and feelings you are having right now, but I can tell you a bit about the experience of grieving. Grieving is, first of all, a process. It takes time; it cannot be rushed. Each of us handles loss in our own way, and there is no right or wrong way to grieve. While each experience of mourning is unique, there are, nevertheless, some similarities in the process. One of those similarities is that there seem to be certain phases that we all go though as we grieve.

Right now you may be feeling numb, confused, and disorganized. You may feel that things are not real, that this is a dream, or that your loved one will return. These experiences characterize the first stage of grief. This part of grieving doesn't usually last very long, but it helps you get through what you have to get through.

The second phase is where you end up doing most of your work. Work? Yes, mourning is work; you may not be doing any heavy labor, but grieving requires a lot of mental labor and readjustment. The trauma of a major loss can also be thought of as a kind of wound. If you use these two analogies, you can see that you'll probably need extra sleep (even afternoon naps), good nutrition (to help you heal), and exercise (even a short walk around the block or moving your hands and legs). Your emotions may run the gamut from deep sadness, to anger, to irritability, to anxiousness, to depression. (You should not assume that what you are experiencing at this point is clinical depression—feeling bad is simply one of the aspects of grieving.) You may feel that you are losing control or going crazy. Don't worry. There is no one way to mourn, and these are all normal reactions to grieving.

Another aspect of this stage of grief is the experience of "secondary losses." You will find yourself mourning not only your primary loss, but all the other little losses connected to it. When one woman's only son was murdered, for example, she not only mourned her son but the fact that there would be no one to look after her in her old age. These losses are painful, but they are also a part of the process of mourning.

Sometimes people have experiences of seeing or feeling the person who died. In the medical community, these are called hallucinations, but these experiences are often encouraging and comforting. They remind us of our belief that there is life after death and that both the living and the dead are part of the "communion of saints" in which all believers share.

The final phase of mourning is called the "re-establishment phase." This describes the point in your mourning where you feel you are ready to reenter the world. If you have lost a spouse, you may feel like dating again. Or you may find that you are motivated to do volunteer work for a worthwhile cause. Your energy won't be so tied up with your emotions, and you'll be ready to give to others. It may help you to know that this phase *will* come; you *will* feel better eventually.

Remember, everyone is different and everyone goes through the process of mourning in various degrees and lengths. There is no right or wrong way to grieve. Many people do most of their grief work in a year or two, but it varies considerably. Allow yourself the same grace and love our Lord Jesus gives to you.

We want to be with you on your journey and offer comfort, support, and love. We will be in touch.

Recovery from grief is not a station you arrive at,
but a manner of traveling.

DR. IVAN G. MATTERN

Common Myths About Grief

"Be gracious to me, O Lord, for I am in distress...."

PSALM 31:9

- All bereaved people grieve in the same way.
- It takes two months to get over your grief.
- Once grief is resolved, it never comes up again.
- You and your family will eventually be just the same as you were before the death of a loved one.
- It's not appropriate to feel sorry for yourself.
- There is no reason to be angry at your deceased loved one.
- Children need to be protected from grief and death.
- You will have no relationship with your loved one after her or his death.
- Once a loved one has died, it is better not to focus on her or him, but to put her or him in the past and go on with your life.

(Taken from *How to Go on Living When Someone You Love Dies,* by Therese A. Rando, Ph.D., Bantam, 1988.)

These first two weeks after the death of your loved one (or other major loss) are confusing and hectic. You may encounter myths like the ones above or others which are often painful and create unrealistic expectations in your grieving process. In the weeks and months ahead, we will be exploring these myths and learning more about the grieving process together.

When you receive these monthly letters, you may feel that some touch you and find yourself saying, "Yes! That's exactly how I feel." Other letters may not seem to apply to you. Other letters may hit so close to home that you find it difficult to read them. Please, just be open to the possibilities of healing. If the letters don't seem to fit right now, lay them aside and reread them at a later time.

We are hoping that through these letters and personal visits we can journey with you offering comfort and support. Many people are praying for you. May you be strengthened by these prayers.

You and Your Emotions

There is a sacredness in tears.
They are not the mark of weakness but of power.
They speak more eloquently than ten thousand tongues.
They are messengers of overwhelming grief, of deep contrition,
and of unspeakable love.

WASHINGTON IRVING

Even when a major loss is expected, we are rarely able to anticipate the full impact it will have on our lives. Often, it leaves your life in complete upheaval. Emotions and feelings are helter-skelter. Tears are mixed with anger. Sadness and loneliness seem overwhelming.

Know that it is okay to cry. After all, Jesus wept when his friend died. Know that it is okay to be angry. Jesus, too, was angry when he threw the money-changers out of the Temple. Feelings aren't good or bad; they just are. It's how you deal with your feelings that is most important.

If you are feeling guilty about something you did or didn't do, now is the perfect time to sit down and write a letter (even to one who is no longer living), say a prayer, or speak with a trusted friend or a clergyperson. Not expressing your emotions allows them to have control over you. Besides, you can waste a lot of your energy trying to keep them bottled up. Here are some other suggestions for coping with your emotions and dealing with the stress of change:

1. Exercising offers a physical and mental release of tensions. Try a walk around the block, a game of golf, or whatever exercise you enjoy.

2. Crying.

3. Talking about your feelings with a trusted friend, counselor, or pastor.

4. Writing your thoughts on paper and expressing your feelings to the person who died, to a doctor, to God, etc. Then you may choose to destroy your writing or place it in a secure place.

5. Praying—for yourself in coping with the necessary adjustments or for your loved one, if you have lost someone to death.

6. Meditating and relaxing can offer you a brief respite from your emotions and obsessive thoughts and allow your body to heal.

7. Drawing, dancing, singing, or any other type of creative expression can help. Make up a song and sing it as loud as you can or paint or color the emotions inside of you.

8. Watching a funny movie can offer a diversion from your grief work for awhile, and laughter allows for the release of tension.

9. Thanking God for the support you have received, for friends, for books, etc. An attitude of thankfulness can be difficult at the beginning but will be an important aspect of living later.

Enough Faith?

I pray that, according to the riches of his glory,
Christ may grant that you may be strengthened in your inner being
with power through his spirit,
and that Christ may dwell in your hearts through faith,
as you are being rooted and grounded in love.

EPHESIANS 3:16-17

"We are accustomed to thinking that if we just had enough faith, we would not have any doubts. Some soldiers are accustomed to thinking that if they just had enough bravery, they would not have any fears in battle. Some grieving people are accustomed to thinking that if they just had enough faith, they would not feel any sorrow. All of these 'accustomed' ways of thinking are unhelpful. In contrast, faith as courage suggests that faith is trusting God in spite of one's doubts, that bravery is action in spite of one's fears, and that faith is hope in a new tomorrow in spite of one's present sorrow. Sometimes faith is the courage to trust in spite of feeling to the contrary."

(Taken from *Grief and Growth: Pastoral Resources for Emotional and Spiritual Growth*, by R. S. Sullende, Paulist Press, 1985.)

After a major loss, it is not uncommon to question our faith. We may ask why this has occurred, we may feel angry at God, or we may feel nothing at all toward God. Such feelings are normal. True faith, as R. S. Sullender reminds us, is not a matter of *feeling,* but of the *courage* to go on believing and hoping.

Our thoughts and prayers are with you.

For everything there is a season,
and a time for every matter under heaven. . . .
a time to weep, and a time to laugh;
a time to mourn, and a time to dance. . . .

ECCLESIASTES 3:1-8

Working With Your Grieving

How long must I bear pain in my soul,
and have sorrow in my heart all the day?

PSALM 13:2

Your life has been changed forever. This is a reality that takes time to absorb fully. Those who are grieving often feel emotional and social isolation, anger, and loss of vigor for life. Try not to be too hard on yourself.

One exercise you can do to connect with some of the life, energy, and the resources of the relationship that you had with your loved one is to close your eyes and, instead of seeing the person who died as small and distant, see the person life-size. Instead of seeing *(her/him)* far away; see *(her/him)* close beside you. Instead of seeing *(her/him)* being still, see *(her/him)* moving.

You cannot replace the person you loved, but you can preserve the benefits and the qualities of the relationship. Maybe there was warmth, intimacy, and deep friendship. Maybe there was intelligence, humor, and liveliness. Maybe you appreciate yourself more because of your relationship. Whatever it is, take those qualities and values that were present in your relationship in the past and imagine what form those values and qualities might take in your future, as they continue to live in you.

You may want to try writing a letter to the person who died answering the following questions:

What qualities do I miss most about you?
What will I miss about our relationship?
What do I wish I hadn't said?
What do I wish I would have said?

What do I wish I would not have done?

What do I wish I would have done?

What is the hardest thing I have to deal with?

What is one special memory I have of you?

What are some ways you will continue to live on in me?

We pray these suggestions will be helpful for you and allow you to feel the love of the person who died.

Returning to "Normal"

Likewise the Spirit helps us in our weakness;
for we do not know how to pray as we ought,
but that very Spirit intercedes with sighs too deep for words.
And God, who searches the heart,
knows what is the mind of the Spirit . . . .

ROMANS 8:26-27

What's "normal"? Normal is different for you than for your friends because of what you have experienced. Death has a way of changing people, often making them stronger and wiser. Your sense of "normal" will change as you pass through the grieving experience, and it will be different from month to month.

Although your thoughts may be different from some of your friends, they may be normal for someone who is grieving. You may find yourself angrier or more irritable. You may worry more about money than others do. You may find you cry more easily or feel like being alone more often.

These emotions can catch you off-guard. You may be out shopping, catch a glimpse of someone who looks like your loved one, and feel like running away. Or you may hear a certain song that brings back strong memories for you. Returning to church may bring back many memories, including memories of the funeral. Anything can be a trigger and set you off crying, feeling confused, or feeling like you need to run. Know that this is a common part of grief. Take a couple deep breaths, cry if you need to, step out for a moment or two, or do whatever you need to do to center yourself. These feelings are real, and it is important to acknowledge that they are there. It will be difficult at first, thinking you are seeing your loved one everywhere you go, for example, but it does get easier.

You may find it difficult going back to work, back to your regular activities, back to social get-togethers, or back to church. Sometimes people don't know what to say to you, so they avoid you. Sometimes friends or family members will say things to you that hurt you. Of course, in most cases, they don't mean any harm; they simply don't know the right thing to say. As you deal with these painful experiences, you will become stronger, and each step of the pain will lead you through grieving and back to life.

We really do need each other; that is the way God made us. In the midst of your loss and your pain, may you discover again a sense of community.

> *Behold, God is my salvation, I will trust, and will not be afraid;*
> *for the Lord God is my strength and my song,*
> *and he has become my salvation.*
>
> ―――――――
>
> ISAIAH 12:2

I Know There's Life After Death, Right?

You may have always believed that there was life after death, but now you're not sure. Or maybe you believed that there was life after death, and this particular death made you feel all the more sure of it.

Our faith has a lot to say about death—in the teaching of the prophets, in the Apostles' Creed, and in reality of Jesus' own death and resurrection. Now, even scientists are conducting research with people who claim that they have died and come back to life. Some people have claimed that in near-death experiences, they have left their body and found themselves hovering over their "dead" body. Their experiences vary, but many describe an overwhelming sense of love and reassurance.

If you should feel the presence of the person who died, or experience them in your dreams, know that you are not going crazy. Such experiences remind us of our belief that there is life after death, and that both the living and the dead share in the "communion of saints" of which all believers are a part. Accept these experiences as a source of comfort. If, on the other hand, you have dreams that replay themselves over and over or have nightmares, talk with someone who can help you interpret your dreams so you can move forward into a restful night's sleep.

Praying for the person who has died can allow you to continue to express your love for her or him, while at the same time beginning to let *(her/him)* go.

> *But we do not want you to be uninformed, brothers and sisters,*
> *about those who have died so that you may not grieve as others*
> *who have no hope. For since we believe that Jesus died and rose again,*
> *even so, through Jesus, God will bring with him those who have died.*
>
> ―――――――
>
> 1 THESSALONIANS 4:13-14

Support Groups

Blessed be the God and Father of our Lord Jesus Christ,
the Father of mercies and the God of all consolation,
who consoles us in all our affliction,
so that we may be able to console those who are in any affliction
with the consolation with which we ourselves are consoled by God.

2 CORINTHIANS 1:3-4

Congratulations! You've made it this far. You still need a lot of tender loving care—be gentle with yourself. Being with others who have gone through the same thing can be very comforting. That is why support groups have become so popular. You may find your friends are sympathetic initially, but as time goes on, they may become impatient that you are not "getting over this." Others who are grieving know that it takes time—that you can't just get over it. You need to tell your story and be listened to. Reaching out for help and assurance is not a sign of weakness. We are in communion with one another to help and serve each other.

If you attend a group and feel uncomfortable with what is being presented, or if it doesn't make sense to you, don't give up . . . try it again. A good rule of thumb is to try something new three times.

Here is a list of support groups you may find helpful:

(Note to bereavement minister: Check the following pages for lists of support groups which may be helpful: 73, 132, 136, 169, 185, 194, 214, 220, 239, 245, 266, 269; then add your research about local groups (see page 17).

Dealing With Criticism

Do you sometimes worry about what others will think about your decisions? Many who have suffered a loss do.

They think things like:

- "I could really use a vacation, but I'm afraid people will think that I'm not really grieving."
- "I feel I'm ready to take off my wedding ring, but I'll feel disloyal if I do."
- "If I'm having fun with my other children, will people think I'm not grieving the child who died?"

There is no right or wrong way to do any of these things. There are people who think they "know" exactly how you should feel or act, and they'll probably tell you: If you grieve too long, you're not strong enough, and if you don't grieve long enough, then you didn't love that person.

Here are just a few suggestions on coping with criticism from yourself and others:

1. Realize that you may be oversensitive at this time. You may be reading into people's statements and actions, feelings that aren't there. You may be thinking people are talking about you when they really aren't.

2. Determine right and wrong for yourself and don't let others force it on you. Only you have the right to determine how bad you will feel.

3. There are only two people to please—God and yourself. Follow God's will to the best of your ability (nobody else knows God's will for your life, except you). You are the only one to assume responsibility for your health and happiness, and you don't need others to determine how you should do this.

(Suggestions taken from *Don't Take My Grief Away*, by Doug Manning, Harper San Francisco, 1984.)

What it really comes down to is this: There are no right or wrong ways to grieve.

You are an individual who experienced a loss of a relationship unlike anyone else's.

Only you can determine how you are going to live.

Just be yourself—if other people are talking about you, let others talk!

More About Exercise and Nutrition

*Beloved, I pray that all may go well with you
and that you may be in good health,
just as it is well with your soul.*

3 JOHN 1:2

Nutrition

If you followed the suggestions offered earlier, you probably have been eating foods higher in protein these last weeks or months. Now, it's time to return to the daily recommendations of the USDA food pyramid:

    6-11 servings of carbohydrates (bread, pasta, rice, and cereal)
    2-4 servings of the fruit group
    3-5 servings of the vegetable group
    2-3 servings of the dairy group
    3-4 servings of the protein group (meat, poultry, fish, nuts, dry beans, eggs)

Exercise

If exercise hasn't been part of your regular routine, you may want to consider starting.

Walking is a great form of exercise. It is easy on the joints, helps clear the mind, and helps in overall conditioning. Start slowly, adding small increments of time each week until you're walking 15-30 minutes or longer each day. Research has shown that mental capacity increases with exercise, especially for older people.

Here are some additional suggestions for exercise. Check with your physician first, especially if you have medical problems.

1. Do it!

2. Warm up for two to five minutes preceding and cool down for three to five minutes following aerobic exercise.

3. Monitor your heart rate to stay within your target heart rate zone. To figure out your target heart rate zone:

   a. Begin with 220 and subtract your age

   b. Multiply the number from (a.) by 0.65

   c. Multiply the number from (a.) by 0.75

   You should keep your pulse between these two numbers.

   Example: you are 70 years old.
   a. 200 - 70 = 150
   b. 150 x 0.65 = 97
   c. 150 x 0.75 = 112

   You should keep your pulse rate between 97 and 112 beats per minute during exercise.

   You can check your pulse rate for a full 15 seconds during your exercise and multiply by 4 to find your beats per minute.

4. Exercise for 20 minutes four times per week or 30 minutes three times per week.

5. Think noncompetitive thoughts: "calm," "relaxed," "steady."

6. Drink plenty of water before and after exercise.

7. Try different exercises and activities for variety.

(Suggestions taken from *Health and Fitness Excellence,* by Dr. Robert Cooper, Houghton Mifflin, 1989.)

How Will I Know I'm Feeling Better?

I walked a mile with pleasure; She chattered all the way,
But left me none the wiser. For all she had to say.
I walked a mile with sorrow; And ne'er a word said she;
But, oh, the things I learned from her, When Sorrow walked with me!

ROBERT BROWNING HAMILTON

The best answer to your question, "How will I know when I am feeling better?" is one only you can answer for yourself. You'll probably find you can now get through a conversation about your loved one without crying. The pain of the loss is less intense. Seeing someone who talks, walks, or looks like your loved one doesn't upset you like it did in the beginning. Your ability to enjoy the holidays again, to start having more energy and less irritability, and to be able to reinvest your emotions back into life again indicate you are on your way. You may feel as though you take one step forward and two steps back, but you will gradually move ahead.

As you journey on, you'll probably experience something called "anniversary reactions." On the anniversary of the day your loved one died, for example, you may feel sad, irritable, and restless. This is normal, and anniversary reactions may happen for some time into the future. You may also experience deep sadness when special events such as a graduation, baptism, or wedding take place, even far in the future; these are times when you will naturally wish your loved one could be with you. Your unconscious mind keeps track of these events, even if you aren't conscious of them. It is important to acknowledge these feelings. You may want to do something special; for example, place a flower on the altar in memory of your loved one during a special ceremony.

As you continue on, it is important to reflect on some questions that can shape and guide your future such as:

- What have I learned from this experience?
- How have I changed?
- What is my future?
- Where have I seen God working?

Praise God for the physical and mental strength to come downthis long hard path. May God live in and through your life, transforming it into his glory.

May those who sow in tears reap with shouts of joy.
Those who go out weeping, bearing the seed for sowing,
shall come home with shouts of joy, carrying their sheaves.

PSALM 126:5-6

A Special Note

Send a special personalized note, poem, or prayer.

Getting Involved Again

*There is no better exercise for your heart
than reaching down and helping to lift someone up.*

ANONYMOUS

You may be starting to want to be involved in activities again. Maybe you have lost contact with friends, family, and your church community. It is difficult sometimes to reconnect those old ties, but most people find that they are readily welcomed back. Or maybe you're ready to try something entirely new.

There are a number of recreational, social, and employment possibilities for your involvement and *(name of church)* offers a number of opportunities for involvement.

There are also a number of activities going on here in our community. (Note to bereavement minister: add your research about local activities (see page 17)).

You may also be interested in knowing about Elderhostel. Elderhostel is a nonprofit educational organization offering inexpensive, short-term academic programs hosted by educational institutions around the world. Individuals 55 years of age and older are eligible; those participating may bring an accompanying spouse or companion of any age. Write Elderhostel, 75 Federal Street, Boston, MA 02110 (1-617-426-7788) for more information.

We hope you find this information useful in your planning. If you have any questions or concerns, please contact Father/Pastor _____ or a member of the bereavement ministry team.

*Experiencing a great sorrow is like entering a cave.
We are overwhelmed by the darkness, the loneliness, the homesickness.
Sad thoughts, like bats, flutter about us in the gloom.
We feel that there is no escape from the prison-house of pain.
But God in his loving kindness has set on the invisible wall
the lamp of faith—whose beams shall guide us back to the sunlit world
where work and friends and service await us.*

HELEN KELLER

The Journey Continues

Most of the more intense reactions of grief subside within 6 to 12 months.
However, the saying "once bereaved, always bereaved" still remains true.
There are some parts of the loss that will continue to be with the griever
until she or he dies.

THERESE RANDO

The journey continues. We hope that these letters and contacts have been helpful during this past year. This year has been a time of many changes for you. Some may have been very painful. Some may have been good. Our prayer is that this year has been a healing journey for you.

In early Christianity, the day on which an individual died was celebrated as his *dies natalis,* the "day of birth" into the divine world. You have experienced a death—either of a loved one or something else important to you. You may not feel like celebrating this experience just yet, but perhaps you can see ways in which this has been a new birth. Now is a time to reflect on the gifts God has given you, including the love of God reflected through your loved one, blessings of friends, and hope and faith in life everlasting.

At this point, our letter ministry will end, but our contacts with you on special days will continue throughout this coming year.

Please let us know of ways that we can continue to support you. Thank you for the privilege of being able to come into your home through visits and letters. God bless you as the journey of life and love continues.

These, then, are my last words to you:
Be not afraid of life.
Believe that life is worth living, and
Your belief will help create the fact.

WILLIAM JAMES

Grieving Children

Setting Up a Program of Bereavement Care for Grieving Children

Children are often forgotten during the grieving process. Yet children also experience deep grief, and they need our help in working through it. Of course, in many cases a grieving child will have parents and siblings experiencing grief from the same loss, and in those cases you will need to coordinate your care of the entire family. When you are working with a grieving family, you will need to support the adults, while also enabling them to meet the needs of their grieving children. (To that end, we have included Initial Packet materials for the parents of the grieving child as well as for the child.) You may find it helpful to have some conversations together with the whole family, but children also need to have their own individual grief addressed.

If possible, encourage inclusion of children in the grieving process from the very beginning. It can be very meaningful to children to be included in preparing and even participating in the funeral.

Initial Contact

You should make an initial visit to the grieving child as soon as possible. The following materials are designed to be given to the parents of the grieving child at your initial visit:

Children's Developmental Responses to Death	(page 55 and page 56, 57-58, or 59-62)
Children Need Help With the Grieving Process	(page 63)
Suggested Activities for You and Your Child	(pages 64-65)
Suggested Reading for Parents on Children's Grieving	(pages 66-67)

Choosing Books for Children on Death   (page 68)
Suggested Reading for Children on Death   (pages 69-70
                                                          or 71-72)

Support Groups and Organizations for Grieving
    Children and Teens   (page 73)

(Please note that there are variations depending on the age of the young person.)

The following materials are designed to be given to the grieving child at your initial visit:

Physical Symptoms of Grieving for Grade-Schoolers   (page 74)
Taking Care of Yourself   (page 75)
Prayer   (page 76)
Meditation   (pages 77-78)
Suggested Reading for Children on
Death   (pages 69-70
                                                          or 71-72)

Support Groups and Organizations for Grieving
    Children and Teens   (page 73)

If the grieving child is not yet in school, "Prechooler's Page" (page 79) should be given at your initial visit.

Monthly Messages

In addition, the following Monthly Messages should be used during the first year of bereavement (see pages 19-21 for instructions on incorporating these messages into personalized letters or otherwise including them in bereavement care):

You and Your Emotions	(page 80)	1 month after loss
Drawing My Emotions	(page 82)	2 months after loss
When We Die, We Go to Heaven, Right?	(page 83)	3 months after loss
Making a Memory Book	(page 84)	4 months after loss
Write a Letter	(page 85)	5 months after loss
Returning to "Normal"	(page 43)	6 months after loss
Complete the Sentences	(page 86)	7 months after loss
Write Your Own Poem or Story About the Person Who Died	(page 87)	8 months after loss
Draw the Person Who Died	(page 87)	9 months after loss
How Will I Know When I'm Feeling Better?	(page 87)	10 months after loss
Create a Ritual	(page 88)	11 months after loss
The Journey Continues	(page 88)	one year after loss

Ongoing Visitation

Please note that children benefit from having consistent contact with familiar people. While you might have a team of bereavement ministers who take turns visiting grieving adults, you should try to have the same bereavement minister(s) work consistently with each child.

Four- to Seven-Year-Olds

Four- to seven-year-olds will benefit from a couple of visits, the first one to two weeks after the death and another anywhere from three to six months later.

A meeting in the home is most appropriate. Bring colors, markers, chalk, or paint and paper and ask the child to draw a picture of the person who died. Suggest that she or he add herself or himself to the picture. Or the child may want to draw a picture of the funeral. Ask her or him to tell you about it.

You may want to show the pictures on page 79 to the child and ask her or him to point to the face that shows the way the child feels right now, the way she or he feels when thinking about the person who died, the way she or he feels when visiting the cemetery, etc.

Bring along a book on grieving (see book list on pages 69-70) that the child can keep until your next visit, and have her or his parents read it to her or him.

Encourage the child to draw more pictures, and tell the child you would like to see her or him next time you visit.

Seven- to Fourteen-Year-Olds

Present the child with the Initial Packet materials one to two weeks after the death. Go through the material together and explain to the child that she or he will be receiving letters, poems, or memory sheets in the mail once a month which talk about grieving.

Try to make an appointment every three months with the child, unless you sense a need for more time. Making an appointment to go to a park or restaurant may be fun for the child and allow her or him to express emotions she or he may not be able to express around other family members.

At the three-month appointment, go over the second month's mailing on "Drawing My Emotions" and the current month's mailing "When We Die, We Go to Heaven, Right?" Have the child draw a picture of heaven and the person who died. Have fun dreaming up what she or he thinks heaven will be like. How will she or he get around? By motorcycle? By flying? What will she or he be wearing? What will she or he be singing? What will she or he be doing?

Bring along a folder marked "My Memory Book" with empty pages for the child to put in favorite pictures of her or his loved one. The child can then place pictures she or he has already drawn in the folder and be ready for the following months' mailings. Encourage her or him to work on it before your next visit.

At the six-month appointment, go over the child's "Memory Book" and the Monthly Messages for months four through six. If the child has received a special item that belonged to her or his loved one, have her or him share it with you.

At the nine-month appointment, you may or may not need to make a visit with the child.

At the twelve-month appointment or anniversary visit, try to make a final appointment with the child (if you plan to end bereavement care at this time) as close as possible to the anniversary of the day the person died. Talk about "anniversary reactions" with her or him, explaining that she or he will probably feel sad or think about the person a lot more around this time, maybe for the rest of her or his life. She or he will probably also feel sadness at major events such as confirmation and graduation.

You may wish to go through the ritual that the child developed (Monthly Message for the eleventh month—"Create a Ritual") unless the family has decided to observe this ritual together privately.

Children's Developmental Responses to Death

*If handled with warmth and understanding,
a child's early experience with the death of someone loved
can by an opportunity to learn about life and living
as well as death and dying.*

DR. ALAN D. WOLFELT

Major factors influencing the child's response to death include the following:

1. The relationship with the person who has died—the "meaning of death."
2. The nature of the death—when, how, and where the person died.
3. The child's own personality and previous experiences with death.
4. The child's chronological and developmental age.
5. The availability of family/social/community support.
6. Most important, the behavior, attitudes, and responsiveness of parents and other significant adults in the child's environment.

(Taken from *Helping Children Cope with Grief,* by Alan D. Wolfelt, Ph.D., Accelerated Development, 1983.)

Children's Developmental Responses to Death

Children Three Years Old and Younger

Infants and toddlers do not intellectually comprehend the death of a loved one, but they do know that someone important is gone, and they miss certain elements like the person's smell and voice. As Dr. Wolfelt says, "If children are old enough to love, they are old enough to grieve."

They can also sense the emotions of the caregiver and may respond by becoming more fussy, by eating more or eating less, waking up in the middle of the night, reacting physically by having more colds, diarrhea, etc. They may regress, and children who were once potty-trained may need to start wearing diapers again, or become more clingy. It just means that the child is upset by the death; eventually, they will return to their old patterns.

What you can do:

1. Keep as regular a schedule as you can.

2. Comfort them with singing, rocking, cuddling, or reading stories together.

3. If at all possible, don't try to wean them from the bottle or the breast at this time, start a new child care arrangement, move them from the crib to the bed, or start potty-training.

Children's Developmental Responses to Death

Four- to Seven-Year-Olds

Preschoolers up through first-graders have difficulty with the concept of time. A child may be told, "Daddy is dead and is gone forever," but she or he may think of "forever" as being no different than a few hours and may shortly ask again where Daddy is.

Children this age think dead people keep doing the same things they did on earth like eating or going to the bathroom and may worry about them. They may think the person can feel them walk over the top of the grave.

Preschoolers often view death like sleep and therefore think they can wake them up. Play sometimes revolves around being dead and acting it out.

Sometimes children will "see" or sense the person who died around them. You may hear remarks such as "I talked with Grandpa the other day."

They also use magical thinking and assume that if you wish or pray for someone to come back to life they will. They may have wished that person dead at one point and then believe that their thoughts somehow resulted in that person's death.

They will be fearful and uncertain about whether they will die, who will take care of them, who will die next, how they will live without their mother or father, etc. They may display these fears through behaviors such as hitting and demanding, and hoarding food or toys. They may have trouble sleeping and eating. They may have physical reactions to the death such as stomachaches, headaches, rashes, and increase in colds or an aggravation of their allergies.

You may also see regressive behaviors such as baby talking, clinging, inability to control their bladder and bowels, and thumb-sucking.

What you can do:

1. Be consistent with your answers when a child has asked for the twelfth time that day, "Where's Daddy?" Use words like "dead," "died," or "killed." Euphemisms such as "gone on a trip," "went away," "resting," "we lost him," or "sleeping" can be confusing for children. Children can sometimes become fearful about going to sleep at night, linking sleep with death.

2. When children ask about the body and how it can eat, go to the bathroom, etc., provide them with simple answers such as "When someone dies, the eyes don't see any more, and the person can't eat."

3. Playing is a way for children to express themselves. They may act out "dying" or "dead" as a natural way of expressing their emotions and dealing with the death. Allow such play to go on.

4. Sometimes children will experience the person who died by either seeing them, hearing them, feeling them, or smelling them. Often they are told by others that they must be seeing things. Instead, take them seriously and ask them questions about what the person said, what she or he looked like, etc. Often, these experiences are wonderful and comforting for children. They remind us of our belief that there is life after death and that the living and the dead are both part of the "communion of saints."

5. Ask your child to pray for the person who died. Occasionally share your memories of that person.

6. If your child thinks that she or he "wished" the person dead, reassure her or him that wishing does not make people die, no matter how angry we are.

7. If your child is fearful about who will take care of her or him, listen to those fears and validate them by confirming that those are scary feelings. Then reassure her or him that she or he will be taken care of—and by whom, and when.

8. If your child is exhibiting hitting or biting behaviors, explain that it is not okay to hurt other people, and remove the child from the other children. If you notice other changes in sleeping or eating, such as thumb-sucking, etc., just let it go. Provide comfort and reassure the child, and eventually these behaviors will disappear.

9. If the child is experiencing more colds, stomachaches, etc., try to not rush her or him to the doctor. Instead, provide lots of comfort in the form of hot water bottles, cuddling on the couch and reading stories, singing gentle songs, more blankets if they're cold, etc.

10. Read stories about grieving together (see book list on pages 69-70).

11. Last, save something that belonged to the person who died that your child could appreciate now (sometimes clothing that still has the scent of the person who died is comforting) and maybe also something she or he could appreciate when she or he grows up.

Children's Developmental Responses to Death

Seven- to Fourteen-Year-Olds

First- through third-graders are just beginning to view death as final. They know that death can happen to young and old and that death has many different causes, but they don't believe that it will happen to anyone they love or to them. They have an active fantasy life and are often curious about what happens to the body after death. They may also personify death as a person, like the "bogeyman," and think they can hide from him.

First- through third-graders may still be able to describe seeing, hearing, or smelling the person who has died. Once they start to transition over into the adult world, they may experience the person who died more in their dreams.

Third- through eighth-graders are making the transition into the adult view of death. They understand that death is final and irreversible. They are also curious about death and what happens to the body, but they are beginning to have a better understanding of biology and how the body works.

They may begin by thinking that death is connected to being bad, and then later begin to see that people died for different reasons. They may, however, still believe that their thinking caused the death (as in "wishing" their brother dead) or that they could have prevented an accident from happening.

They may find it difficult to concentrate on their school work and find their grades slipping. They may lack energy to go out with friends or participate in their extracurricular activities. That is a normal part of grieving because of the emotional energy required to heal.

You may find them "acting out" their grieving or regressing to previous behaviors they had as young children such as becoming afraid of the dark, throwing tantrums, having nightmares, clinging, thumb-sucking, wetting the bed, or being afraid of new places and new experiences.

They may become aggressive and rebellious and become the "bad" child, thinking they somehow deserve to be punished. Or they may try to become the "perfect" child. Both are ways to try to overcome the helpless feeling they are experiencing.

They may be fearful about who will take care of them, what will happen if the other parent dies, where will the money come from, etc. As a physical expression of their fears, they may talk nonstop, or hoard toys or food in trying to gain some control over their lives.

They may have difficulty sleeping and difficulty with eating. They may experience headaches, stomachaches, rashes, symptoms of the illness the person who died had, difficulty breathing, and aggravation of their allergies.

What you can do:

1. If the children are curious about what happens to the body after death, give them concrete answers: "The body cannot breathe or walk or talk anymore." Sometimes what they dream up in their head is scarier than reality. Relate the dying to nature and how all things have to die at some time. You can talk to the child about the "spiritual body" that goes to heaven when a person dies.

2. Children may report to an adult that they have spoken to a loved one who is dead. They are often told, "You can't be talking to Grandma. You must be hearing things." These experiences, however, can be wonderful and comforting for children, and unless they feel openness in the adults around them, they probably won't want to talk about it.

3. Ask your child to pray for the person who died and share memories together about the person, sad and happy.

4. Children grieve in cycles or "doses." Don't be surprised if the child is sad and crying one minute and the next minute she or he is out playing. They can only take so much at a time.

5. If your child thinks that she or he "wished" the person dead or could have somehow prevented the death, reassure her or him that being angry and having thoughts about that person dying didn't cause the death. If the child feels guilty, thinking she or he could have somehow prevented the death, help her or him go through the events before the death and look at the reality of the situation. If the child feels guilty because the loved one died before she or he could apologize after a fight, have her or him write a letter to that person. Pray with the child, asking God for forgiveness and asking the person who died to forgive the child. Sometimes writing a letter to the person who died provides a good release of emotions and a sense that the person is listening. Burning the letter can have a powerful effect on the child as a symbol of her or his thoughts going up to the person who died.

6. Reassure her or him that she or he will be taken care of, that you are in good health (if you are), that there will be enough money for clothes and food and toys (if there is), etc.

7. Withdrawing from people and depression can be a natural part of the grieving process. But if you observe constant sadness, extreme withdrawal from family and friends, severe anger or listlessness, or use of alcohol or drugs, especially if persistent, seek professionals who are knowledgeable in the area of grieving.

8. "Acting-out" behaviors and rebelliousness need attention. Telling your child to "grow up" or "straighten up" when you see regressive behaviors will not help. All these behaviors are normal, and it is a way for children to deal with their sense of helplessness. Instead, listen to them, acknowledge their scary feelings, their guilty feelings, their sad feelings, even their feelings of relief (especially after a long illness) and tell them about your own feelings.

9. Model "good grieving." Show children that it's okay to cry and feel sad when you talk about the person who died. Tell them it's okay to have angry feelings that the person who died had to leave so soon, etc. Don't assume they don't want to talk about the person who died because it will upset them. At points, it may seem that's all they want to talk about. Let them talk for hours if they need to. Restate in your own words what your child is saying to let her or him know you are listening: "You're angry that daddy had to die." Don't immediately rush in and try to make them feel better. Your gift of listening will aid in their recovery.

10. Buy your child a notebook or journal in which to write down her or his thoughts and feelings. Putting emotions down on paper is very therapeutic. (Your bereavement minister can provide a set of reflections that may be useful in journaling.)

11. Emotions during this time may run high, and children's feelings will fluctuate from being sad, to being silly with their friends, to angry, etc. Your child may not be sure how to feel. Reassure her or him that she or he is not going crazy. It's a normal part of the process of grieving.

12. Try not to push the child into a premature adult role by suggesting that she or he become the "woman" or the "man" of the house. The child may need to do extra chores to help out, but she or he shouldn't have the responsibilities that the person who died had.

13. If you can't think of anything to talk about or your words don't seem to be coming out right, just hold or hug your child. She or he needs to feel your physical support.

14. Acknowledge physical reactions to grieving such as the stomachaches, headaches, etc. If they are having trouble sleeping, try using relaxing music or progressive relaxation. If they are having trouble eating, don't force them. Rashes, stomachaches, headaches, etc., will eventually go away. Explain to them that these are normal reactions that many children have after someone has died. Reassure them that they are normal and okay.

15. Read to them or get them books to read on grieving.

16. If a children's support group is available in the area, sign them up, if it's okay with them. Being around other children who have had someone die is a very comforting and "normalizing" experience.

17. Let your child know it's okay to laugh. Children may think that they didn't love the one who died or that they are being disrespectful if they can laugh. Remind your child that it's okay and that she or he may need to take a break from mourning.

18. Let your child have something that belonged to the person who died. A piece of clothing that smells like the person, favorite piece of jewelry, a painting, etc., will acknowledge that you thought of the child.

19. Accept your child's friends. They can help your child sort out feelings, keep your child company, and keep her or him busy. One exception, of course, is if you suspect your child's friends of aiding your child through buying alcohol or drugs, which will interfere and delay the grieving process.

20. If your child is away at school, try to include her or him in the funeral services. A child's grieving process may be extended if she or he isn't able to participate.

Children Need Help With the Grieving Process

Here are a few things to keep in mind as you help your child through her or his grief:

1. Children worry about the emotions and behavior of their parents. ("Daddy, why don't you stop smoking?")

2. Children do not necessarily stay focused on the loss. They may be grieving one minute and laughing and playing the next. They may say things that are surprising and unnerving. Parents may interpret this as a seeming lack of concern or love. They can be remarkably honest and straightforward about the death, which may trigger more grief by the parents.

3. Children may grieve intensely without giving much evidence of it. They may be trying to suppress their own emotions. They may daydream. Some grieve privately. They may avoid new attachments. Others may become overly friendly and inappropriate. They become difficult to understand. They may have physical symptoms or a variety of accidents, cuts, and bruises to seek attention. They may regress to behavior they had previously outgrown.

4. Children's grief may be expressed through angry outbursts, fights, poor grades, or other ways of calling attention to themselves. They may be angry that they are being left alone. If parents are distracted because of their own grief, children may become preoccupied with meeting their own needs.

For children mourning the loss of a sibling:

1. The loss of a sibling brings about fear and insecurity. The surviving children may become clinging and demanding. They might worry about their own death or the death of their parents. ("Am I next?")

2. Children may feel a strong sense of "survivor guilt" or direct guilt if they feel they did something to cause the death. A history of pre-existing conflict with a sibling also predisposes children to guilt. They may consciously or subconsciously identify their feelings of anger as contributing to their sibling's death.

3. The parental idealization and preoccupation with the memory of the dead sibling may cause a child to feel unloved. A child may feel her or his life is being lived in the shadow of the one who was lost.

4. The child may overidentify with the deceased sibling and try to take on her or his characteristics or meet expectations reserved for the child. She or he may see her or his sibling as all "good" and herself or himself as "bad."

(Taken from "Children Need Help with the Grieving Process," by Val Farmer, 1988.)

Suggested Activities for You and Your Child

Here some suggestions for activities which may help both you and your child in working through the grieving process.

1. Take a nature walk. Look at dead and living things and talk about the difference.

2. Make a follow-up visit to the funeral home or cemetery to talk about the events that took place there. You will need to check with the funeral director.

3. Share your own feelings (it helps the child not feel alone in her or his own feelings) and your personal faith.

4. If the child is angry, help her or him direct these feelings by
   - painting or coloring
   - writing about these feelings, perhaps in a journal (Your bereavement minister can provide a set of reflections that may be useful in journaling.)
   - working with clay
   - making bread together
   - pounding nails to make a birdhouse
   - doing some type of physical exercise like going for a walk, bowling, swimming, tennis

5. If there are regrets,
   - record a message to the person who died (speaking feelings out loud is helpful)
   - write a letter
   - draw, color, or paint
   - write a note tied to a balloon and let it go into the sky

6. Include lots of hugging and loving touch.

7. Select and talk about a special keepsake of the person who died.

8. Look through photographs together.

9. Put together a scrapbook about the person who died. Write down her or his favorite foods, color, things she or he did, things that made you laugh or made you mad, what she or he was good at or not so good at, what she or he always said to you, and things you miss and don't miss about that person.

10. View home movies of the person who died.

11. Try the game, "I remember when. . . ."

12. Make up a play about the person who died.

13. Talk about dreams and draw them out.

14. Read a good book about death together.

(These suggestions adapted from *The Grieving Child*, by Helen Fitzgerald, Simon & Schuster, 1992.)

Suggested Reading for Parents on Children's Grieving

There are several resources you can use in locating these titles: your local library (and inter-library loan system), your church library, bookstores, your bereavement minister's personal library, local support groups' lending libraries, hospices, and funeral homes.

Remember, if a book doesn't seem to make sense right now, try reading it again later.

About Dying. S. B. Stein. Walker and Co., 1974.

Adolescence and Death. J. McNeil and C. Corr, eds. Springer, 1986.

Adolescents and Death. G. L. Baxter and W. Stuart.

Are You Sad Too? Helping Children Deal with Loss & Death. D. Seibert. ETR, 1993.

Bereaved Children & Teens: A Support Guide for Parents & Professionals. E. A. Grollman, ed. Beacon, 1995.

Books to Help Children Cope with Separation & Loss, 2nd Edition. J. E. Bernstein. R.R. Bowker Company, 1983.

A Child's Parent Dies: Studies in Childhood Bereavement. E. Furman. Yale University Press, 1974.

Childhood & Death. H. Wass and C. Corr, eds. Hemisphere, 1984.

Children Are Not Paperdolls: A Visit with Bereaved Siblings. E. Levy. Counseling Consultants, 1982.

Children Mourning, Mourning Children. K. Doka, ed. Hospice Foundation of America, 1995.

Comforting Those Who Grieve. D. Manning. HarperSan Francisco, 1987.

Don't Take My Grief Away: What to Do When You Lose a Loved One. D. Manning. HarperSan Francisco, 1984.

For Those Who Live: Helping Children Cope with the Death of a Brother or Sister. K. LaTour. K. Latour, 1983.

Grief in Children: A Handbook for Adults. A. Dyregrov. Taylor and Francis, 1991.

The Grieving Child: A Parent's Guide. H. Fitzgerald. Simon & Schuster, 1992.

Helping Children Cope with Death. R. Dodd. Herald, 1984.

Helping Children Cope with Death: Guidelines and Resources. H. Wass and C. Corr, eds. Hemisphere, 1984.

Helping Children Cope with Grief. A. Wolfedt. Accel Develop., 1983.

Helping Children Cope with Separation and Loss. C. L. Jarratt. Harvard Common Press, 1994.

Helping Children Grieve. T. Huntley. Augsburg Fortress, 1991.

How Do We Tell the Children: A Parent's Guide to Helping Children Understand and Cope when Someone Dies. D. Schaefer and C. Lyons. Newmarket Press, 1988.

How It Feels When A Parent Dies. J. Krementz. Knopf, 1982.

I Had a Friend Named Peter: Talking to Children about the Death of a Friend. J. Cohn. Morrow, 1987.

Kid's Book About Death and Dying. E. Rofes. Little, 1985.

Learning to Say Good-Bye: When a Child's Parent Dies. E. LeShan. Avon, 1978.

Life & Loss: A Guide to Help Grieving Children. L. Goldman. Accel Develop., 1994.

Lifetimes: The Beautiful Way to Explain Death to Children. B. Mellonie and R. Ingpen. Bantam, 1983.

On Life After Death. E. Kubler-Ross. Celestial Arts, 1991.

One Hundred Fifty Facts about Grieving Children. E. Linn. Pub. Mark., 1990.

Questions and Answers on Death and Dying. E. Kubler-Ross. Macmillan, 1993.

Sad But O.K. My Daddy Died Today: A Child's View of Death. B. Juneau. Blue Dolphin Publishing, 1988.

The Seasons of Grief: Helping Children Grow Through Loss. D. Gaffney. Plume, 1988.

The Secret Places: The Story of a Child's Adventure with Grief. J. Campbell. Centering Corporation, 1992.

Should the Children Know? Encounters with Death in the Lives of Children. M. Rudolph. Schocken Books, 1978.

Talking About Death: A Dialogue Between Parent and Child. E. A. Grollman. Beacon, 1991.

Tell Me About Death, Tell Me About Funerals. E. Corley. Grammatical Sci., 1973.

Tell Me Papa. J. Johnson and M. Johnson. Center for Thanatology, 1980.

Tell Me Papa: A Family Book for Children's Questions about Death and Funerals. (Grades 2-7) J. Johnson and M. Johnson. Centering Corporation, 1978.

Telling a Child About Death. E. N. Jackson. Hawthorn Books, 1965.

Unspoken Grief: Coping with Childhood Sibling Loss. H. Rosen. Lexington Books, 1986.

When A Parent Is Very Sick. E. LeShan. Joy Street Books, 1986.

Choosing Books
for Children on Death

Good books can help children to identify and express their feelings. Dr. Stephen A. Timm, a child psychologist, shares these thoughts about choosing books for children:

- Allow for unhurried reading and for pauses with questions and discussion.

- Choose books with real characters rather than educational books that speak only to the intellect.

- Choose books that use realistic terms.

- Pick a story that portrays adults responding effectively to the child's loss.

- Choose a story that provides hope.

(Taken from "Magic News," a publication by Dr. Stephen Timm, Fargo, N.D.)

Suggested Reading For Three- to Seven-Year-Olds on Grief

There are several resources you can use in locating these titles: your local library (and inter-library loan system), your church library, bookstores, your bereavement minister's personal library, local support groups' lending libraries, hospices, and funeral homes.

Remember, if a book doesn't seem to make sense right now, try reading it again later.

General

Aarvy Aardvark Finds Hope: A Read-Aloud Story for People of All Ages. D. O'Toole. Compassion, 1989.

About Dying. S. B. Stein. Walker & Co., 1984.

A Bunch of Balloons: A Book-Workbook for Grieving Children. D. Ferguson. Centering Corporation, 1992. (Grade 1-6).

Fall of Freddie the Leaf. L. Buscaglia. C. B. Slack, 1982.

Giving Tree. S. Silverstein. Harper & Row, 1964.

Life and Death in Third Grade. M. Burns and C. Burns. Empey Enterprises, 1987.

Lifetimes: The Beautiful Way to Explain Death to Children. B. Mellonie and R. Ingpen. Bantam, 1983.

Tell Me Papa: A Family Book for Children's Questions About Death and Funerals. J. Johnson and M. Johnson. Centering Corporation, 1987.

Thumpy's Story: A Story of Love and Grief Shared. N. Dodge. 1986.

Velveteen Rabbit. M. Williams. Knopf, 1983.

Waterbugs and Dragonflies. D. Stickney. 1982.

When I Die, Will I Get Better? J. Breebaart and P. Breebaart. Bedrick Books, 1993.

When Someone Very Special Dies: Children Can Learn to Cope with Grief. M. Heegaard. Woodland Press, 1988.

Loss of a Parent

After Charlotte's Mom Died. C. Spelman. A. Whitman, 1996.

The Day Before Christmas. E. Bunting. Clarion Books, 1992.

Everett Anderson's Good-bye. L. Clifton. Holt, Rinehart, & Winston, 1983.

My Daddy Died: When Someone You Love Dies and You Need to Tell a Child. R. Andersen. Andersen Enterprises, 1994.

My Mom Is Dying: A Child's Diary. J. McNamara. Augsburg Fortress, 1994.

The Princess in the Kitchen Garden. A. Heymans. Farrar, Straus & Giroux, 1993.

Saying Goodbye to Daddy. J. Vigna. A. Whitman, 1991.

When My Dad Died: A Child's View of Death. J. Hammond. Cranbrook, 1980.

When My Mommy Died: A Child's View of Death. J. Hammond. Cranbrook, 1980.

Loss of a Grandparent

Allison's Grandfather. L. Peavy. American Printing House, 1984.

Another Christmas. S. Roth. Morrow Junior Books, 1992.

Christmas Moon. D. Cazet. Bradbury Press, 1984.

Come Back, Grandma. S. Limb. Knopf, 1994.

Eleanor, Arthur, and Claire. D. Engel. Macmillan, 1992.

Fox Song. J. Bruchac. Philomel Books, 1993.

Grandad Bill's Song. J. Yolen. Philomel Books, 1994.

Grandpa's Chair. T. Thornton and S. Thornton. Multnomah Press, 1987.

The Happy Funeral. Eve Bunting. Harper & Row, 1982.

Looking for Atlantis. C. Thompson. Knopf, 1994.

My Grandpa Died Today. J. Fassler. Human Sciences Press, 1971.

My Grandson Lew. C. Zolotow. HarperCollins, 1974.

Nana Upstairs and Nana Downstairs. T. dePaola. Penguin, 1978.

Pop's Secret. M. Townsend and A. Stern. Addison-Wesley, 1980.

Saying Good-bye to Grandma. J. Thomas. Clarion Books, 1988.

Talking About Death. E. Grollman. Beacon, 1991.

The Two of Them. A. Brandenberg. Greenwillow Books, 1979.

Waiting for the Whales. S. McFarlane. Philomel Books, 1993.

What Happened When Grandma Died. P. Barker. Concordia, 1984.

When Grandpa Died. M. Stevens and K. Ualand. Children's Press, 1979.

Loss of a Sibling

A Birthday Present for Daniel: A Child's Story of Loss. J. Rothman. Prometheus Books, 1996.

Children Are Not Paper Dolls: A Visit with Bereaved Siblings. E. Linn. Pub. Mark., 1982.

Last Week My Brother Anthony Died. M. Hickman. 1984.

No New Baby: For Boys and Girls Whose Expected Sibling Dies. M. Gryte. Centering Corporation, 1988.

Where's Jess? J. Johnson and M. Johnson. Centering Corporation, 1982.

Loss of a Friend

I Had a Friend Named Peter: Talking to Children About the Death of a Friend. J. Cohn. Morrow, 1987.

Suggested Reading For Seven- to Fourteen-Year-Olds on Grief

There are several resources you can use in locating these titles: your local library (and inter-library loan system), your church library, bookstores, your bereavement minister's personal library, local support groups' lending libraries, hospices, and funeral homes.

Remember, if a book doesn't seem to make sense right now, try reading it again later.

General

Am I Still A Sister? A. Sims. Big A, 1993.

Death Is Natural. L. Pringle.

Geranium Morning: A Book About Grief. S. Powell, Lerner Group, 1991. (Grades 1-4)

Grover. V. Cleaver and B. Cleaver. New American Library, 1975.

Growing Up When Someone You Know Has Died. R. Schenkerman. Bar For At-Risk, 1993.

The Kid's Book About Death and Dying/By and For Kids. E. Rofes. Little, Brown, 1985.

Life and Death. H. Zim. Morrow, 1970.

Life and Death in Third Grade. M. Burns and C. Burns. Empey Enterprises, 1987.

Living with Death. M. Cera. Good Apple, 1991. (Grades 1-4)

Missing May: A Novel. C. Rylant. Orchard Books, 1992.

My Guardian Angel in My Mourning. R. Shay. CSSOH, 1996.

A Taste of Blackberries. D. Smith. T. Y. Crowell, 1973.

Tell Me About Death, Tell Me About Funerals. E. Corley. Grammatical Sci., 1973.

The Three Birds: A Story for Children About the Loss of a Loved One. M. Van den Berg. Imagination Press, 1994.

Thumpy's Story: A Story of Love and Grief Shared. N. Dodge. 1986.

Walk Two Moons. S. Creech. HarperCollins, 1994.

What Do They Do in Heaven All Day? S. Thomas. Our Family Lines, 1995.

What Makes Me Feel This Way. E. LeShan. Macmillan, 1974.

When Someone Very Special Dies: Children Can Learn to Cope with Grief. M. Heegaard. Woodland Press, 1988.

When Someone You Love Dies. W. Coleman. Augsburg Fortress, 1994.

When Someone You Love Dies: An Explanation of Death for Children. R. Dodd. Abingdon Press, 1986.

When Something Terrible Happens: Children Can Learn to Cope with Grief Workbook, M. Heegard. Woodland Press, 1992.

Loss of a Parent

How it Feels When a Parent Dies. J. Krementz. Knopf, Inc., 1981.

Learning to Say Good-bye: When a Parent Dies. E. LeShan. Avon Books, 1976.

Mama's Going to Buy You a Mocking Bird. J. Little. Puffin Books, 1986.

My Daddy Died Today: A Child's View of Death, B. Juneau. Dolphin Publishing, 1988.

My Mom Is Dying: A Child's Diary. J. McNamara. Augsburg Fortress, 1994.

Pennies for the Piper. S. McLean. Farrar, Strauss & Giroux, 1993.

When My Mommy Died: A Child's View of Death. J. Hammond. Cranbrook Publishing, 1980.

Loss of a Grandparent

Annie and the Old One. M. Miles. Little, 1972.

Blackberries in the Dark. M. Jukes. Knopf, 1995.

Grandpa's Berries: A Story to Help Children Understand Grief and Loss. J. Dickerson. Cherubic Press, 1995.

My Grandmother's Cookie Jar. M. Miller. Price Stern Sloan, 1987.

The Remembering Box. E. Clifford. Houghton Mifflin, 1985.

So Long, Grandpa. E. Donnelly. Crown Publishing, 1981.

What Happened When Grandma Died. P. Barker. Concordia, 1984.

What Will We Do Without a Grandpa? C. Nelson. Heather Hill, 1995.

Who Will Take Care of Me? P. Hermes. Harcourt Brace Jovanovich, 1983.

Why Did Grandma Have to Die? K. Randle. Bookcraft, 1987.

Why Did Grandpa Die? B. Hazen. Western, 1985.

Loss of a Sibling

All Shining in the Spring: The Story of a Baby Who Died. L. Blackburn. Centering Corporation, 1989.

Beat the Turtle Drum. C. Greene. Viking Press, 1976.

The Magic Moth. V. Lee.

A Summer to Die. L. Lowry. Houghton Mifflin, 1977.

Tawny. C. Carner. Macmillan, 1978.

Loss of a Friend

Timothy Duck: The Story of the Death of a Friend. L. Blackburn. Centering Corporation, 1989.

# *Support Groups and Organizations for Grieving Children and Teens*

It is one of the most beautiful compensations of this life
that no man can seriously help another
without helping himself.

RALPH WALDO EMERSON

Rainbows
1111 Tower Rd.
Schaumburg, IL 60173
1-708-310-1880

(Newsletters, information, and referral for children and adults grieving painful transitions such as death and divorce. Information for schools, churches, and social agencies.)

Twinless Twin Support Group
c/o Dr. Brandt
11220 St. Joe Rd.
Fort Wayne, IN 46835-9737
1-219-627-5414

(Newsletters, guidelines, and assistance in starting local group, referral, phone support, pen pals, and conferences for those who have lost a twin.)

Physical Symptoms of Grieving for Grade-Schoolers

Right now you may be feeling funny. Lots of kids have physical feelings after somebody they loved has died. Some kids have:

- Headaches
- Stomachaches
- Difficulty sleeping
- Difficulty eating (eating too much or eating too little)
- Skin rashes
- Difficulty breathing or shortness of breath
- Allergies that get worse
- Nervous feelings or trembling
- Nightmares
- Low energy and a feeling of tiredness
- Tightness in their throat
- Muscles feeling weak

(Adapted from *Healing the Bereaved Child*, by Alan Wolfelt, Ph.D., Companion Press, 1996.)

If you have any of these physical feelings, don't worry. This is just the way the body sometimes expresses your emotions. It's also okay if you don't feel any of these physical feelings. Everybody is different. Eventually, these bodily feelings will go away. It helps to talk to somebody about the way your body is feeling and about your emotions. It also helps to cuddle or snuggle with a parent or favorite aunt or uncle. Holding hands or giving a big hug to someone can make you feel better and calm you down, as well as making the other person feel great.

If you have a bad or funny feeling that won't go away, just tell your mom or dad.

And Jesus took the children in his arms,
put his hands on them and blessed them.

MARK 10:16

Taking Care of Yourself

Here are some things that may help you as you deal with your loss:

1. Exercising. This allows you to let go of sad thoughts and feelings. Try walking around the block, rollerblading, or any other type of exercise you enjoy.

2. Crying.

3. Talking about your feelings with a parent, trusted friend, counselor, or your priest or minister.

4. Journaling. This just means writing your thoughts on paper. (Your bereavement minister can give you some reflections that may help you in journaling.) You may also want to write a letter to the person who died; then you may choose either to put it in a safe place or destroy it.

5. Praying—for the person who died and for yourself in coping with all the changes in your life.

6. Meditating and relaxing. These can offer you a time-out from your thoughts and emotions and allow you to heal.

7. Drawing, dancing, singing, or any other type of creative activity. Make up a song and sing it as loud as you can. Or paint the emotions inside of you.

8. Watching a funny movie. This offers another time-out from your emotions, and it feels good to laugh again.

9. Thanking God for the support you've received from friends and family, for books that have helped, etc. An attitude of thankfulness can be hard at first, but it will be important for the rest of your life.

10. Reading, reading, reading. The more you know about grieving and understand how other people have gone through it, the better.

11. Attending a healing service. That may sound "hokey," and God does hear your prayers when you pray alone, but God also works when two or more are gathered in his name. Prayers for help, prayers for healing, prayers for understanding can be very helpful when you're questioning your faith, when you just can't pray anymore, or when you just need support.

12. Making a "feel-good" box for those days when you're feeling especially down. Find a unique or pretty box and put stuff in there that is important to you or makes you feel special. Examples are: pictures, a card that has a great picture on it, a piece of jewelry, pieces of paper with special sayings or Bible passages on it, etc.

Prayer

Do all this in prayer, asking for God's help.
Pray on every occasion, as the Spirit leads.

EPHESIANS 6:18

What is prayer? Prayer is simply talking to God. We can talk to God using prayers like those said in church, or prayer can be like talking to a friend. When you talk with a friend, you talk for awhile and your friend listens. When your friend talks, you listen. Sometimes you want to be alone with your friend so you can share stories you don't want others to hear, so you may go to your bedroom, go for a walk, or go out to a restaurant. That's what it is like with God too.

You can talk to God anytime you like: at school, at home, at your sporting events, anywhere. Sometimes going for a walk in nature helps. Or having a special place in your home or bedroom may help you concentrate on God better.

Try the following:

1. Set a table with a candle, a picture of nature, a book, a cross, a picture of Jesus, or whatever you find peaceful.

2. Talk to God about whatever is troubling you. Share your feelings with God, draw a picture, or write in your journal. (Your bereavement minister can give you some reflections that may help you in journaling.)

3. Listen to God. It's hard to listen when you are around a lot of noise, so you might want to try turning off the television or radio. Then close your eyes and find the quiet place inside your heart where you can enter into this love-filled room and see God waiting for you. He has been eagerly awaiting your visit and has something to say to you. What do you hear?

4. Thank God for listening. Know that God hears your prayers and answers them in a way that God knows is best for you and for others. Remember, God is not the great "wish-giver" in the sky who gives you what you want. Talking to God, or praying, is having a friendship with God, a friendship like one with earthly friends, only better.

Meditation

May my meditation be pleasing to God, for rejoice in the Lord.

PSALM 104:34

What is meditation? Meditation is a way of quieting your body, your thoughts, and your feelings to hear God. It allows you to gain insight or wisdom about yourself and others and bring peace to your life. Meditation as a tool can improve your concentration and give you control over your emotions so they don't have control over you.

Start by practicing two to three minutes at the beginning, then work your way up. You can probably work your way up to five to ten minutes if you're in early grade school, ten to twenty minutes if you're in late grade school, and twenty to thirty minutes if you're in junior high or high school. Set a timer and make a chart for yourself keeping track of your progress. Some days will be harder than others and you may even fall asleep, which is okay.

If you're feeling restless before meditating, try stretching your back by bending forward, backward, and from side-to-side.

While you're meditating, if thoughts creep into your mind either let them pass through or write them down on a slip of paper. Then go back to concentrating on the exercise.

You can make up your own words to chant such as "love," "peace," "kindness," etc., or try using images from nature. The following exercise is one way to meditate. You may find it hard to read this sheet and meditate at the same time. If so, you may want to record the following instructions on tape. Then play it back so you can simply listen to the instructions instead of reading them. Or you could have someone else read the instructions to you.

> Start by sitting in an upright position (this can be in a chair or on the floor), uncross your legs (unless you are on the floor), and let your arms rest lightly on your lap. Close your eyes and take three deep breaths, breathing in through your nose and blowing out through your mouth. Starting with your feet, curl your toes and hold, 1, 2, 3, and relax. Slowly, work your way up from your feet, tightening each group of muscles to a count of three, and then relaxing. When you get to your head, scrunch

your entire face and hold to the count of three and relax. Take three more deep breaths, breathing in through your nose and out through your mouth, monitoring your body and making sure all your muscles are relaxed.

Next focus on the spot between your eyebrows. Concentrate on this area and imagine yourself breathing in through this spot in your forehead—breathing in the breath of God and blowing out anger. Breathe in peace and blow out fear. Breathe in love and blow out guilt. Next move your attention to your heart, and imagine yourself breathing in through this spot. Breathe in the breath of God and blow out anger. Breathe in peace and blow out fear. Breathe in love and blow out guilt. Still concentrating on your heart center, ask God your question or just "be" in God's presence. Listen for your answer. Remember it may not be what you think it should. Then, thank God before you go.

When you have finished meditating, begin by feeling your feet on the floor and your buttocks on the chair (or the floor, if you are sitting on the floor). Feel your fingers and start to move them and when you are ready, you can open your eyes.

You may want to write about your experience of meditating in a journal.

Preschooler's Page

Monthly Messages

You and Your Emotions

Death can turn your life upside-down. One minute you are sad and lonely; the next minute you're angry. Your emotions go back and forth, and sometimes they feel overwhelming. This is normal for people who are grieving! No matter what you're feeling, it is okay.

People are all different, and people will grieve in different ways and for different lengths of time. It is important to express your emotions in some way so you have control over your emotions rather than your emotions having control over you. Here are a few things to remember about emotions:

1. You are not your emotions. Your emotions and feelings come and go.

2. Feelings aren't good or bad; they just are.

3. It is okay to feel sad and cry. Even Jesus cried when his friend died. (John 11:35)

4. It is okay to feel anger. Many of the prophets of the Bible and even Jesus felt angry.

5. Know it is okay to feel happy, laugh, and have fun. You can't be sad all the time, and sometimes you just need to get your mind off the work of grieving and have fun with friends.

6. It's okay to feel guilty. You may have had a fight with the person who died or wished that person dead. Your wishing cannot kill anybody. Maybe you wished you had spent more time with the person or done what they asked you to do. If you are having a hard time with feelings of this kind, talk to God, to your parents, to a trusted friend, to your priest or minister, or try writing a letter to the person who died.

7. It's okay to feel afraid. You may be afraid because you're not sure who will take care of you or where the money will come from or if you'll have enough money for clothes or food. Sit down with your parent or trusted adult and discuss your concerns. Don't waste your needed energy in worrying.

> Look at the birds: they do not plant seeds, gather a harvest and put it in barns; yet your Father in heaven takes care of them! Aren't you worth much more than birds? Can any of you live a bit longer by worrying about it?.... So do not worry about tomorrow; it will have enough worries of it's own. There is no need to add to the troubles each day brings.
> —Matthew 6:26, 27, 34

8. It's okay to feel these feelings in your body. God built our bodies to handle stress. Look again at the sheet titled "Physical Symptoms of Grieving for Grade-Schoolers."

9. You may find that you actually feel relieved if a death ends a long illness or other difficult situation. This feeling can be hard to admit, but it's normal.

10. It's okay to feel worried or very scared. These feelings will pass, but they are uncomfortable. Try to be near people who you trust and ask for physical touch like hugs, cuddling, or holding hands.

11. It's okay not to feel anything. You may play with friends, laugh, and have fun after you hear about a death. It's one way people deal with a big shock.

12. Look at your "Taking Care of Yourself" sheet in your packet to help give you more ideas on handling your emotions.

For everything there is a season,
and a time for every matter under heaven . . .
a time to weep, and a time to laugh;
a time to mourn, and a time to dance. . . .

ECCLESIASTES 3:1-8

Drawing My Emotions

This is what I look like when I feel angry.
It's okay to feel angry.

I am angry about _____.

This is what I look like when I feel sad.
It's okay to feel sad.

I am sad about _____.

This is what I look like when I feel happy.
It's okay to feel happy.

I am happy about _____.

When We Die, We Go to Heaven, Right?

As Christians, we believe that after our physical bodies die, our souls go to heaven to be with God. What do you think heaven looks like? Draw a picture of heaven and how you think the person who died may be eating, sleeping, working, playing, traveling, and praying. What do you think they will look like? What do you think they will be wearing? Who else will be with that person?

Making a Memory Book

Answer the questions in the spaces provided or make your own special "book" by writing your answers out on sheets of paper and then stapling them together or placing them in a folder. If you make a memory book, you may want to include photos or other things.

The full name of the person who died_____

Where was that person born?_____

When was that person born?_____

When did that person die?_____

How old was the person when she/he died?_____

What was the person's favorite color?_____

What was the person's favorite story?_____

What was your favorite thing to do with the person?_____

_____

I liked the way the person used to_____

_____

I still think about that person when _____

_____

One special memory I have of the person who died is_____

_____

Put your favorite picture of the person who died here.

Write a Letter

Try writing a letter to the person who died. You may want to tell that person how much you miss her or him, how angry you are, or how you wish that she or he could be at your next activity. You may want to thank her or him or say you're sorry. Include whatever you want to say. This can be your good-bye letter.

Dear _____,

_____

_____

_____

_____

_____

_____

_____

_____

_____

_____

_____

_____

_____

_____

_____

_____

_____

_____

Complete the Sentences

I get angry when _____

_____

I am scared that _____

_____

I wish _____

_____

I am happy that _____

_____

My friends say _____

_____

The biggest challenge I continue to face is _____

_____

_____

The loss I have experienced has changed me by _____

_____

_____

The hardest thing I have to deal with is _____

_____

_____

Ways you will continue to live on in me are _____

_____

_____

Write Your Own Poem or Story
About the Person Who Died

Think back over your memories of your loved one, the experience of losing them, the funeral, or what you have experienced since then. Write a poem or story that expresses your feelings . . .

Draw the Person Who Died

Draw the person who died, using colored markers, paint, or chalk. Or draw something that reminds you of the person or represents the person to you.

How Will I Know When I'm Feeling Better?

The best answer to your question, "How will I know I am feeling better?" is one only you can answer because we are all so different. You will probably find you can talk about the person who died and not cry. You can see someone who looks like the person who died, or walks or talks like the person, but it doesn't upset you like it did at the beginning.

You are able to enjoy the holidays again. You are starting to have more energy and you are not as crabby. You will be able to start up new activities and feel like you can put yourself into them again. Some days you will still feel as though you are not really getting any better, but it is normal to feel that way.

As the months go by, you will probably experience something called "anniversary reactions." That just means that on the anniversary of the day that your loved one died, you may feel grumpy, sad, or restless. This is normal, and lots of kids feel this way. You may have these feelings for a long time or you may not. You can even have them a long time later like when you are confirmed or at your graduation. You may even have those kinds of feelings when you get married or have a baby and you wish your loved one could have been there to be with you. It doesn't happen to everybody, but just keep it in the back of your mind that it can happen and that you are not weird if it does.

You can do something on those special days such as placing a flower on the altar in memory of the person who died, keeping yourself busy by being with friends, or spending the time writing, drawing, or painting your feelings.

There are two important questions to answer as you continue in your journey of grieving:

What have I learned from this experience?
Where have I seen God working?

Create a Ritual

Maybe you would like to do something special to remember the person who died. Would you like to read a poem, go through your scrapbook, sing a song, play the person's favorite music, show some of your art work or dance? Maybe each person in your family could share a special memory she or he has of the person who died and light a candle.

Whatever you do, memories will be shared and memories will be built as you remember together.

Why don't you tell someone about your ideas?

The Journey Continues

This year for you has been a time of many feelings and many changes for you—some very painful and some perhaps good. I hope that these letters and visits have been helpful during this past year.

As Christians, we believe that God is always with us and helps us, and in the end God's love can help us get through even very hard times. God gives us many gifts, including family, friends, and a feeling of hope. Now would be a good time to think about the gifts God has given you.

At this point, you will stop getting letters as often, but you will still get one or two throughout this coming year.

Please let me know of ways that we can continue to support you. Thank you for the privilege of being able to come into your home through visits and letters. God bless you as your journey of life and love continues.

Grieving Teenagers

Setting Up a Program of Bereavement Care for Grieving Teenagers

Teens are often forgotten during the grieving process. This is a time when many are pulling away from their family and becoming independent adults; some have already left for college. Yet teens also experience deep grief—sometimes even deeper than the adults around them—and they need our help in working through it. Of course, in many cases a grieving teen will have parents and siblings experiencing grief from the same loss, and in those cases you will need to coordinate your care of the entire family. When you are working with a grieving family, you will need to support the adults, while also enabling them to meet the needs of their grieving teenagers. (To that end, we have included Initial Packet materials for the parents of the grieving teen.) You may find it helpful to have some conversations together with the whole family, but teens also need to have their own individual grief addressed.

If possible, encourage the inclusion of teens in the grieving process from the very beginning. It can be very meaningful to teens to be included in preparing and even participating in the funeral.

Initial Contact

As soon as possible, send the grieving teen a personalized "Initial Bereavement Letter," which includes information about the bereavement program and the monthly letters she or he will be getting. Let the teen know you would like to include her or him in your regular visits. This note or letter, on a special bereavement card or a note card with the church letterhead, should be sent out as soon as you hear about the news of the death. Include condolences about the loss, acknowledge that it may seem like a dream and be confusing, and tell the teen that you will try to make contact with her or him one to two weeks after the death.

If the clergy person performing the ceremony makes contact with the child at the funeral, you may not need to write this letter. Just let the young person know that you will be making a bereavement visit one to two weeks after the funeral.

After your letter has been received, you should call to set up an initial visit. At your initial visit, give the following materials to the parents of the grieving teen:

Teenagers' Developmental Responses to Death	(pages 93-95)
Teens Need Help With the Grieving Process	(page 96)
Suggested Activities for You and Your Teen	(page 97)
Suggested Reading for Parents on Teens' Grieving	(page 98)
Suggested Reading for Teens on Grief	(pages 99-101)
Support Groups and Organizations for Grieving Children and Teens	(page 73)

Also at your initial visit, give the following materials to the grieving teen:

Taking Care of Yourself	(page 102)
Prayer	(page 103)
Meditation	(pages 104-105)
Physical Symptoms of Grieving for Teens	(pages 106-107)
Exercise and Eating Right	(page 108)
Getting to Sleep	(page 32)
Suggested Reading for Teens on Grief	(pages 99-101)
Support Groups and Organizations for Grieving Children and Teens	(page 73)

Monthly Messages

In addition to visitation, the following Monthly Messages should be used during the first year of bereavement care (see pages 19-21 for instructions on incorporating these messages into personalized letters or otherwise including them in bereavement care):

The Grieving Process	(page 38)	2 weeks after loss
You and Your Emotions	(page 109)	1 month after loss
Enough Faith?	(page 41)	2 months after loss
Anger	(page 110)	
Guilt	(page 111)	3 months after loss
I Know There's Life After Death, Right?	(page 44)	4 months after loss
Working With Your Grieving	(page 42)	5 months after loss

Ongoing Visitation

Please note that teens benefit from having consistent contact with familiar people. While you might have a team of bereavement ministers who take turns visiting grieving adults, you should try to have the same bereavement minister(s) work consistently with each teen.

Present the teen with the appropriate Initial Packet materials one to two weeks after the death. Go through the material together and explain to her or him that she or he will be receiving letters every month talking about grieving and that she or he may want to keep this folder for her or his work on grief. Make available any of the material from pages 115-283 that you think might be helpful, including "Reflections for Journaling."

Try to make an appointment with the teen every three months, unless you detect a need for more time. Making an appointment to go to a park or out to a restaurant may allow the teen to express emotions that she or he wouldn't be able to express around her or his family.

At the three-month appointment, go over the previous three months' mailings on feelings: "You and Your Emotions," "Anger," and "Guilt." Ask how she or he is feeling: angry or guilty, afraid, or even happy? Tell her or him again about the range of feelings and remind her or him that anything is okay, except using drugs, alcohol, or violence to cover up the pain. If the teen has been using "Reflections for Journaling," ask about these reflections.

At the six-month appointment, go over the previous months' materials on "I Know There's Life After Death, Right?" "Working With Your Grieving," and "Returning to 'Normal.'" Ask the teen about her or his understanding of heaven and whether she or he is able to picture her or his loved one there.

Don't be afraid to say, "I don't know." Teens appreciate honest answers and honest struggles.

Explain to them that sometimes around six months, people will experience a period where they go back through the emotions they felt earlier except it won't be as painful and won't last as long.

At the nine-month appointment, you may or may not need to make a visit with the teen.

At the twelve-month appointment or anniversary visit, try to make a final appointment with the teen (if you plan to end bereavement care at this time) as close as possible to the anniversary of the day the person died. Talk about "anniversary reactions" with her or him, explaining that she or he will probably feel sad or think about the person a lot more around this time, maybe for the rest of her or his life. She or he will probably also feel sadness when there are major events in her or his life such as confirmation, graduation, a wedding, or the birth of a new baby.

You may wish to go through the ritual that the teen developed (Monthly Message for the eleventh month—"Create a Ritual") unless the family has decided to observe this ritual together privately.

# *Teenagers' Developmental Responses to Death*

Teenagers recognize that death comes to everyone and everything living. They have the thinking skills to question the meaning of life, but they have difficulty believing that death will happen to them.

They may experience seeing, hearing, smelling, or feeling the person who died. Often the deceased will be experienced in their dreams. Such experiences can be upsetting, but for most, they are comforting.

Teens may become angry at God and question their faith. They tend to be self-focused, and they may act out and become angry that life is unfair. Male teens, in particular, tend to have angry outbursts.

Teens are in the developmental process of pulling away from their parents, and arguments are common. If the deceased died after such an argument or other unfinished business, they may feel guilty. They may feel guilt, thinking they could have prevented the death in some way.

Their grades may suffer because of their inability to concentrate. Their energy will probably be low. They may sleep more or lack energy to go out with friends or participate in extracurricular activities. That is a normal part of grieving because of the emotional energy required to heal.

They may regress to behaviors they exhibited as children such as thumb-sucking, twisting their hair, becoming afraid of the dark, having nightmares, etc. They may start withdrawing. Their patterns of eating and sleeping may change. They may try using drugs or alcohol to numb themselves from the experience of grief. They may become sexually promiscuous (this is more common among girls). They may not want to leave home, though that is a normal developmental step, and they may suffer from a damaged self-esteem.

They may become fearful regarding the well-being of the family, the health of the remaining parent, finances, or their own care. They may become fearful of becoming intimate with someone else and question what the future will hold for them.

Physically, they may experience headaches, stomachaches, heart palpitations, symptoms of the person who died, rashes, more colds and infections, breathing difficulties, and exaggerated allergy symptoms.

What you can do:

1. Ask your teen to pray for the person who died and share memories together about the person—including both good and bad times.

2. Reassure your teen that she or he will be taken care of, that you are in good health (if you are), that there will be enough money for clothes and food (if there is), etc.

3. If your teen thinks that she or he "wished" the person dead or could have somehow prevented the death, reassure her or him that being angry and having thoughts about that person dying didn't cause the death. If your teen feels guilty, thinking she or he could have somehow prevented the death, help her or him go through the events before the death and look at the reality of the situation. If your teen feels guilty because the loved one died after an argument took place, suggest writing a letter to the loved one. Pray with your teen, asking God for forgiveness and asking the person who died to forgive her or him. Sometimes writing a letter to the person who died provides a good release of emotions and a sense that the person is listening. Burning the letter can have a powerful effect on the teen if it is done as a symbol of her or his thoughts going up to the person who died.

4. Withdrawing from people and depression can be a natural part of the grieving process. But, if their withdrawal and depression (being constantly sad, withdrawl from family and friends, absence of pleasure in what they used to find fun, being constantly angry or irritable, lack of concern for how they look, seeming tired and being unable to sleep, relying on alcohol or drugs), or even constant activity so they can't settle down or stand to be left alone, lasts for months you may want to seek professional services that are knowledgeable in the area of grieving.

5. Acting-out behaviors and rebelliousness still need appropriate consequences. Telling your teen to "grow up" or "straighten up" when you see regressive behaviors will not help. All these behaviors are normal, and it is a way for your teen to deal with their sense of helplessness. Instead, listen to them, acknowledge their scary feelings, their guilty feelings, their sad feelings, even their feelings of relief (especially after a long illness), and tell them about your own feelings.

6. Teens may sense the presence of the person who died. People generally don't talk about these kinds of experiences, but they are common. Be respectful toward your teen and acknowledge that other people have had those kinds of experiences and that they are normal.

7. Model "good grieving" for teens. Show them it's okay to cry and feel sad when you talk about the person who died. Tell them it's okay to have angry feelings that the person who died had to leave so soon. Don't assume they don't want to talk about the person who died because it will upset them. At points, it may seem that's all they want to talk about. Let them talk for hours if they need to. Restate in your own words what your teen is saying to let them know you are listening: "You're angry that Dad had to die." Don't immediately rush in and try to make them feel better. Your gift of listening will aid in their recovery.

8. Buy your teen a notebook or journal to record her or his thoughts and feelings. Putting emotions down on paper is very therapeutic. (Your bereavement minister can provide a set of reflections that may be helpful in journaling.)

9. Emotions during this time may run high, and their feelings will fluctuate from being sad, to being silly with their friends, to being angry, etc. Your teen may not be sure how to feel. Reassure her or him that she or he isn't going crazy. These feelings are a normal part of the process of grieving.

10. Try not to push them into a premature adult role by becoming the "woman" or the "man" of the house. They may need to do extra chores to help out, but they shouldn't have the responsibilities of the person who died.

11. If you can't think of anything to talk about or your words don't seem to be coming out right some days, just offer a hug. Your teen needs to feel your physical support.

12. Acknowledge physical reactions to grieving such as stomachaches, headaches, etc. Rashes, stomachaches, headaches, etc., will eventually go away. If your teen is having trouble sleeping, try using relaxing music or progressive relaxation. If she or he is having trouble eating, ignore it. Explain that these are normal reactions that many young people have after someone has died. Reassure her or him that they are normal and okay.

13. Encourage them to read books on grieving.

14. If there is a young persons' support group available in the area, encourage your teen to sign up. Being around other teens who have had someone die is a very comforting and "normalizing" experience.

15. Let your teen know it's okay to laugh. She or he may think that she or he didn't love the one who has died or that laughter is disrespectful. Tell her or him that it's okay and that we all need to take a break from mourning sometimes.

16. Let your teen have something that belonged to the person who died. A piece of clothing, favorite piece of jewelry, painting, etc., will acknowledge that you thought of your teenager.

17. Accept your teen's friends. They will help your teen sort out her or his feelings, keep her or him company, and keep her or him busy. One exception, of course, is if you suspect your teen's friends of aiding your teen through buying alcohol or drugs, which will interfere and delay the grieving process.

18. If your teenager is away at school or college, try to include her or him in the funeral services. Her or his grieving process may be extended if she or he is not able to participate.

Teens Need Help With the Grieving Process

Here are a few things to keep in mind as you help your teen through her or his grief:

1. Teens may be concerned about their parents if their parents are grieving too.

2. Teens will not necessarily stay focused on the loss. They may be grieving one minute and laughing and playing the next. They may say things that are surprising and unnerving. Parents may interpret this as a seeming lack of concern or love.

3. Teens may grieve intensely without giving much evidence of it. They may be trying to suppress their own emotions. They may daydream. Some grieve privately. They may avoid new attachments. Others may become overly friendly and inappropriate. They may regress to behavior they had previously outgrown.

4. Teens' grief may be expressed through angry outbursts, fights, poor grades, or other ways of calling attention to themselves. They may be angry that they are being left alone. If parents are distracted because of their own grief, teens may become preoccupied with meeting their own needs. A teenager may try to replace the loss through addictive distractions.

For teens mourning the loss of a sibling:

1. The loss of a sibling brings about fear and insecurity. The surviving teen may become clinging and demanding. The teen might worry about her or his own death or the death of her or his parents. ("Am I next?")

2. A teen may feel a strong sense of "survivor guilt," or direct guilt if the teen feels she or he did something to cause the death. A history of pre-existing conflict with a sibling also predisposes a teen to guilt. she or he may consciously or subconsciously identify her or his feelings of anger as contributing to her or his sibling's death.

3. The parental idealization and preoccupation with the memory of a dead sibling may cause a teen to feel unloved. A teen may feel her or his life is being lived in the shadow of the one who was lost.

4. The teen may overidentify with the deceased sibling and try to take on her or his characteristics or meet expectations reserved for the child. She or he may see her or his sibling as all "good" and herself or himself as "bad."

_____

(Adapted from "Children Need Help with the Grieving Process," by Val Farmer, 1988.)

Suggested Activities for You and Your Teen

Here some suggestions for activities which may help both you and your teen in working through the grieving process.

1. Be available to your teen. Taking a walk together can be a good way to allow for sharing of feelings.

2. Make a follow-up visit to the funeral home or cemetery.

3. Share your own feelings and your personal faith.

4. If the teen is angry,
    - encourage her or him to express these feelings by journaling, painting, or working with clay. (Your bereavement minister can provide a set of reflections that may be helpful in journaling.)
    - bake bread or do some other creative activity together.
    - do some type of physical exercise like going for a walk, bowling, swimming, tennis.

5. If she or he has regrets, encourage her or him to vocalize these feelings, perhaps by writing a letter to the person who died.

6. Include lots of hugging and loving touch.

7. Select and talk about a special keepsake of the person who died.

8. Look through photographs together.

9. Put together a scrapbook about the person who died. Write down her or his favorite foods, color, things she or he did, things that made you laugh or made you mad, what she or he was good at or not so good at, what she or he always said to you, and things you miss and don't miss about that person.

10. View together home movies of the person who died.

11. Talk with your teen about your favorite memories of the person who has died.

12. Talk about dreams and draw them out.

13. Read together a good book about death.

(Adapted from *The Grieving Child*, by Helen Fitzgerald, Simon & Schuster, 1992.)

Suggested Reading for Parents on Teens' Grieving

There are several resources you can use in locating these titles: your local library (and inter-library loan system), your church library, bookstores, your bereavement minister's personal library, local support groups' lending libraries, hospices, and funeral homes.

Remember, if a book doesn't seem to make sense right now, try reading it again later.

About Dying. S. B. Stein. Walker and Co., 1974.

Adolescence and Death. J. McNeil and C. Corr, eds. Springer, 1986.

Are You Sad Too? Helping Children Deal with Loss & Death. D. Seibert. ETR Association, 1993.

Bereaved Children & Teens: A Support Guide for Parents & Professionals. E. A. Grollman, ed. Beacon Press, 1995.

Comforting Those Who Grieve. D. Manning. HarperSan Francisco, 1987.

Don't Take My Grief Away: What to Do When You Lose a Loved One. D. Manning. HarperSanFrancisco, 1984.

For Those Who Live: Helping Children Cope with the Death of a Brother or Sister. K. LaTour. K. Latour, 1990.

How It Feels When A Parent Dies. J. Krementz. Knopf, 1982.

Learning to Say Good-Bye When a Parent Dies. E. LeShan. MacMillan, 1976.

Life & Loss: A Guide to Help Grieving Children. L. Goldman. Accel Develop., 1994.

On Life After Death. E. Kubler-Ross. Celestial Arts, 1991.

Straight Talk About Death for Teenagers: How to Cope with Losing Someone You Love. E. A. Grollman. Beacon Press, 1989.

Talking About Death: A Dialogue Between Parent and Child. E. A. Grollman. Beacon Press, 1991.

Teenagers Talk About Grief. J. Kolp. Baker, 1990.

Suggested Reading for Teens on Grief

There are several resources you can use in locating these titles: your local library (and inter-library loan system), your church library, bookstores, your bereavement minister's personal library, local support groups' lending libraries, hospices, and funeral homes.

Remember, if a book doesn't seem to make sense right now, try reading it again later.

General

Coping with Separation and Loss as a Young Adult. L. LeGrand. 1986.

Death Be Not Proud. J. Gunther. Harper, 1949.

A Death in the Family. J. Agee. Bantam, 1969.

Death is Hard to Live With: Teenagers Talk About How They Cope with Loss. J. Bode. Dell, 1995.

The Death of Ivan Ilych. L. Tolstoy. New American Library, 1960.

Driver's Ed. C. Cooney. Delacorte Press, 1994.

Fire In My Heart Ice In My Veins: A Journal for Teenagers Experiencing a Loss. E. Traisman. Centering Corporation, 1992.

Flowers for the Ones You've Known: Letters from Bereaved Teenagers. J. Sieff and E. Traisman, eds. Centering Corporation, 1995.

A Grief Observed. C. S. Lewis. Bantam, 1976.

How It Feels When a Parent Dies. J. Krementz. Knopf, 1986.

Hunter in the Dark. N. Hughes. Atheneum, 1984.

I Heard the Owl Call My Name. M. Craven. Dell, 1973.

It's Not Fair! Through Grief to Healing. K. Dockrey. Womans Mission Union, 1992.

Little Men. L. Alcott. G.K. Hall, 1995.

Little Women. L. Alcott. Courage Books, 1995.

Living with Death—Middle School. J. Bisnignano. Good Apple, 1991.

Loss: And Loss to Cope with It. J. Berstein. Clarion, 1977.

Ordinary People. J. Guest. G.K. Hall, 1981.

Part of Me Died, Too: Stories of Creative Survival among Bereaved Children and Teenagers. V. Fry. Dutton, 1995.

The Red Badge of Courage. S. Crane. Bantam, 1985.

Shira: A Legacy of Courage. S. Grollman. Doubleday, 1988.

Straight Talk About Death for Teenagers: How to Cope with Losing Someone You Love. E. Grollman. Beacon Press, 1993.

Straight Talk about Death with Young People. R. Watts. Westminister, 1975.

The Sunday Doll. M. Shura. Dodd, Mead, 1988.

Teenagers Face to Face with Bereavement. K. Gravelle and C. Haskins. Julian Messner, 1989.

Too Old to Cry, Too Young to Die. E. Pendleton. Thomas Nelson, 1980.

When Someone You Love Dies: An Explanation of Death for Children. R. Dodd. Abingdon Press, 1986.

Loss of a Parent

Carly's Buck. C. Adler. Clarion, 1987.

The Ceremony of Innocence. J. Highwater. Harper and Row, 1985.

Cowboys Don't Cry. M. Halvorson. Delacorte Press, 1985.

Crazy Lady! J. Conly. HarperCollins, 1993.

The Eagle Kite: A Novel. P. Fox. Orchard Books, 1995.

Earth Shine. T. Nelson. Orchard Books, 1994.

Everything You Need to Know When a Parent Dies. F. Bratman. Rosen Group, 1995.

Flip-Flop Girl. K Paterson. Dutton, 1994.

The Garden Is Doing Fine. C. Farley. Atheneum, 1975.

Learning to Say Good-bye: When a Parent Dies. E. LeShan. Macmillan, 1976.

Of Love and Death and Other Journeys. I. Holland. Lippincott, 1975.

Recovering From the Loss of a Parent. K. Donnelly. Dodd, Mead, 1987.

A Season In-Between. J. Greenberg. Farrar, 1979.

Sometimes I Don't Love My Mother. H. Colman. Morrow, 1977.

Tell Me Everything. C. Coman. Farrar, Straus, and Giroux, 1992.

There Are Two Kinds of Terrible. P. Mann. Doubleday, 1977.

Tiger Eyes. J. Blume. Bradbury, 1981.

What My Sister Remembered. M. Sachs. Dutton, 1992.

When the Phone Rang. H. Mazer. Scholastic, Inc., 1985.

Where the Lilies Bloom. B. Cleaver and V. Cleaver. HarperCollins, 1991.

Loss of a Sibling

Adams Cross. A. Mead. Farrar, Straus, and Giroux, 1996.

Annie and the Sand Dobbies: A Story about Death for Children and Parents. J. Coburn. Seabury, 1964.

Beat the Turtle Drum. C. Green. Viking, 1976.

Chinese Handcuffs. C. Crutcher. Greenwillow, 1989.

The Family Project. S. Ellis. McElderry, 1988.

Losing Someone You Love: When a Brother or Sister Dies. E. Richter. Putnam, 1986.

Memory. M. Mahy. McElderry, 1988.

Mick Harte was Here. B. Park. Knopf, 1995.

Night Kites. M. Kerr. Harper and Row, 1986.

Phoenix Rising: Or How to Survive Your Life. C. Grant. Atheneum, 1989.

Probably Still Nick Swansen. V. Wolff. H. Holt, 1988.

Remembering Mog. C. Rodowsky. Farrar, Straus, and Giroux, 1996.

The Stone Pony. P. Calvert. Dutton, 1983.

Striking Out. W. Weaver. Harper Collins, 1993.

A Summer to Die. L. Lowry. Houghton Mifflin, 1977.

Tunnel Vision. F. Arrick. Bradbury, 1980.

Loss of a Friend

A Begonia for Miss Applebaum. P. Zindel. Harper and Row, 1989.

The Bumblebee Flies Anyway. R. Cormier. Pantheon, 1983.

Close Enough to Touch. R. Peck. Delacorte Press, 1981.

Coping with Suicide. J. Smith. Rosen Group, 1990.

A Gathering of Days: A New England Girl's Journal. Scribner, 1979.

Music From a Place Called Half Moon. J. Oughton. Houghton Mifflin, 1995.

Say Goodnight, Gracie. J. Deaver. Harper and Row, 1988.

When Heros Die. P. Durant. Anthem, 1992.

Loss of a Grandparent

After the Rain. N. Mazer. G.K. Hall, 1989.

Gold Star Sister. C. Murphy. Lodestar Books, 1994.

I'll Get There, It Better Be Worth the Trip. J. Donovan. Harper and Row, 1969.

A Ring of Endless Light. M. L'Engle. Farrar, Straus, and Giroux, 1980.

Unlived Affections. G. Shannon. Harper and Row, 1989.

You Shouldn't Have to Say Good-bye. P. Hermes. Harcourt Brace Jovanovich, 1982.

Taking Care of Yourself

Here are some things that may help you as you deal with your loss:

1. Exercising. This allows you to let go of sad thoughts and feelings. Try walking around the block, rollerblading, or any other type of exercise you enjoy.

2. Crying.

3. Talking about your feelings with a parent, trusted friend, counselor. or your priest or minister.

4. Journaling. This just means writing your thoughts on paper. (Your bereavement minister can provide a set of reflections that may help you in journaling.) You may also want to write a letter to the person who died; then you may choose either to put it in a safe place or destroy it.

5. Praying—for the person who died and for yourself in coping with all the changes in your life.

6. Meditating and relaxing. These can offer you a time-out from your thoughts and emotions and allow you to heal.

7. Drawing, dancing, singing or any other type of creative activity. Make up a song and sing it as loud as you can. Or paint the emotions inside of you.

8. Watching a funny movie. This offers another time-out from your emotions, and it feels good to laugh again.

9. Thanking God for the support you've received from friends and family, for books that have helped, etc. An attitude of thankfulness can be hard at first, but it will be important for the rest of your life.

10. Reading, reading, reading. The more you know about grieving and understand how other people have gone through it, the better.

11. Attending a healing service. That may sound "hokey," and God does hear your prayers when you pray alone, but God also works when two or more are gathered in his name. Prayers for help, prayers for healing, prayers for understanding can be very helpful when you're questioning your faith, when you just can't pray anymore, or when you just need support.

12. Making a "feel good" box for those days when you're feeling especially down. Find a unique or pretty box and put stuff in there that is important to you or makes you feel special. Examples are: pictures, a card that has a great picture on it, a piece of jewelry, pieces of paper with special sayings or Bible passages on it, etc.

Prayer

Do all this in prayer, asking for God's help.
Pray on every occasion, as the Spirit leads.

EPHESIANS 6:18

What is prayer? Prayer is simply talking to God. We can talk to God using prayers like those said in church, or prayer can be like talking to a friend. When you talk with a friend, you talk for awhile and your friend listens. When your friend talks, you listen. Sometimes you want to be alone with your friend so you can share stories you don't want others to hear, so you may go to your bedroom, go for a walk, or go out to a restaurant. That's what it is like with God too.

You can talk to God anytime you like: at school, at home, at your sporting events, anywhere. Sometimes going for a walk in nature helps. Or having a special place in your home or bedroom may help you concentrate on God better.

Try the following:

1. Set a table with a candle, a picture of nature, a book, a cross, a picture of Jesus, or something you find peaceful.

2. Talk to God about whatever is troubling you. Share your feelings with God, draw a picture, or write in your journal. (Your bereavement minister can provide a set of reflections that may help you in journaling.)

3. Listen to God. It's hard to listen when you are around a lot of noise, so you might want to try turning off the television or radio. Then close your eyes and find the quiet place inside your heart where you can enter into this love-filled room and see God waiting for you. He has been eagerly awaiting your visit and has something to say to you. What do you hear?

4. Thank God for listening. Know that God hears your prayers and answers them in a way that God knows is best for you and for others. Remember, God is not the great "wish-giver" in the sky who gives you what you want. Talking to God, or praying, is having a friendship with God, a friendship like one with earthly friends, only better.

Meditation

May my meditation be pleasing to God, for
I rejoice in the Lord.

PSALM 104:34

What is meditation? Meditation is a way of quieting your body, your thoughts, and your feelings to hear God. It allows you to gain insight or wisdom about yourself and others and bring peace to your life. Meditation as a tool can improve your concentration and give you control over your emotions so they don't have control over you.

Start by practicing two to three minutes at the beginning, then work your way up. You can probably work your way up to five to ten minutes if you're in early grade school, ten to twenty minutes if you're in late grade school, and twenty to thirty minutes if you're in junior high or high school. Set a timer and make a chart for yourself keeping track of your progress. Some days will be harder than others and you may even fall asleep, which is okay.

If you're feeling restless before meditating, try stretching your back by bending forward, backward, and from side-to-side.

While you're meditating, if thoughts creep into your mind either let them pass through or write them down on a slip of paper. Then go back to concentrating on the exercise.

You can make up your own words to chant such as "love," "peace," "kindness," etc., or try using images from nature. The following exercise is one way to meditate. You may find it hard to read this sheet and meditate at the same time. If so, you may want to record the following instructions on tape. Then play it back so you can simply listen to the instructions instead of reading them. Or you could have someone else read the instructions to you.

Start by sitting in an upright position (this can be in a chair or on the floor), uncross your legs (unless you are on the floor) and let your arms rest lightly on your lap. Close your eyes and take three deep breaths, breathing in through your nose and blowing out through your mouth. Starting with your feet, curl your toes and hold, 1, 2, 3, and relax. Slowly, work your way up from your feet, tightening each group of muscles to a count of three, and then relaxing. When you get to your head, scrunch your entire face and hold to the count of three and relax. Take three more deep breaths, breathing in through your nose and out through your mouth, monitoring your body and making sure all your muscles are relaxed.

Next focus on the spot between your eyebrows. Concentrate on this area and imagine yourself breathing in through this spot in your forehead—breathing in the breath of God and blowing out anger. Breathe in peace and blow out fear. Breathe in love and blow out guilt. Next move your attention to your heart, and imagine yourself breathing in through this spot. Breathe in the breath of God and blow out anger. Breathe in peace and blow out fear. Breathe in love and blow out guilt. Still concentrating on your heart center, ask God your question or just "be" in God's presence. Listen for your answer. Remember it may not be what you think it should. Then, thank God before you go.

When you have finished meditating, begin by feeling your feet on the floor and your buttocks on the chair (or the floor, if you are sitting on the floor). Feel your fingers and start to move them, and when you are ready, you can open your eyes.

You may want to write about your experience of meditating in a journal.

Physical Symptoms of Grieving for Teens

Right now, you may be feeling a lot of different physical pains that are different from ever before. You may feel as though you are going crazy at times, but this is all a *normal* part of grieving.

Grieving is work. The exhaustion from grieving is similar to a heavy physical workout. Often symptoms from grieving are mistakenly identified as simply physical. Some complaints are as follows:

chest pains or heart problems

dizziness

dry mouth

empty feeling in the stomach

fatigue

feeling of "something stuck in the throat"

headache

inability to sleep

loss of sexual desire or having an overly active sexual desire

loss of weight

nausea and vomiting

oversensitivity to noise

pain

purposeless activity

shortness of breath

trembling

uncontrollable sighing and sobbing

weakness in the muscles

various gastrointestinal symptoms: constipation, diarrhea, or excessive gas

Any of these symptoms can be a *normal* part of the grieving process; it is one way the body physically expresses its emotions. If one or more of these symptoms persist or become very uncomfortable, please make an appointment or have an adult make an appointment for you with your physician. Tell your doctor that someone close to you has died. You may even want to bring this sheet along with you.

If you are on medication from your doctor, continue to take it without fail. If necessary, use simple things like aspirin, acetaminophen, and ibuprofen for headaches and other aches and pains. Avoid using sleeping medications that you can purchase at the drug store. These drugs may only interfere with your sleep and your overall work that needs to be done with grieving. Meditation, relaxation, and sleeping information is included in your packet. There are a lot of relaxation tapes and CDs that you may want to try. Look at your local music store or ask the bereavement minister who has given you this information.

Come to me,
all you that are weary and are carrying heavy burdens,
and I will give you rest.

MATTHEW 11:28

Exercise and Eating Right

Grieving often affects physical well-being. You may not be sleeping well at night, or you may be rerunning events over in your mind and feeling especially tired. A nap during the day is okay, or, even better, try the techniques for getting to sleep that are listed in your packet.

Emotional shock is like physical shock—your body needs rest to recover. Your energy will come back in time. If you find yourself a few months down the road wanting only to sleep, arrange with a friend a time that she or he can call you to get you up.

Eating Right

Eating right is a hard thing to do right now, especially with your ongoing activities. Maybe you have lost your appetite. Try these two things:

1. Take a multi-vitamin every day. It can't replace a good meal, but it can help fill in the gaps.

2. Eat foods that are high in protein since your body is in a state of repair. Try an extra glass of milk a day, an extra serving of cheese or peanut butter, or maybe an extra hamburger, at least for the next six to eight months.

Exercising

Do whatever you can. It's a great release for emotions such as anger, guilt, anxiety, or restlessness. It will also give you more energy. Exercising can also relieve mild depression and improve your mood. Here are some ideas:

- go walk the dog
- go running
- go swimming
- play soccer
- play basketball
- play baseball
- go rollerblading
- go skateboarding

- go biking
- try some volleyball
- play football
- walk on the treadmill
- do some stretches in front of the TV
- play softball
- go for a walk in the park
- try some aerobics

Monthly Messages

You and Your Emotions

Death is such a big upheaval in a person's life. One minute you are sad and lonely; the next minute you're angry. Your emotions are helter-skelter, and sometimes they feel overwhelming. Know that it is a *normal* part of grieving. Know that no matter what your feeling, it is okay.

People are all different, and people will grieve in different ways and for different lengths of time. It is important to express your emotions in some way so you have control over your emotions rather than your emotions having control over you. When your emotions are controlling you, you may drink too much, take drugs, or use violence. These are unhealthy ways to deal with the pain. Eventually, you need to deal with it and going through the pain is the only way to learn and grow. Here are a few things to remember about emotions:

1. You are not your emotions. Your emotions and feelings come and go.

2. Feelings aren't good or bad, they just are.

3. It's okay to feel sad and cry. Even Jesus cried when his friend died. (John 11:35)

4. It's okay to feel anger. Many of the prophets of the Bible and even Jesus felt angry.

5. It's okay to feel happy, laugh, and have fun. You can't be sad all the time, and sometimes you just need to get your mind off the work of grieving and have fun with friends.

6. It's okay to feel guilty. You may have had a fight with the person who died or wished that person dead. Your wishing cannot kill anybody. Maybe you wished you had spent more time with the person or done what they asked you to do. If you are having a hard time with feelings of this kind, talk to God, to your parents, to a trusted friend, to your priest or minister, or try writing a letter to the person who died.

7. It's okay to feel afraid. You may be afraid because you're not sure who will take care of you or where the money will come from or if you'll have enough money for clothes or food. Sit down with your parent or trusted adult and discuss your concerns. Don't waste your needed energy in worrying.

Look at the birds: they do not plant seeds, gather a harvest and put it in barns; yet your Father in heaven takes care of them! Aren't you worth much more than birds? Can any of you live a bit longer by worrying about it? . . . So do not worry about tomorrow; it will have enough worries of it's own. There is no need to add to the troubles each day brings.
—Matthew 6:26, 27, 34

8. It's okay to feel these feelings in your body. God built our bodies to handle stress. Look again at the sheet titled "Physical Symptoms of Grieving for Teens."

9. You may find that you actually feel relieved if a death ends a long illness or other difficult situation. This feeling can be hard to admit, but it's normal.

10. It's okay to feel disorganized or panicked. You may even experience anxiety attacks. These will pass, but they are uncomfortable. Try to be near people who you trust and ask for physical touch like hugs, cuddling, or holding hands.

11. It's okay to not feel anything. You may go out with friends, laugh, and have fun after you hear about a death. It's one way your emotional self protects itself from a big shock.

12. Look at your "Taking Care of Yourself" sheet in your packet to help give you more ideas on handling your emotions.

For everything there is a season,
and a time for every matter under heaven . . .
a time to weep, and a time to laugh;
a time to mourn, and a time to dance. . . .

ECCLESIASTES 3:1-8

Anger

In last month's letter ("You and Your Emotions"), we talked about anger. Anger is one of those emotions we don't like to talk about because it doesn't seem "Christian." We tend to think that Christians don't get angry. But if we look at the examples in the Bible, you'll see that God's messengers (the prophets) get angry at God, curse God, and blame Him. Even God's own son, Jesus, threw the money changers out of the temple (Matthew 21:12). Maybe you, too, have had feelings of anger related to the loss you have experienced.

Are you angry at yourself for having a fight with your loved one before she or he died and now you won't have a chance to say you're sorry? Are you angry at the hospital, the doctor, or the nurses because they didn't give your loved one the care she or he needed? Maybe you're angry at family or friends for saying things that hurt you or your family. Maybe you're angry at the person who died wishing she or he had tried harder or taken better care of herself or himself. Maybe you're angry at your situation, feeling that you shouldn't have to be going through this. You just wanted to have fun and be a teenager, but now you have more responsibilities than you wanted. Or maybe you're angry that your loved one won't be at your graduation, your wedding, your prom. Maybe you're even angry at God for taking that person away from you, or not working a miracle. Whatever you're angry about, it's okay. Anger is just an emotion, but it carries a lot of energy. It's your choice to decide how you will direct that energy to be used positively.

The Bible gives us a helpful suggestion about balancing anger:

"Be angry, but do not sin; do not let the sun go down on your anger, and do not make room for the devil" (Ephesians 4:26).

Here are some other ideas on handling anger:

1. "You always have the choice of how intense your anger will be, how long it will last, and what you are going to do with it."

(From *Prescription for Anger*, by G. Hankins, Princess Publications, 1988.

2. Use humor. It's hard to laugh and be angry at the same time.
3. Use "I" messages. Instead of saying, for example, "You make me so angry," say, "I get angry when I can't finish my sentences."
4. Take deep breaths.
5. Count to ten.
6. Use positive self-talk. "I can do this. I can stay in control."
7. Reframe the situation. Look at the situation from a different perspective.

(Adapted from *Prescription for Anger*, by G. Hankins. Princess Publications, 1988)

Guilt

In last month's letter we talked about anger. This month we'll talk about guilt. After someone dies, we often feel guilty. Why? Because we're human, and we make mistakes. There are things we wish we had said: "I wish I would have told him I was sorry before he died!" There are things we wish we had done: "I should have cut the grass more like he always wanted me to." "I could have given her a ride home, but she refused. I should have made her come with me." "I was supposed to have gone with them that night. Now they're all dead, except me. Why am I still alive?" "I should have spent more time with him."

We blame ourselves, our family, our friends, the doctors and nurses, or the clergy. We "could have" or "should have" ourselves into a depression.

It might help you to try to imagine seeing things from the perspective of the one who has died. Do you think that person is blaming you for your decision? Do you think that person still holds a grudge against you because of a fight you had with her or him? Or do you think the person has a more eternal perspective of love, and forgiveness?

Jesus often talks about healing and forgiveness. These are two powerful parts of God's love. As Christians we are called to forgive one another, as God in Christ forgave us (Colossians 3:13). Jesus was asked how many times should we forgive? The answer was "seventy times seven" (Matthew 18:22). What he meant, or course, is that we need to learn to forgive over and over again.

If you are blaming yourself or others, you may need to look at the reality of the situation. Everyone did what she or he could at the time and thought was best at that particular moment. Maybe it wasn't what you would do now in hindsight, but hindsight is meant for you to learn from, not to blame or accuse you. Whatever it is, ask God for forgiveness, ask forgiveness from the person who died, and forgive other people.

Writing a letter to the person who died is one way you can say the things you didn't get to say before that person died. Tell the person how much you miss her or him, how angry you are that she or he couldn't be with you longer, thank them, and most importantly pray for them. Sometimes it's helpful to talk with someone else like your clergyperson or a counselor. When you are able to forgive and be forgiven, it will move you forward on your road to healing.

> *The Lord is merciful and loving,*
> *slow to become angry and full of constant love. . . .*
> ———————
> PSALM 103:8

Writing a Letter

You may find it helpful to write a letter to the person who died. You may want to tell that person how much you miss her or him, how angry you are, or how you wish she or he could be at your next activity. You may want to thank her or him or say you're sorry. Include whatever you want to. Think of this as your good-bye letter.

Making a Memory Book

It may help you to create a "memory book" honoring the loved one you've lost. Answer the questions below, or include other information that you think is important. You may also want to include photos or other memorabilia.

- When was that person born?
- When did that person die?
- How old was the person when she or he died?
- What was the person's favorite thing?
- What was the person's favorite story?
- What was your favorite thing to do with the person who died?
- What are your strongest memories of the person?
- What especially reminds you of her or him?

How Will I Know I'm Feeling Better?

The best answer to your question, "How will I know I am feeling better?" is one only you can answer because we are all so different. You will probably find you can talk about the person who died and not cry. You can see someone who looks like the person who died, or walks or talks like the person, but it doesn't upset you like it did at the beginning.

You are able to enjoy holidays and special events again. You are starting to have more energy, and you are not as crabby. You will be able to start up new activities and feel like you can put yourself into them again. Some days you will still feel as though you are not really getting any better, but it is normal to feel that way.

As the months go by, you will probably experience something called "anniversary reactions." That just means that on the anniversary of the day that your loved one died, you may feel grumpy, sad, or restless. This is normal, and lots of kids feel this way. You may have these feelings for a long time or you may not. You can even have them a long time later like when you are confirmed, or at your graduation. You may even have those kind of feelings when you get married or have a baby and you wish your loved one could have been there to be with you. It doesn't happen to everybody, but just keep it in the back of your mind that it can happen and that you are not weird if it does.

You can do something on those special days such as placing a flower on the altar in memory of the person who died, keeping yourself busy by being with friends, or spending the time writing, drawing, or painting your feelings.

There are two important questions to answer as you continue in your journey of grieving:

What have I learned from this experience?
Where have I seen God working?

You may want to stop and think about your answers to these questions.

Create a Ritual

You may find it helpful to create a special ritual honoring the person who died. You could read a poem, go through your scrapbook, sing a song, play the person's favorite music, or show some of your artwork or dance. Maybe each person in your family could share a special memory she or he of the person who died and light a candle.

Whatever you do, memories will be shared and memories will be built as you remember together.

Perhaps you could share your ideas for an anniversary ritual with a parent or other family member.

Part III

SUPPLEMENTAL RESOURCES

Resources for Holidays and Special Days

Including Special Days in a Program of Bereavement Care

Holidays and special anniversary days such as the day a loved one died, a wedding anniversary, and birthdays are days that need extra attention and care. Depending on the circumstance, certain holidays tend to be particularly difficult. If a parent is grieving a young child, for example, Halloween may be a difficult day. If a spouse has died, Valentine's Day will be hard.

Pages 122-124 offer material which can be included in letters or personal notes at the appropriate times. Also consider scheduling visitation on or near these special days.

Here are additional ideas for the holidays that you can develop as unique symbols of ongoing care:

Valentine's Day

- hand-delivered vase of carnations donated by a florist
- crocheted heart bookmarks
- specially wrapped bag of candy
- handmade valentines

Mother's Day (especially for those dealing with infertility, the death of a child, or the death of a mother)

- carnations
- balloons

Father's Day (especially for those dealing with infertility, the death of a child, or the death of a father)
- plant
- a small tree

Easter
- cross or butterfly that has been crocheted, woven, needlepointed, or other type of craft
- tissue paper art of a cross or butterfly
- stained-glass cross or butterfly

Halloween (especially for those dealing with the death of a child)
- hand-painted pumpkin
- specially wrapped Halloween candy

Christmas
- star that has been crocheted, woven, needlepointed, or other type of craft
- hand-delivered sprig of holly, Christmas cactus, etc.

Messages for Special Days

"Special Days" (page 119) is meant to be personalized and sent before the first important anniversary after the loss. "Suggestions for Handling the Holidays and Special Days" (page 120), which is designed to be given as a handout, is geared especially toward the holidays which are usually celebrated with family: Easter, Thanksgiving, and especially Christmas. You might send this page at the start of the first major holiday season after the loss.

The "Special Day Messages" (pages 122-124) are intended to be sent on those important days which can be difficult for those who are grieving—a wedding anniversary, a birthday, or important holidays.

Also remember to send out a special note on Mother's Day, Father's Day, and Halloween if a child has died.

Special Days

Throughout the year, we celebrate special days to remember the lives of others, our lives, our church, our community, and our nation—birthdays, anniversaries, baptisms, promotions, dates of death, graduations, etc. As you are grieving your loss, these days can bring strong emotions and memories, both happy and sad. You may find yourself especially sad or weepy, unable to sleep, and irritable. It's important to acknowledge these feelings and allow yourself to feel them; they are God-given and life-sustaining. You may feel like being alone at home, you may want to be around other people, or you may want to get out of the house. Whatever your response is, it is okay.

Those who have worked through these "special days" have suggested the following:

- burning a candle for that person at the supper table
- buying flowers for yourself
- eating out with a friend
- being able to share about your loved one
- reaching out to others who are lonely

These are ways to love and take care of yourself as well as honor and celebrate the occasion.

Incline your ear, O Lord, and answer me,
for I am poor and needy.
Preserve my life, for I am devoted to you,
save your servant who trusts in you.
You are my God; be gracious to me, O Lord,
for to you, O Lord, I lift up my soul.
For you, O Lord, are good and forgiving,
abounding in steadfast love to all who call on you.
Give ear, O Lord, to my prayer;
listen to my cry of supplication.
In the day of my trouble I call on you,
for you will answer me.

PSALM 86:1-7

Suggestions for Handling the Holidays and Special Days

Holidays and special days like birthdays, wedding anniversaries, and the anniversary of your loved one's death can be difficult. Here are some suggestions that may be helpful:

1. Allow yourself to feel your emotions on your special day; don't feel that you need to just "get over it." You may want to write them down in a journal or draw them on paper. Take time for reflection.

2. Call a friend and see if she or he can spend some of the day with you. You may feel like getting out of the house, going out for dinner, or having a picnic. Call a friend who is a good listener.

3. Take time and share memories with your family of the loved one who died.

   - light a candle in honor of her or him

   - set out a picture and tell stories of her or his life

   - watch a home video together

   - look through a photo album together or make a family memory book

4. Plan ahead to help you set limits and do what is meaningful for you and your family during the holidays. You may want to ask yourself:

   - "Is this something I do out of habit or do I really enjoy it?"

   - "Can I share the job with someone else?"
     (Example: Decorating your home can be taken over by an older child or maybe a niece or nephew.)

   - "Who will take over the role traditionally assigned to the person who died?" (Example: carving the turkey or ham)

   - "Can someone else do my gift shopping?"

   - "Do I want to exchange gifts at Christmas with my friends and relatives or is there another day like Thanksgiving or Epiphany that would be easier?"

   - "Can someone else help with the housecleaning or could I even afford someone to come in and clean the house?"

   - "Can I send out Christmas cards at Epiphany?" (Note: If you do send out Christmas cards and not everyone has heard of your loved one's death, insert a memorial card to let them know.) You may want to plan ahead and work on Christmas cards gradually: address the envelopes in October, stuff them in November, and send them out just after Thanksgiving.

- "Should I buy some new clothes?"

5. Try the following cooking ideas for the holidays:
    - reduce the number of dishes you make
    - ask your guests to bring a dish to share
    - go to someone else's house for dinner
    - go out to eat

6. Be open to good experiences that the holidays may bring. Live in the present. Remember, past holidays weren't perfect.

7. Don't avoid long-standing traditions. Children often find comfort in them. On the other hand, new traditions say you are still a family.

8. Provide your children with extra amounts of attention, praise, and emotional support.

9. Children imitate behavior. If they see you are crying and expressing your sadness at the death of your loved one, they will know they have the freedom to do the same.

10. Do something for someone else. Reaching out to someone else who is in need can help with your feelings of helplessness and hopelessness. Give a donation in memory of your loved one. Give food to the needy. Invite someone else who is alone to join in the holiday meal and festivities.

11. Allow yourself to feel joy. You are not betraying your loved one. You may want to read the following books for more ideas:

Carpenter, P. *Away for the Holidays.* PCA Publishing, P.O. Box 16066, Minneapolis, MN 55416, 1-612-927-5270.

Conley, B. *Handling the Holidays.* Thum Printing, P.O. Box A, Elburn, IL 60119, 1-312-365-6414.

Miller, J. *How Will I Get Through the Holidays? 12 Ideas For Those Whose Loved One Has Died.* Willowgreen Publishing, 1996.

Special Day Messages

Valentine's Day

This note comes to wish you a happy Valentine's Day and to let you know that we are thinking about you and praying for you.

This day may be difficult for you. Don't be surprised if you find yourself feeling more emotional. If the tears come, let them come. You have known the love of the person who died, and that love was a special love.

One of the unique and special things about our Christian faith is that we meet and find God in one another. There were ways that you found the love of God in your loved one and she or he found the love of God in you. In John 5:20 we find these words: "The Father loves the Son." In John 11, when Jesus described his relationship to Lazarus, it says: "Jesus wept. So the Jews said, 'See how he loved him!'" In John 20:2, John is described as "the one whom Jesus loved." And in Jesus' farewell conversation with his disciples, we find these words: "For the Father himself loves you, because you have loved me and have believed that I came from the Father."

It is natural for you to grieve the loss of this love.

Remember on this day celebrating love that God's love for you has not ended. God loves us tenderly and affectionately. He puts his arms around us, and he holds us.

May this love from God be yours on this Valentine's Day and each day.

Easter

The Easter message is, "He is risen!" At Easter, we celebrate more than an empty tomb; we focus on the life, the energy, and the hope that is released by God through the resurrection of his son Jesus Christ.

Easter is a natural time for you to remember your loved one. It is because of Easter and the message of the resurrection that your loved one is still your loved one; death does not change that. Certainly through her or his death, your relationship has changed, but that does not stop her or him from being a part of you.

Hope comes from God. Not only did God give us life, but he gave us Jesus, who loves you and your loved one and all of us. The cross teaches us about that love, and the resurrection teaches us that not even death can overcome it. God always has the last word; death does not.

May you know the love of this God who loved your loved one and continues to love her or him and continues to love you. May this hope that is Christ Jesus be yours in these days. May the life, the energy, and the hope of God give you the courage and the strength for today and the days ahead. God bless you at this Easter time. Remember that you are loved.

Blessed be the God and Father of our Lord Jesus Christ!
By his great mercy he has given us a new birth into a living hope
through the resurrection of Jesus Christ from the dead,
and into an inheritance that is imperishable, undefiled, and unfading,
kept in heaven for you, who are being protected by the power of God
through faith for a salvation ready to be revealed in the last time.

1 PETER 1:3-5

Thanksgiving

Thanksgiving can be a difficult time when you're grieving a loss. Our prayer is that you would know the love that God has for you and the ways in which his love has sustained you through your loss. May this be a time to give thanks to God for the love that he shared with you through your loved one.

The apostle Paul invites us to "give thanks in all circumstances"—not *for* all circumstances, but *in* all circumstances, reminding us that even in difficult times, we have been given good things.

In another place, Paul writes, "Do not worry about anything, but in everything by prayer and supplication with thanksgiving let your requests be made known to God. And the peace of God, which surpasses all understanding, will guard your hearts and your minds in Christ Jesus."

May the peace of God "guard your heart and mind" in these days of Thanksgiving.

Christmas

Christmas can be the hardest time of year when you are grieving a loss. The decorations and celebrations, which are supposed to make you feel festive, only remind you of your loss. In a season of love and togetherness, you can somehow feel very *alone*.

The Christmas message is that "God is with us." He came to become one of us in Jesus Christ. In this season, we celebrate the fact and the faith that God loved us so much that he was born among of us.

123

And yet, even at the first Christmas, there was a reminder of death. One of the gifts that the wise men brought to the baby Jesus was the gift of myrrh, a perfume that was used to prepare a dead body for burial. Part of the plan of God from the very beginning was that this baby born in Bethlehem would eventually show his love through death. It is through this birth, death, and resurrection of this Jesus that we celebrate life even in the midst of death.

May the love that was born in Bethlehem in Jesus the Christ be born in you today.

But the angel said to them, "Do not be afraid; for see—
I am bringing you good news of great joy for all the people:
to you is born this day in the city of David a Savior,
who is the Messiah, the Lord."

LUKE 2:10-11

Resources for Special Circumstances

Death of a Spouse

Setting Up a Program of Bereavement Care After the Death of a Spouse

The loss of a spouse creates not only grief, but a crisis in the business of everyday life. If there are young children in the home, immediate questions will arise concerning the ongoing functioning of the household. If the couple was older, the grieving spouse may find herself or himself living alone—perhaps for the first time. It is especially important to address practical concerns in addition to issues of grief resolution.

Here are some specific issues to keep in mind:

Women

1. Uncertain identity—Women over 50 years of age probably have spent most of their lives working in the home while their husbands earned most or all of the household income. They may have tied up their identity with their spouses and may be unsure how to be an "I" instead of a "we."

2. Financial insecurity—Within five years, a widow's income is reduced by 44%, on average. Widows who must enter the job market are often unprepared for jobs that pay more than minimum wage.

3. Fear—Women tend to have more fear of their financial security, crime, living alone, and being taken advantage of in the marketplace. If you sense this concern, make available "Safety Tips When You Live Alone" (pages 256-261).

4. House maintenance—Women often have less experience with roofing, mechanical, electrical, and plumbing problems.

5. Dating—There are more older women than men, and "the rules have changed."

Men

1. Household chores—Men often have questions regarding shopping, cleaning, and cooking.

2. Relational support—If the man has spent most of his time on his career and has relegated the making of friends to his wife, her death may leave him friendless and unable to form new friendships.

3. Communication—Men may have difficulty talking about their feelings and even allowing them to surface.

_____

(From *The Grief Adjustment Guide,* by Greeson, Hollingsworth, and Washburn.)

Of course, those who have lost a spouse also have important similarities, and all express the need for companionship.

Initial Contact

As suggested on page 19, you should make an initial visit to the grieving person as soon as possible. At this visit, give the grieving person an Initial Packet, varying the materials for men and women.

The following materials are designed to be given at your initial visit to a woman who has lost a spouse:

Physical Symptoms of Grieving	(page 29)
Exercise and Nutrition	(page 30)
Getting to Sleep	(page 32)
Suggested Reading After a Major Loss	(page 34)
Finances—What to Do in the First Month	(pages 128-129)
Suggested Reading—Finances and Employment	(pages 130-131)
Suggested Reading for Widows	(pages 133-134)
Support Groups for Those Who Have Been Widowed	(page 132)

The following materials are designed to be given at your initial visit to a man who has lost a spouse:

Physical Symptoms of Grieving	(page 29)
Exercise and Nutrition	(page 30)
Getting to Sleep	(page 32)
Suggested Reading After a Major Loss	(page 34)
Finances—What to Do in the First Month	(pages 128-129)
Support Groups and Organizations for Widowers	(page 136)
Suggested Reading for Widowers	(page 135)

Monthly Messages

In addition, the following Monthly Messages should be used during the first year of bereavement (see pages 19-21 for instructions on incorporating these messages into personalized letters or otherwise including them in bereavement care):

The Grieving Process	(page 38)	2 weeks after loss
Common Myths About Grief	(page 39)	1 month after loss
You and Your Emotions	(page 40)	2 months after loss
Enough Faith?	(page 41)	
Working With Your Grieving	(page 42)	3 months after loss
Returning to "Normal"	(page 43)	4 months after loss
I Know There's Life After Death, Right?	(page 44)	5 months after loss
Support Groups	(page 45)	6 months after loss
Dealing With Criticism	(page 45)	7 months after loss
On Your Own	(page 137 or 138)	

(There are two variations of this letter: the first one is intended for those under 60; the second is intended for those 60 or over.)

More About Exercise and Nutrition	(page 46)	8 months after loss
How Will I Know I'm Feeling Better?	(page 48)	9 months after loss
A Special Note	(page 49)	10 months after loss
Getting Involved Again	(page 49)	11 months after loss
The Journey Continues	(page 50)	one year after loss

Also add "Messages for Special Days" on pages 122-124 and Bereavement Surveys on pages 303-304 as appropriate.

Ongoing Visitation

See suggestions for visitation on page 21.

Finances—What to Do in the First Month

1. First:

   - Don't throw anything away, even if it looks unimportant.

   - In the first few days and weeks after a major loss, try not to make any major decisions such as selling your home, moving, making a major investment, loaning money, or buying insurance.

   - Have a trusted friend help you.

   - If it is worrying you, make finances a matter of prayer.

2. Next, locate these important papers:

   ___ Bank books

   ___ Certificates of deposit

   ___ Car title

   ___ Real estate deeds

   ___ Insurance policies

   ___ Spouse's birth certificate

   ___ Minor children's birth certificates

   ___ Copies of your tax returns for the last 7 years

   ___ W-2 forms from the past year

   ___ Will (Check with your lawyer or banker if you cannot find it. If you have no will, call the probate clerk in your county. Check under local government listings.)

   ___ Spouse's and your social security cards

   ___ Marriage certificate

   ___ Military discharge papers

   ___ Stock certificates

   ___ Copies of the death certificate (at least 20)

3. Then, organize and pay your bills

   First, pay your mortgage, your health and property insurance, and utilities.

   You may want to wait to pay the full amount of other bills until you have a clearer picture of your finances. These include funeral directors, doctors, hospitals, or other creditors. Write them a letter advising them that you intend to pay but that you need time to determine your financial status. Send along a token payment.

   Be aware of phony claims. If you are not familiar with a bill, write the creditor asking for a proof of the claim.

4. Make appointments to see your financial planner, accountant, and lawyer.

If you do not have an attorney, find one who specializes in "probate" law. He or she should be able to explain things easily to you. Ask friends and family for references, or contact any of these three agencies for a reference.

American Bar Association (ABA)
Lawyers Referral and Information Service
1155 East 60th St.
Chicago, IL 60637
312-332-1111 (9 AM to 5 PM Central Time)

National Legal Aid and Defenders Association
1625 K Street, NW
8th Floor
Washington, DC 20006
202-452-0620 (9 AM to 5:30 PM Eastern Time)
(A clearinghouse of organizations for people who are unable to pay.)

National Resource Center for Consumers of Legal Service
3254 Jones Court, NW
Washington, DC 20007
202-338-0714 (9 AM to 5 PM Eastern Time)

Remember that lawyers charge by the hour, so try to have your papers sorted out before your appointment and bring them along.

5. Open a new bank account in your name.

6. In some states, bank accounts and safety deposit boxes are frozen upon a death. Get proper authorization to have the assets or other property released.

7. Notify all insurance companies of the death and file claims.

8. Call Social Security (and the Veterans' Administration, if applicable) to apply for benefits. (Look under United States Government in your phone book.)

———
(Adapted from *On Your Own*, by Armstrong & Donahue, Dearborn Financial Publishing, Inc., 1993.)

9. Once you have taken care of the most pressing financial matters, you will need to create a new budget for yourself. There are books listed under "Suggested Reading—Finances and Employment" which can help with this.

Suggested Reading

Finances and Employment

There are several resources you can use in locating these titles: your local library (and inter-library loan system), bookstores, your bereavement minister's personal library, your church library, and local support groups' lending libraries.

Remember, if a book doesn't seem to make sense right now, try reading it again later.

The 100 Best Jobs for the 1990s and Beyond. C. Kleiman. Dearborn Financial Publishing, 1992.

Beating the Street. P. Lynch. Simon and Schuster, 1993.

Better Late Than Never: Financial Aid for Older Women Seeking Education and Training. Woman's Equity Action League.

The Budget Kit: The Common Cent$ Money Management Workbook. J. Lawrence. Dearborn Financial Publishing, 1993.

Can I Trust You With My Money? The Little Book of Financial Wizardry. N. Gonce. Book Partners, 1996.

Dividends Don't Lie. G. Weiss and J. Lowe. Dearborn Financial Publishing, 1988.

Everything Your Heirs Need to Know: Your Assets, Family History and Final Wishes. D. Magee. Dearborn Financial Publishing, 1991.

Federal Tax Guide for Survivors, Executors, and Administrators (Internal Revenue Service Publication No. 559.) U.S. Department of the Treasury. Government Printing Office.

Finding the Facts: A Woman's Housing Primer (Publication No. 696.) League of Women Voters of the United States.

Home Filing Made Easy! M. Martin and J. Michael. Dearborn Financial Publishing, 1993.

How To Not Get Conned. National Criminal Justice Reference Service.

How To Sell Your Home Without Losing Your Shirt. J. Werner. Houseworks Press, 1995.

Job-Finding Techniques for Mature Women. U.S. Department of Labor. U.S. Government Printing Office.

Kiplinger's Invest Your Way to Wealth. T. Miller. Kiplinger, 1991.

Making Money Last: Financial Clarity for the Surviving Spouse. K. Demetriou. Kendall-Hunt, 1996.

Marshall Loeb's Money Guide. M. Loeb. Little, Brown, 1993.

On Your Own: A Widows' Passage to Emotional and Financial Well-Being. A. Armstrong and M. Donahue. Dearborn Financial Publishing, 1993.

One Up On Wall Street. P. Lynch. Simon and Schuster, 1989.

Our Money, Our Selves. G. Wall. Consumer Reports Books, 1992.

A Second Start. J. Brown, LLB and C. Baldwin. Simon and Schuster, 1986.

The Sex of the Dollar. A. Blau. Simon and Schuster, 1988.

Sleep Tight Money. L. Krause. Simon and Schuster, 1987.

Terry Savage Talks Money. T. Savage. Dearborn Financial Publishing, 1990.

What Color Is Your Parachute? R. Bolles. Ten Speed Press, 1970-1993.

What to Do When Your Spouse Dies: Decisions to Make - Legal and Financial Considerations - Planning Ahead. D. Gibberman. Commerce, 1991.

A Woman's Guide to Social Security (Social Security Administration Publication No. 10127). U.S. Department of Health, Education, and Welfare. Government Printing Office.

Women and Money. A. Jones-Lee. Barron's Educational Series, 1991.

Your Financial Plan. Money Management Institute.

Support Groups for Those Who Have Been Widowed

Widowed Persons Service
c/o American Association of Retired Persons
601 East Street NW
Washington, DC 20049
1-202-434-2260
1-202-434-6474 (FAX)
(A non-age related service. Trained peer counseling, referrals, publications, and conventions.)

Widowed Information and Consultation Services (WICS)
P.O. Box 66896
Seattle, WA 98166
1-206-241-5650
1-206-241-1139
(Support and information after the death of a spouse.)

Society of Military Widows (SMW)
5535 Hempstead Way
Springfield, VA 22151
1-703-750-1342
1-703-354-4380 (FAX)
(This service provides legislative information and social activities.)

National Association of Military Widows
4023 - 25th Road North
Arlington, VA 22207
1-703-527-4565
(Learn about survivor benefits for military widows.)

THEOS Foundation (They Help Each Other Spiritually)
322 Boulevard of the Allies, Ste. 105
Pittsburgh, PA 15222-1919
1-412-471-7779
1-412-471-7782 (FAX)
(*Survivors Outreach* magazine, educational groups, and conventions.)

Suggested Reading for Widows

There are several resources you can use in locating these titles: your local library (and inter-library loan system), your church library, bookstores, your bereavement minister's personal library, local support groups' lending libraries, hospices, and funeral homes.

Remember, if a book doesn't seem to make sense right now, try reading it again later.

After the Flowers: Life Beyond Widowhood. A. Daniels. Fithian, 1996.

All Alone: Surviving the Loss of Your Spouse. K. Buntin. Desert, 1995.

Being a Widow. L. Caine. Viking Penguin, 1990.

But I Never Thought He'd Die: Practical Help for Widows. M. Nye. Westminster John Knox, 1978.

Companion Through the Darkness: Inner Dialogues on Grief. S. Ericsson. HarperSan Francisco, 1993.

Coping with Life after Your Mate Dies. D. Cushenberry and R.C. Cushenberry. Baker, 1997.

Coping with Separation and Loss as a Young Adult. L. LaGrand. Charles C. Thomas, Publisher, 1989.

DAWN - Divorced and Widowed Women's News Founder: Sharon Grinage.

Dear Lord, I Can't Do It All. B. Reed. Concordia, 1991.

Does Anybody Else Hurt This Bad and Live? C. Eneroth. Otis, 1991.

Doors Close, Doors Open: Widows Grieving & Growing. M. Lieberman. Putnam, 1996.

Fran & Jesus on the Job. M. Whekchel. Tyndale, 1993.

I'm Grieving As Fast As I Can: How Young Widows & Widowers Can Cope & Heal. L. Feinberg. New Horizon, 1994.

Instantly a Widow. R. Sissom. Discovery House, 1990.

The Lessons of Love: Rediscovering our Passion for Life When it all seems too hard to take. M. Beattie. Walker & Company, 1995.

Letter To My Husband: Notes About Mourning and Recovery. J. Truman. Viking Penguin, 1987.

Letters To My Husband. F. Brooks. Hall-Sloane, 1993.

Living Alone. H. Anderson and F. Gardner. Westminister John Knox Press, 1997.

Being a Widow. L. Caine. Viking Penguin, 1990.

Living Through Personal Crisis. A. K. Stearns. Thomas More, 1984.

Living With An Empty Chair. R. Temes. New Horizon, 1992.

More Power to You! The Personal Protection Handbook for Women. S. Koumanelis. Round Lake, 1993.

The Nevertheless Principle. M. West. Chosen Books, 1986.

Older Bereaved Spouses. D. Lund. Hemisphere Publishing, 1989.

Parents Without Partners Sourcebook. S. L. Atlas.

A Practical Guide to Prepare for & Survive Widowhood. R. Carpenter. Carpenter Ventures.

Rest Stops for Single Mothers: Devotions to Encourage You on Your Journey. S. Osborne and L. Moses. Broadman, 1995.

Starting Over: Help for Young Widows and Widowers. A. R. Nudel. Dodd, Mead, 1986.

Suddenly Alone. P. Gates. HarperCollins, 1990.

Suddenly Single! A Lifeline for Anyone Who Has Lost a Love. H. J. Larson and S. Larson. Halo Books, 1993.

Suddenly Single Mom: A Practical Guide to Self-Sufficient Survival. T. Terry. TJ Terry, 1996.

Survival Handbook for Widows (and for relatives and friends who want to understand). R. J. Loewinsohn. Scott, Foresman and Company and the American Association of Retired Persons, 1984.

The Suddenly Single Mother's Survival Guide. L. Kite. Mills Sanderson, 1991.

Turning Your World Right Side Up. J. Smoke. Focus on the Family, 1995.

When Your Spouse Dies. C. Curry. Ave Maria Press, 1990.

Widow. L. Caine. Bantam, 1974.

The Widows' Guide to Life. I. Fisher and B. Lane. Prentice-Hall, 1981.

The Widow's Handbook: A Guide for Living. C. Foehner and C. Cozart. Fulcrum, 1988.

Suggested Reading for Widowers

There are several resources you can use in locating these titles: your local library (and inter-library loan system), your church library, bookstores, your bereavement minister's personal library, local support groups' lending libraries, hospices, and funeral homes.

Remember, if a book doesn't seem to make sense right now, try reading it again later.

All Alone: Surviving the Loss of Your Spouse. K. Buntin. Desert Books, 1995.

Companion Through the Darkness: Inner Dialogues on Grief. S. Ericsson. Harper San Francisco, 1993.

Coping with Life after Your Mate Dies. D. Cushenberry and R. C. Cushenberry. Baker, 1997.

Coping with Separation and Loss as a Young Adult. L. LaGrand. Charles C. Thomas, Publisher, 1989.

Cowbells and Courage. P. Page. Centering Corporation, 1993.

The Death of a Wife: Reflections for a Grieving Husband. R. Vogt. ACTA, 1996.

Does Anybody Else Hurt This Bad and Live? C. Eneroth. Otis, 1991.

I'm Grieving As Fast As I Can: How Young Widows & Widowers Can Cope & Heal. L. Feinberg. New Horizon, 1994.

The Lessons of Love: Rediscovering our Passion for Life When it all seems too hard to take. M. Beattie. Walker & Company, 1995.

Living Alone. H. Anderson and F. Gardner. Westminister John Knox Press, 1997.

Living Through Personal Crisis. A. K. Stearns. Thomas More, 1984.

A Look in the Mirror: A Handbook for Widowers. E. Ames. Centering Corporation, 1995.

Older Bereaved Spouses. D. Lund. Hemisphere, 1989.

Parents Without Partners Sourcebook. S. L. Atlas.

She Never Said Good-Bye: One Man's Journey Through Grief. R. Dykstra. Shaw, 1989.

Starting Over: Help for Young Widows and Widowers. A. R. Nudel. Dodd, Mead, 1986.

Suddenly Single! A Lifeline for Anyone Who Has Lost a Love. H. J. Larson and S. Larson. Halo Books, 1993.

Turning Your World Right Side Up. J. Smoke. Focus on the Family, 1995.

When Your Spouse Dies. C. Curry. Ave Maria Press, 1990.

Why Her, Why Now?: A Man's Journey Through Love & Death & Grief. L. Elmer. Signal Elm Press, 1994.

Widowed. P. Jebb. St. Bedes, 1984.

Widower: When Men Are Left Alone. S. Campbell and P. Silverman. Baywood, 1995.

Support Groups and Organizations for Widowers

It is one of the most beautiful compensations of this life
that no man can seriously help another
without helping himself.

RALPH WALDO EMERSON

Widowed Persons Service (WPS)
c/o American Association of Retired Persons
601 East St. NW
Washington, DC 20049
1-202-434-2260
1-202-434-6474 (FAX)
(A non-age related service. Trained peer counseling, referrals, publications, and conventions.)

Widowed Information and Consultation Services (WICS)
P.O. Box 66896
Seattle, WA 98166
1-206-241-5650
1-206-241-1139
(Support and information after the death of a spouse.)

THEOS Foundation (They Help Each Other Spiritually)
322 Boulevard of the Allies, Ste. 105
Pittsburgh, PA 15222-3510
1-412-471-7779
1-412-471-7782 (FAX)
(*Survivors Outreach* magazine, educational groups, and conventions.)

Monthly Messages

On Your Own (for those under 60)

Living alone was not your choice.
But you do have the choice how you will continue to live.

RONALD C. STARENKO

It can be difficult moving from being a "we" to an "I," especially after many years of marriage. Being alone can bring challenges, joys, and loneliness.

You may have experienced the disappearance of some of your closest friends or been surprised by others whom you least expected to give you support. Our closest friends sometimes feel they need to give us answers when we ask questions like "Why me?" instead of just listening. Or they may simply not understand what you're going through or what grief is about; they may think you'll get over it in a couple weeks. Or it may be that even though you are friends, you have never shared your deepest feelings, and now that you are vulnerable and needing to express feelings of sadness, anger, etc., they are not sure how to handle it.

At this point, you may be wishing you had some companionship. Perhaps you have felt like a fifth wheel at a gathering or party; perhaps you just miss the sound of a (woman's/man's) voice or the touch of a hand.

You may be considering dating or have already gone out on a date. When you think about dating again, try to bring to it a mindset of friendliness and adventure. You may not feel like starting over again and may even feel awkward and resentful. You may not even feel like dating after taking care of a spouse through a long illness. But remember, it can be stimulating to make a new friend. When love is given away, more love is generated.

Many widows and widowers have been surprised and sometimes felt ashamed by their revived interest in sex. But after many years of having close physical contact—whether it be a quick kiss or the passions of your bedroom—you knew you had a sense of belonging and a feeling of being attractive. Being interested in dating and perhaps remarriage can be a testimony to your wonderful marriage.

But remember, there is no right or wrong way to feel or mourn. Some people will be ready to date sooner than others, and you may never have the urge to get married again. There is no right time to get involved; you should simply wait until you are ready—whether in three months or in three years.

One question that often comes up is, "Should I stop wearing my wedding ring?" This is an individual decision, and there is no right or wrong time, but if you are considering dating it can be confusing to your date if you leave your ring on. You may want to try moving it to your other hand, giving it to one of your children, wearing it on a chain, or remaking it into a different ring. Another practical question that is frequently asked is, "What should I do with the pictures of my wife/husband?" You may want to display only one picture and move the others to your children's rooms or put them in a family album.

If you are feeling eager to meet some new people, consider the following possibilities:

- support groups
- single groups
- volunteer activities (even if you work full-time, a couple hours volunteering can put you in contact with new and interesting people)
- church
- classes at a university or college
- a college-sponsored tour
- chartered day trips offered through a travel agency that goes to museums, skiing, shopping, etc.
- cruises
- athletic clubs
- local necessities: grocery shopping, library, restaurants, coffee shops

Starting a new life can be scary. It will be a challenge, but remember: it can also be an adventure!

> *"The hour is coming, indeed it has come, when you will be scattered,*
> *each one to his home, and you will leave me alone.*
> *Yet I am not alone because the Father is with me."*
> _____
> JOHN 16:32

On Your Own (for those over 60)

> *Living alone was not your choice.*
> *But you do have the choice how you will continue to live.*
> _____
> RONALD C. STARENKO

It can be difficult moving from being a "we" to an "I," especially after many years of marriage. It may be hard to think of yourself as a single person. You have probably experienced some of your friends not calling anymore and been surprised by others whom you least expected to give you support.

You may find yourself longing for companionship. After years of being sexually active, touched, and caressed you may be feeling the need for a partner to share these moments, or you may just be longing to hear a (*woman's/man's*) voice again, to have a dance, dinner, or a movie partner, and/or go out on a date. Perhaps you have felt like a fifth wheel at a gathering or party.

Don't rule out the possibility of finding new romance. When you think about dating again, try to bring to it the mindset of friendliness and adventure. You may not feel like starting over again and may even feel awkward and resentful. You may feel tired after taking care of a spouse through a long illness. But remember, it can be stimulating to make a new friend. Being interested in dating and perhaps remarriage can be a testimony to your wonderful marriage.

One question that often comes up is, "Should I take off my wedding ring?" It is an individual decision, and there is no right or wrong time, but if you are considering dating, it may be confusing to your date if you leave your ring on. You may want to try moving it to your other hand, giving it to one of your children, wearing it on a chain, or remaking it into a different ring. Another practical question that is frequently asked is, "What should I do with the pictures of my wife/husband?" You may want to display only one picture and move the others to your children's rooms or put them in a family album.

Above all, remember there is no right or wrong way to feel or mourn. Some people will be ready to date sooner than others; some may never have the urge to get married again. There is no right time to get involved; you should simply wait until you are ready—whether in three months or in three years.

If you are feeling eager to meet some new people, consider the following possibilities:

- support groups
- volunteer activities
- church
- classes at a university or college
- a college-sponsored tour
- chartered day trips offered through a travel agency that goes to museums, skiing, shopping, etc.
- cruises
- local necessities: grocery shopping, library, restaurants, coffee shops

On the other hand, being on your own can offer more freedom to seek out new activities that weren't possible before, e.g., more time to spend with your children or grandchildren, to volunteer, to travel, to learn, to try a new craft, hobby, or take up an artistic talent (many great works of art, literature, poetry, etc., were done after the age of 60). Your creative energy can also be directed into love and service to others

Another concern you might have is one of health. "Who will look after me when I am sick?" If your children are close by and are willing to help you, that can be a real blessing. But if you have no children or your children are far away, what can you do?

1. Call the church office and let us know if you are sick, even if it's same-day surgery. There is no need to suffer alone.

2. Develop a signal with your neighbor such as opening a shade or a curtain, or give a two-jingle ring on the telephone at 7 a.m. to let the other person know you are okay

3. Let friends know what they can do for you. Often friends are very willing to drop off a thermos of chicken-noodle soup, talk on the phone, or pick up a flower for you.

4. Local hospitals might have a free service where a volunteer from the hospital will call you every day to make sure you are okay.

Starting a new life can be scary. It will be a challenge, but remember: it can also be an adventure!

"The hour is coming, indeed it has come, when you will be scattered,
each one to his home, and you will leave me alone.
Yet I am not alone because the Father is with me."

JOHN 16:32

Death of a Parent

Setting Up a Program of Bereavement Care for Those Grieving the Death of a Parent

Special concerns of adult children who lose a parent include the following:

1. They may not want to get close to anyone emotionally for fear of that person dying or deserting them and reawakening the painful loss.

2. They may experience what Katherine Donnelly, in her book *Recovering from the Loss of a Parent,* calls "birthday syndrome." When a parent dies at a particular age, the son or daughter may begin to get anxious and even develop symptoms related to the parent's illness as she or he approaches the age at which the parent died. For example, a son whose father died of a heart attack at age 49 may become increasingly anxious with each birthday until he is able to successfully pass through his 49th year.

3. They may experience a dreadful sense of being alone. They may see someone resembling the parent walking down the street or in a restaurant and burst into tears.

4. They may experience battles with siblings. Tempers can flare, fuses can be short, and disagreements can block the grieving process. There may be power struggles over possessions. Old jealousies and grievances can emerge, and adult children can revert to the same roles they had as children. In such instances, it may be helpful to offer gentle reminders that the disputed possessions are not a substitute for the parent. Often parents can be the glue that holds children together and once they have died the family disbands.

5. They may also experience what Katherine Donnelly calls the "caretaker syndrome." Adult children caring for ill parents sometimes wish their mother or father would die because of their resentment over how the parent has changed their life. They may have felt locked in and forced to do things for the parent. Then once the parent has died, they feel guilty. The "should haves" and "shouldn't haves" can often debilitate children.

- "I shouldn't have yelled at dad for. . . ."
- "I should have been there more for mother. . . ."

Encourage them that they did the best they could at the time and that what they did or didn't do was not unusual or wrong. Writing a letter of repentance to the dead parent is often very healing and offers a form of catharsis.

6. If the surviving parent is healthy, financially secure, and independent, the death may be less devastating, though she or he will feel a great deal of aloneness. If, on the other hand, the surviving parent is ill, the child may be thrust into the role of caregiver. One child may feel resentment that the other siblings aren't sharing in the responsibility and may even fantasize about the remaining parent's death. These adult children need community help and resources. Contact your local library, government assistance programs, churches, nursing homes, hospice, United Way agencies, and others for help.

Initial Contact

Immediately after the death, send out a personalized "Grieving the Death of a Parent" letter (page 143). Individualize this letter, using the parent's name and appropriate details.

After your letter has been received, you should call to set up an initial visit to the grieving person. At this visit, you should remind the grieving person that reactions to the death of a parent can vary but that she or he should take her or his own grieving process seriously. The following materials are designed to be given at your initial visit:

Physical Symptoms of Grieving	(page 29)
Exercise and Nutrition	(page 30)
Getting to Sleep	(page 32)
Suggested Reading After a Major Loss	(page 34)
Suggested Reading After the Death of a Parent	(page 144)

Monthly Messages

In addition, the following Monthly Messages should be sent during the first few months of bereavement (see pages 19-21 for instructions on incorporating these messages into personalized letters or otherwise including them in bereavement care):

The Grieving Process	(page 38)	2 weeks after loss
Common Myths About Grief	(page 39)	1 month after loss
You and Your Emotions	(page 40)	2 months after loss
Enough Faith?	(page 41)	
Working With Your Grieving	(page 42)	3 months after loss

Depending on the relationship of parent and child, also send out some or all of the following Monthly Messages (see pages 19-21 for instructions on incorporating these messages into personalized letters or otherwise including them in bereavement care):

Returning to "Normal"	(page 43)	4 months after loss
I Know There's Life After Death, Right?	(page 44)	5 months after loss
Dealing With Criticism	(page 45)	6 months after loss
How Will I Know I'm Feeling Better?	(page 48)	8 months after loss
A Special Note	(page 49)	10 months after loss
The Journey Continues	(page 50)	one year after loss

Also remember to send Special Day Messages on the parent's birthday, the anniversary of the death, Christmas, etc.

Ongoing Visitation

Further visitation will depend on the nature of the relationship of parent and child. See suggestions for visitation on page 21.

Please note: you may come in contact with those whose parents are still living, but are chronically ill or aging. In these cases, you may want to make available "Suggested Reading on Issues Related to Aging Parents" (page 265) and "Support Groups for Those Caring for the Chronically Ill or Aging" (page 266).

Grieving the Death of a Parent

(A personalized letter with this material should be sent immediately after the death.)

When a *(mother/father)* dies, it can be very difficult to say good-bye. Sometimes there are just no words to describe the sorrow or measure the pain. The words of Paul to the Romans may be comforting to you:

"Likewise the Spirit helps us in our weakness; for we do not know how to pray as we ought, but the Spirit himself intercedes for us with sighs too deep for words."

Know we are thinking about and praying for you.

Suggested Reading After the Death of a Parent

There are several resources you can use in locating these titles: your local library (and inter-library loan system), your church library, bookstores, your bereavement minister's personal library, local support groups' lending libraries, hospices, and funeral homes.

Remember, if a book doesn't seem to make sense right now, try reading it again later.

Coping When a Parent Dies. J. Grossshandler-Smith. Rosen, 1994.

How It Feels When A Parent Dies. J. Krementh. Peter Smith, 1993.

Learning to Say Goodbye When a Parent Dies. E. Le Shan. Avon, 1978.

Letters from Motherless Daughters: Words of Courage, Grief, and Healing. H. Edelman. Addison-Wesley, 1995.

Losing A Parent: Passage to a New Way of Living. A. Kennedy. HarperSanFrancisco, 1991.

The Loss That is Lost Forever: The Lifelong Impact of the Early Death of a Mother or Father. M. Harris. NAL-Dutton, 1995.

Making Peace With Your Parents. H. Bloomfield. Ballantine, 1983.

Motherless Daughters: The Legacy of Loss. H. Edelman. Addison-Wesley, 1994.

On Grieving the Death of a Father. H. Smith. Augsburg Fortress, 1994.

The Orphaned Adult. M. D. Angel. Human Services Press, 1987.

Recovering from the Loss of a Parent. K. Donnelly. Berkely, 1993.

Surviving the Loss of a Parent: A Guide for Adults. L. Akner and C. Whitney. Morrow, 1993.

When Parents Die: A Guide for Adults. E. Myers. Viking, 1986.

When Your Parent Dies. C. Curry. Ave Maria Press, 1993.

Death After Long-Term and Debilitating Illness

Setting Up a Program of Bereavement Care After Death From a Long-Term and Debilitating Illness

By the time someone has died from AIDS, cancer, or other long-term illness, the family has often gone through many weeks, even years, of emotional turmoil. The family life has been turned upside down, and most of their activities have revolved around the person who was ill.

Marriage relationships often suffer; couples may or may not have turned to counseling or a support group for help with their continuous grieving.

Caregivers have probably had to work against prejudice in themselves and others and fight against "the system" or even doctors and nurses as they wade through institutional red tape. They have probably suffered financially and may even have had to go on some type of governmental assistance.

They have had to watch their loved one become sicker by degrees and stages as the body prepared to die through manifestations of vomiting, lethargy, difficulty breathing, inability to eat or drink, mental confusion, seizures, muscular weakness, delusional thinking, and other symptoms. They may have even feared for their own safety in the case of an infectious disease such as AIDS.

They have probably cried many tears and been very angry at God and others.

All of these experiences can leave caregivers emotionally and physically exhausted, and they may have found their own well-being compromised during the long illness. They need encouragement that they did the best they could at the time and help to focus on the positive aspects of the relationship. If you were able to observe some of these positives—the way they worked hard to bring the person to church, or their diligence in helping the ill person feel good by keeping her or him attractively dressed—it would be encouraging to share these observations with the caregiver.

Often things are said and done in anger and frustration in a long-term care-giving situation. These issues should be brought up and discussed. Guilt can remain an important issue for many caregivers if not explored. Restitution with the deceased, through the writing of a letter, through prayer, through visualization or meditation, can aid the caregiver in healing.

The grieving experience will be varied. Since many have begun grieving as they have watched their loved one die, the grieving process after death may be shorter than usual. But ongoing grief will remain in connection with remembering the person and the dreams for the future that were cut short.

Initial Contact

Immediately after the death, send out a personalized "Grieving a Death After Long-Term and Debilitating Illness" letter (page 147). Individualize this letter as appropriate, including any information you have on local support groups.

After your letter has been received, you should call to set up an initial visit to the grieving person. The following materials are designed to be given at your initial visit:

Physical Symptoms of Grieving	(page 29)
Exercise and Nutrition	(page 30)
Getting to Sleep	(page 32)
Suggested Reading After a Major Loss	(page 34)

Monthly Messages

In addition, the following Monthly Messages should be sent during the first year of bereavement (see pages 19-21 for instructions on incorporating these messages into personalized letters or otherwise including them in bereavement care):

The Grieving Process	(page 38)	2 weeks after loss

Ongoing Visitation

See suggestions for visitation on page 21.

Please note: you may come in contact with those whose loved ones are still living, but are chronically ill or aging. See "Suggested Reading on Issues Related to Aging Parents" (page 265),"Support Groups for Those Caring for the Chronically Ill or Aging" (page 266), "Suggested Reading Related to Ongoing Illness" (page 267), and "Support Groups for Those Dealing With Terminal Illness" (page 269).

Grieving a Death After Long-Term and Debilitating Illness

(A personalized letter with this material should be sent immediately after the death.)

Please know that we are thinking about you at this difficult time. I know that circumstances have not been easy these last few *(weeks, months, years)*. There have probably been many situations where frustration, anger, fear, and worry have had the upper hand. But I'm sure there have also been moments of hope, laughter, strength, joy, and love that have been a part of your life.

Everyone has regrets of some kind or another—the "I should haves" or "I could haves"—but your love, discipline, patience, tolerance, and kindness were real, and *(deceased person's name)* could feel the love behind them. *(She/he)* was fortunate to have someone as caring and loving as you.

(We are/I am) thinking of you and your loss. *(We/I)* will be calling within the next week to make an appointment to see you.

You may also want to get in touch with a support group of people grieving as you are. Check (your local hospital), (your local hospice), Catholic Charities, Lutheran Social Services, United Way, or the Chamber of Commerce for a group near you.

Infertility

Setting Up a Program of Bereavement Care for Those Experiencing Infertility

There are probably couples in your congregation who have been dreaming of having a child. They may have made job choices or even saved up enough money to buy a house with this in mind. They may have begun to talk about a baby with excitement and anticipation. Some of them, however, will find that their dreams do not materialize.

A couple is described as having a medical condition called infertility if they have not been able to conceive after one full year of unprotected sex, or if the woman is unable to carry a pregnancy to live birth. Infertility is a complex experience that involves pain, grief, and isolation, and that requires bereavement care. Because not everyone is familiar with the realities of infertility, we have included some background information below.

Causes of Infertility

Infertility occurs in 12-15 % of the population and is on the rise. It is estimated that 35 % relates to the woman, 35 % relates to the man, and another 20 % to both. In 10 % of cases, no cause for infertility is found. "Sterility" is a term used to describe a diagnosed irreversible physical condition that prevents conception.

Some couples who are able to conceive go on to face the heartbreak of miscarriage. For some couples, repeated miscarriage will thwart their hope of bearing their own biological child.

Infertility Testing

Infertility testing can involve a large number of tests that can take a few months to a few years. These tests can be dehumanizing, embarrassing, and often painful. They can require that the couple leave work for a few hours, or sometimes for several days in a row, and can sometimes continue for months at a time.

Infertility Treatment

Infertility clinics claim that 50-70% of their patients can be treated for infertility. That does not mean that 50-70% of the couples seeking treatment will carry home a baby. Rather it means that 50-70% of the couples will have their problem diagnosed. Statistics suggest that only 13-35% of couples who seek treatment will be able to conceive and carry the pregnancy to term. Even though the chances are low in achieving a live birth, technology still provides hope for couples who wish for a child.

Infertility treatments are usually used in combination with one another, and standard care is changing due to the many recent developments in technology. At this point standard treatments may include any or combinations of the following:

- Pills or injections that stimulate production of eggs or cause the uterine wall to thicken

- Pills or injections that suppress the female reproductive cycle, "giving it a rest" (often used for endometriosis)

- Surgery

- Assisted Reproductive Technologies (ART), which tend to be more expensive, include the following:
  - IUI or AI (IUI = intrauterine insemination, AI = artificial insemination) both involve introducing sperm into a woman's body without intercourse. If donor sperm is used, of course, a number of additional issues come up: finding a donor, the child's genetic connection to only one parent, the child's questions about her or his conception, and bringing a "third party" into the marriage.
  - In vitro fertilization (IVF) involves stimulating the woman to produce several eggs, allowing fertilization to take place in the lab, and then putting the fertilized embryos directly into the uterus where, it is hoped, at least one will implant, creating a pregnancy. "Natural-cycle IVF" uses only the single egg that the woman naturally produces.
  - In Gamete Intrafallopian Transfer (GIFT), the eggs are removed from the ovaries, combined with the sperm, and then transferred to the fallopian tube where it is hoped that at least one will be fertilized, move on to the uterus, and implant, creating a pregnancy; GIFT generally has a higher success rate than IVF.

- In Zygote Intrafallopian Transfer (ZIFT), eggs are allowed to fertilize in the lab and are then placed in the fallopian tube; it is hoped that at least one embryo will then move into the uterus and implant, creating a pregnancy. Statistically, ZIFT offers the greatest chance of pregnancy.

(Taken from *The Infertility Book*, by Carla Harkness, Celestial Acts, 1992, and *How to Be a Successful Fertility Patient*, by Peggy Robin, William Morrow & Co., 1993.)

The Experience of Infertility

Infertility treatments can have several side effects for women:

- Moodiness
- Depression
- Irritability
- Anxiety
- Headaches
- Nausea
- Heart palpitations
- Lightheadedness
- Hot flashes
- Weight gain

Men can experience some of the same symptoms if they are put on hormone therapy.

Of course, the ongoing crisis of infertility has its own effects, apart from drug treatments. Those dealing with infertility may also experience depression, anger, guilt, inadequacy, jealousy, low self-esteem, shame, and resentment. They may have difficulty organizing, concentrating, and making decisions.

Infertility also has an effect on a couple's marriage. Infertility is often the first major crisis the couple has had to face together, since it usually happens relatively early in the marriage. Suddenly, the couple has to grapple with the most essential marital issues, including communication, sexuality, finances, decision making, how to resolve conflict, faith issues, and extended family and friendship issues.

There are important differences in the way that men and women approach infertility. Women tend to verbalize their pain, read about infertility, and establish relationships with other infertile women. Women often see their very identity as women threatened, and they usually take a more active role in the infertility process. Men, on the other hand, are often more stoic and less expressive. They take a more supportive or silent role even though they sometimes feel the same things that their wives do. Men may see themselves failing as a protector and provider: they can't fix the problem; the situation makes their wives unhappy, and they can't protect them from it.

Men tend to leave more of the decisions about infertility up to their wives, which can be a problem if their wives are looking for equal partners in the decision-making process.

Secondary Infertility

Couples who have been able to have one child or more but are unable to conceive or carry another child to term are said to have "secondary infertility."

These couples often feel caught in the middle—neither "fertile" nor "infertile." Testing and treatment tends to be more difficult insofar as their schedules revolve around an already existing child. Financially, it tends to be harder because they are already paying for child-related expenses. Emotionally, they grieve not being able to give their son or daughter another brother or sister and have difficulty at times going to their child's functions and having to deal with other children.

Grieving Infertility

Infertility involves a complex grieving process, creating up to six important losses:

- Control over many aspects of life
- Individual genetic continuity
- Joint conception of a child with one's life partner
- Physical satisfactions of pregnancy and birth
- Emotional gratifications of pregnancy and birth
- The opportunity to parent (depending on whether or not the couple eventually chooses to adopt)

(Taken from *Adopting After Infertility*, by P. I. Johnston, Perspectives Press, 1992.)

Those experiencing infertility mourn these losses in two simultaneous cycles of grieving. One extends from the initial recognition of the problem until resolution. This process can last anywhere from one to twelve years, depending on how long the couple decides to remain in treatment. If a couple is ultimately unable to bear their own biological child, the grieving process will probably last their entire lifetime, just as with any major loss experience.

The other cycle of grieving is centered around the woman's menstrual cycle. The couple begins infertility treatments about a week or so after the woman's last period. She may take shots or pills, with increasing anticipation. Intercourse (which is often a chore) or insemination is planned. Excitement builds with the hope that this time conception has occurred. Then, the women's period starts, and the grief returns: sadness, guilt, anger, shame, maybe even denial. Treatment may be renegotiated with the doctor, and the process starts all over again.

If pregnancy does not occur, a couple will at some point come to feel that they have expended as many of their resources—emotional, physical, and financial—as they can. If they have been able to grieve their losses in such a way that they are able to move on, they will resolve their infertility crisis in one of several ways: they may take a break from infertility treatment, stop treatment altogether and remain childless, or pursue other options such as adoption or foster care (with or without continuing fertility treatments). Of course, such decisions may have to be made again in the future.

What the Church Can Do

Listed below are a number of ways the church can support couples going through the crisis of infertility.

1. Recognize that there are probably infertile couples in your congregation, even if you aren't aware of it.

2. When you find out about their infertility (it is a personal matter and is often difficult for couples to share with others), approach them in person or by letter or phone call to find out whether they might be interested in the Initial Packet materials contained in this book. (See below.) Please do not send any information without their permission.

3. If you know two or more couples who are experiencing infertility, ask each whether they are interested in being put in touch with others who are in the same situation. If they are, introduce the couples to each another.

4. Remember prayers for couples going through infertility on Mother's Day, Father's Day, and at other child-oriented services. "We pray for all the men/women who would like to have children, but are unable to do so."

5. Send "I'm thinking of you" cards to infertile couples on holidays such as Halloween, Christmas, Easter, Mother's Day, and Father's Day, since these holidays tend to be child-centered and hard to cope with. (You may also want to send them "Handling the Holidays or Special Occasions," page 166.)

6. Suggest that they contact a reputable infertility clinic, if they have not done so already.

7. Help the couple make healthy, balanced choices for their lives. (If appropriate, send them "Taking Care of Yourself" pages 162-165.)

8. Remind the couple that even though it may be one or the other's infertility problem, it is still their problem together. Encourage them to support, uplift, and uphold one another during the process, and to go to doctor appointments together.

9. Hold healing services and invite infertile couples. You may even hold a special healing service just for those who are infertile.

10. Support them in their effort to conceive a child and offer empathy for the process of infertility. Acknowledge individual differences in those grieving and experiencing the process of infertility.

11. Offer the sacrament of reconciliation (confession and absolution) when appropriate.

12. Be supportive as they wrestle with social, moral, and ethical choices regarding infertility treatment.

13. Extend guilt- and shame-free counseling, extending love and compassion.

14. Offer them the possibility, when they are ready, of a ritual commemorating the loss of a child through miscarriage or loss of the child they had hoped for. (See pages 282-283.)

15. Last, offer ongoing support and concern about their treatments and testing. They will need to talk to someone who has an understanding heart.

You may find it helpful to do some reading to acquaint yourself further with issues surrounding infertility and ways in which you can minister to those dealing with this kind of grief. Below is a list of suggested reading.

"Child Sacrifice: Returning God's Gift." S. Ackerman. *Bible Review,* June 1993, 20-29.

"Genetic Science and Pastoral Care." M. Cavanagh. *Pastoral Psychology,* 1994, 42(5), 335-344.

"The Impact of Infertility and Treatment Guidelines for Couples Therapy." D. Eunpu. *The American Journal of Family Therapy,* 1995, 23(2), 115-126.

"Infertility: A Crisis With No Resolution." R. Butler and S. Koraleski. *Journal of Mental Health Counseling,* 1990, 12(2), 151-163.

"Infertility: His and Hers." A. Greil, T. Leitko, and K. Porter. *Gender and Society,* 1988, 2(2), 172-195.

"Infertility: An Unanticipated and Prolonged Life Crisis." L. Forrest and M. Gilbert. *Journal of Mental Health Counseling,* 1992, 14(1), 42-57.

"Parents and Children of Reproductive Technology: Chances and Risks for Their Well-Being." H. Colpin. *Community Alternatives,* 1994, 6(1), 49-65.

"Pastoral Care for Infertile Couples." N. Devor. *The Journal of Pastoral Care,* 1994, 48 (4), 355-360.

"Remembrance and Commendation: A Rite to Speak to Losses in Pregnancy." J. Peterman. *Lutheran Partners,* July/August 1988, 21-24.

"Self-Discrepancy As an Important Factor in Addressing Women's Emotional Reactions to Infertility." K. Kikendall. *Professional Psychology: Research and Practice,* 1994, 25(3), 214-219.

"Storm Clouds Are Coming: Ways to Help Couples Reconstruct the Crisis of Infertility." J. Atwood and S. Dobkin. *Contemporary Family Therapy,* 1992, 14 (5), 385-403.

"Strategies for Counseling Infertile Couples." J. Daniluk. *Journal of Counseling and Development,* 1991, 69, 317-320.

Initial Contact

If you encounter couples who indicate their interest in receiving information and support, make an appointment for an initial visit and offer an attractive notebook containing the following materials:

Physical Symptoms of Grieving	(page 29)
Getting to Sleep	(page 32)
Worry-Reduction Techniques	(page 252)
Suggested Reading After a Major Loss	(page 34)
Infertility Myths	(page 156)
The Grieving Process of Infertility	(pages 157-161)
Taking Care of Yourself	(pages 162-165)
Handling the Holidays or Special Occasions	(page 166)
Suggested Reading on Infertility	(pages 167-168)
Support Groups and Organizations Dealing With Infertility	(pages 169-170)

Ongoing Visitation

At the initial visit, also discuss the possibility of regular visits every six months or so. You may want to make available "Relaxation Resources" (pages 253-254) and "Coping With Your Emotions and Managing Stress" (page 262).

On pages 171-172 is a list of suggested reading regarding adoption and childless living. Give this list to the couple if and when you are able to determine that they have begun to consider these options.

A "Ritual for Saying Good-bye" (pages 282-283) may be used if and when the couple ends their attempts to conceive or a fetus is lost before birth. This can be given to the couple for their own private service, or bereavement ministers may offer to participate in or lead the service.

In the case of infertility. a program of letters sent "after two weeks," "after one month," etc., is not appropriate, given the chronic, cyclical nature of this grief experience. You should, however, contact couples again if you are aware of particular disappointments in their infertility treatment. A short note expressing your support on Mother's Day and Father's Day may also be much appreciated.

Infertility Myths

Unfortunately, many commonly held beliefs about infertility simply aren't true. Perhaps you've heard some of the following.

1. "Just relax and you'll get pregnant!" or "You're trying too hard."

   Fact: Psychological and emotional stress result from infertility, but do not cause infertility.

2. "When you adopt, you'll get pregnant!"

   Fact: Pregnancy occurs in only 5% of couples after an adoption, the same as for infertile couples who don't adopt.

3. "You must be having fun trying to make a baby!" or "Practice makes perfect."

   Fact: Sex often deteriorates because of its task orientation and lack of privacy with intimate facts known by physicians and fertility staff.

The Grieving Process of Infertility

The following is a list of emotions typical to the grieving process of infertility. Our suggestion is to read the section that seems to fit your situation right now, referring back to these pages frequently as your emotions change.

There are two types of grieving cycles connected with infertility. One begins with the initial recognition of infertility and lasts until it is resolved in one way or another (for some couples, this can take as long as ten years). The second revolves around monthly hope and disappointment connected with the woman's menstrual cycle.

There are three important points to remember:

1. Acknowledge that men and women will think, and act differently in response to the infertility process. Misunderstanding, frustration, and disappointment often occur when each thinks the other is not responding the way she or he should. Give one another lots of latitude. Love, uphold, and support one another because this is part of your work together.

2. Remember you will grieve differently, not just because of your gender but because of who you are as an individual. It's a given.

3. Your grieving will not move smoothly from one phase to another. You can expect to jump around, regress, and move ahead. It's okay; people's reactions vary.

Surprise/Shock/Denial/Disbelief

[Infertility Process]

"I can't believe this is happening to us!"
Infertile? Not me. I'll probably get
pregnant next month!"

[Monthly Cycle]

"We tried so hard this
month, and I was sure
it was going to happen."

These feelings are normal and typical of the beginning phases of grieving. This may be one of the first times in your married life that things haven't gone as you planned or hoped. Help is available. Consider a medical examination by a fertility specialist if you have been having unprotected intercourse for more than a year without a pregnancy.

At this point, when your monthly cycle ends without a pregnancy, disbelief and denial set in.

Anger

"Why won't God answer our prayers? We've prayed and prayed. I don't think God cares!"

"I did everything right this month! We even skipped the weekend at the cabin so we wouldn't miss treatment. It's not fair!"

"Why can teenage girls, who can't afford a baby, have one so easily, and we who could afford one and love and nurture it can't have a child?! It's not fair!"

Anger is a normal part of the grieving process. You are angry at your sense of helplessness and loss of control. It is most important to acknowledge that you are angry. If anger at the infertility process isn't recognized, it may cause you to blame your spouse and become angry and irritable with her or him. This in turn can cause you to withdraw your support and even stop empathizing with her or him.

You may find you are angry at everything and everyone . . . angry at baby commercials, pregnant women, infertility doctors and nurses, adoption agencies, holidays like Mother's Day and Father's Day, your spouse, yourself, and God.

If you're angry at God, you're not alone. In the Old Testament, God's faithful followers cried out to God to give them a child. Some of their pleas were answered with a child, such as in the story of Hannah (1 Samuel 1 and 2). Others were not. You're right; it's not fair—cry out to God!

Guilt

"What did I do that caused my infertility?"

"I shouldn't have gone to that party the other night where there was so much smoking."

"If my husband/wife had chosen another woman/man, he'd/she'd be a father/mother right now!"

"I'm so sick of all the tests and treatments. I just want to quit, but I'm afraid the next procedure might be the one to give us a baby."

Of course, we have all done things that we are not proud of. As Christians, in fact, we believe that we have all sinned. As you wrestle with infertility, you may have become aware that past actions you have taken have contributed to your infertility. There are two steps to take here. First, ask for and accept forgiveness. God promises that he is always ready to forgive. You may also want to ask for forgiveness from your spouse. If the sacrament of reconciliation (confession and absolution) is a part of your church tradition, you may find this to be a very helpful step.

Second, move on. Accept the forgiveness that you've been given. Do not allow yourself to believe that painful tests or repeated miscarriages are some sort of punishment. If you find yourself with vague, nagging thoughts such as "I'm really not forgiven," or "How worthless I am if I can't make babies"—stop! Resist these negative thoughts and replace them with ones that help you to see yourself as a worthwhile person and worthy of carrying on Christ's vocation into the world. ("Take every thought captive to obey Christ" 2 Corinthians 10:5.)

If you feel it would be helpful, get help from a professional counselor, preferably one familiar with issues of infertility.

Depression

"How can I be a real woman/man?"

"How can I be good at my work when I can't do something as simple as get pregnant?"

"We won't ever be able to have a baby."

"I feel so tired all the time."

This tends to be the longest part of the infertility process, lifting only periodically during each monthly cycle. At this point in your life you are probably around a lot of couples who are having babies: in-laws, coworkers, friends, and others. And if they don't know about your situation or aren't sure what to say, you may hear comments such as "When am I going to be a grandparent?" "Isn't it about time, you two?" "What's wrong, buddy? Do you want me to show you how?" or "You can have our kids!" These can be hurtful comments and may even cause you to pull away from friends and family. If you find this is happening to you, try some of the following suggestions:

1. Talk with your spouse if you've started to shut her or him out. Remember, you need each other for support.

2. Set goals for yourself every day that are easy to attain. This allows you to feel a sense of accomplishment when everything else seems out of control in your life.

3. Remember it's okay to cry at things like diaper and baby clothes commercials. It's also okay to change the channel!

4. If you have to go to a function where there will be friends and family asking a lot of questions, role-play some situations ahead of time. You might "practice" telling a friend that you don't feel like talking about your infertility problems right now, but that you'll let her know when you do.

5. If you have to go to a function where there are children, set a time limit or leave when you feel uncomfortable.

6. Not going to a function is always an option. If you find yourself avoiding all such events, though, you may want to push yourself to get out.

7. If you feel you need to talk to someone other than your spouse about your infertility problems, don't hesitate to call an understanding friend, counselor, or clergy person.

8. Remember that you cannot control your fertility, but you can control your treatment options and how long you will continue.

9. Remember we are New Testament people. In the Old Testament, having children was a way to fulfill the covenant promise given to Abraham (Genesis 12), a way to fulfill God's mandate "to be fruitful and multiply" (Genesis 1:28), and it was a sign of God's pleasure. But we know that we are more than reproductive beings, and, as New Testament people, we know that the kingdom of God is built by adoption—as God adopts us into God's kingdom, through Jesus Christ. In Christ, we are all brothers and sisters to one another and our blessings are in following our call as Christians and sharing our gifts with God's people.

The Losses Infertility Brings

Infertility involves at least six important losses:

- Control over many aspects of life
- Individual genetic continuity
- Joint conception of a child with one's life partner
- Physical satisfactions of pregnancy and birth
- Emotional gratifications of pregnancy and birth
- The opportunity to parent (depending on whether or not you eventually choose to adopt)

It is entirely normal for you to grieve each of these losses as you experience them.

Resolution

"I'm ready to look at adoption now."

"I need to take a break from treatment. Let's take the summer off and then re-evaluate."

At this point you are ready to move on . . . either to make a decision about remaining childless, to try more technology-based treatment, or to look at alternatives such as adoption, foster care, daycare, teaching, etc. It has been difficult, but you have made it as a couple. You have to congratulate yourself that you have made it through—or are making it through—a very difficult experience, hopefully strengthened in your relationship with one another, with your faith renewed and your commitment to Christian service heightened.

Whatever choice you make, God has something special planned for you—as individuals and as a couple. Good things will come your way, things that could not have happened if you had become pregnant as you originally planned. Be open to God's calling.

Before you make this transition, however, it is important to say good-bye to a painful yet strengthening phase of your life through ritual. Your bereavement minister, who has given you this information, has a "Ritual for Saying Good-bye" that may be helpful to you. In this ritual—which you can use formally or informally—you will say good-bye to the child you dreamed of. You have probably often pictured the child you hoped for. Now is the time to allow yourself to visualize that child as fully as you can. Take the time to write that child a letter and tell her or him how painful this has been and how sad you are that you couldn't have shared it with her or him. Next, gather supportive family and friends, with or without clergy, and celebrate your good-bye ritual. This ritual can be a very healing experience that allows you to move on.

From time to time—and perhaps for years into the future—you may experience what are called "anniversary reactions." If you had a miscarriage on April 12th, you may feel sad on many April 12ths and not be able to explain why. Or you may start feeling melancholy in October because that was when you were first diagnosed with infertility. You may also continue to experience unexpected episodes of deep sadness, perhaps when a close friend announces that she is expecting. Don't worry; these experiences are also part of the grieving process, and their intensity will decrease as time goes on.

Meanwhile, celebrate your "moving on." It is now time to move on and strengthen friendships that may have fallen by the wayside, take up a new hobby, renew your commitment to your work, and give thanks for all the good things that life has given you.

Taking Care of Yourself

"Just relax" won't help you get pregnant any faster, but taking care of yourself will aid your body to rebalance itself while going through a stressful time. You are probably familiar with a lot of these suggestions already, but are you practicing them? Try at least one or two.

1. Eat a diet low in fat and high in complex carbohydrates (grains, cereals, pasta). Be sure you are getting adequate protein. Cut down or stop smoking and drinking altogether.

2. In view of a possible pregnancy, women should make sure they get adequate folic acid, through diet or through vitamin supplements. Good sources of folic acid include spinach, whole wheat, wheat bran, romaine lettuce, cabbage, asparagus, kidney beans, lima beans, oranges, bananas, and cantaloupe.

3. Get adequate rest and sleep.

4. Walk briskly, at least 30 minutes a day, to increase your blood circulation and reduce stress.

5. Pray and meditate daily for at least 20 minutes.

   a. If you're too angry to pray, tell God so. Keep the lines of communication open. Try reading the passages from the Bible where other faithful people were angry at God, too. (Psalms 10, 13, 22, 38, 55, 74, 83, 102, and 109)

   b. Try using a mantra (a word or set of words that are repeated over and over) for relaxing meditation. When you start using mantras or verses, don't become discouraged if distracting thoughts come into your mind. There are several ways to deal with distracting thoughts:

   • Keep a piece of paper and a pencil handy to write down what you want to remember.

   • Ask yourself to remember it after your meditation time.

   • Just let the thought go by nonjudgmentally.

   • Bring the disturbing thought before God and ask for guidance.

   • Start with five minutes of meditation and work up to 20-30 minutes.

One variation is to say your mantra to yourself as you breathe in; then, when you blow out, say the word that is the opposite of your mantra. (Example: love—inhale; hate—exhale.) Imagine yourself breathing in the good and breathing out the bad.

Another variation is to fix an image to your mantra and imagine those images moving in and out of your body. (Example: An image for love might be a warm flame; an image for hate may be a twisted black wire. Flame—inhale; wire—exhale.)

You can make up your own mantra or try one of the following:

- "Light"
- "Love"
- "Courage"
- "Hope"
- "Faith"
- "Peace"
- "Be strong and of good courage; neither fear nor be dismayed; for the Lord your God is with you wherever you go" (Joshua 1:9).
- "God is our hope and strength, a very present help in trouble. . . . Be still then, and know that I am God" (Psalm 46:1, 10).
- "Lo, I am with you always, to the close of the age" (Matthew 28:20).
- "They that wait upon the Lord shall renew their strength; they shall mount up with wings as eagles, they shall run and not be weary, they shall walk and not faint" (Isaiah 40:31).
- "Come unto me, all you who labor and are heavy-laden, and I will refresh you" (Matthew 11:28).
- "Let not your heart be troubled. You believe in God, believe also in Me" (John 14:1).
- "Let your hope be a joy to you, be patient in trouble, continue steadfastly in prayer" (Romans 12:12).
- "I can do all things through Christ who strengthens me" (Philippians 4:13).
- "Let the peace of God rule in your hearts" (Colossians 3:15).

6. Attend a healing service. God sometimes gives people unexpected healing. But even if you are not healed miraculously, it may help to remind you that God is listening and that God will guide you in the process of healing. Sometimes, we just need other people to pray for us and support us when we get too tired to pray for ourselves or when we are questioning our faith.

7. Laugh often. Develop a humor library if you can. Collect books, movies, cartoons, or other paraphernalia that you can watch or read when you're feeling especially down. Even if you can only produce a forced smile and sit upright, it will set the physiology of your body in a positive way to help produce positive emotions. Try it for a minute or two.

8. Attend a support group. The group will provide a place from the fertile world that will allow for the expression of pain and isolation that often accompanies infertility. Contact the national infertility support group to find out the closest support group in your area. See the attached sheet for more information.

9. Seek professional counseling if you feel like you need it. Sometimes feelings of inadequacy and depression can affect every arena of your life. Seek a counselor who is experienced in infertility issues.

10. Renew your interest in each other (other than around the fertile time of the woman's cycle!). Dine out together by candlelight, buy each other small gifts, give each other massages, go on bike rides together . . . use your imagination!

11. Make time for your hobbies, volunteer work, sports, artistic endeavors, etc. It's important to find an outlet outside of infertility and your work that will allow you freedom to express your creativity or take your mind off of it.

12. Keep a personal journal of your experiences and feelings. Writing them down on paper helps bring them to your conscious mind where you can deal with them more objectively.

13. List five things you are grateful for every day.

14. Read, read, read. The more knowledge you have about infertility, the more confident you will be in asking questions of your doctor as to what sort of treatment you may be facing. See the "Suggested Reading" list.

15. Educate your family and friends, and be assertive. Most of the time, people are not trying to hurt you, but they don't know any other way to ask their questions or how to talk about your infertility. When they ask, for example, "When are you and Mike going to have a baby?" you may want to respond with something like, "We're having problems trying to conceive. It's a difficult subject, and it's hard to talk about right now. But I'll talk to you about it someday when I'm feeling better." If they keep pressing you, you probably won't feel like talking to them later, but having a few handy lines at the tip of your tongue can save you feelings of anger or bitterness. Sometimes people just won't understand.

16. When talking with your spouse try to avoid accusations and instead use "I" statements. Instead of "You don't care," turn it into "I was disappointed when you couldn't be with me during my test today. I felt like it wasn't important to you, and it really hurt!" Try reflective listening: listen carefully to your spouse and restate for her or him what you heard. For example, "So, you believe . . ." or "It sounds like you feel. . . ." This helps your spouse to know that you are hearing her or him and validating her or his feelings. Avoid using words such as "never" or "always."

17. Relaxation exercises such as deep breathing and progressive relaxation can offer a sense of peace and calm. In progressive relaxation, you begin by tightening your toes, holding them for five seconds, and then releasing the muscles. Work your way up the body, tightening and releasing different muscle groups until you reach your head.

18. Visual imagery can be an effective tool for physical and emotional healing. Take some quiet time and visualize yourself as calm, collected, making wise decisions in your treatment. Visualize your body strong and healthy. Visualize the conception that you hope for, with sperm finding egg and the egg finding a welcoming uterus.

19. Make a "feel good" box for days when you're especially low such as right after you get your period. Find the prettiest box you can and fill it with treasured mementos such as: pretty earrings you wear only once in awhile, a special tea or expensive hot cocoa, uplifting sayings or Bible passages, pictures, a wonderful-smelling sachet, a beautiful painting on a card, or anything that makes you feel good.

20. Find a "prayer partner" or "sponsor" who is not going through infertility but would be sympathetic to your journey. Ask that person if she or he would be willing to stay in touch with you. Make a contract with that person for three, six, or twelve months. During that time the person may send you a card, give you a call, go to appointments with you, pray for you, or somehow express her or his concern and care for you. Don't be afraid to ask your friends. They are often looking for ways to help you, and this would give them an opportunity for ministry.

Handling the Holidays or Special Occasions

Holidays and special occasions can be especially difficult when you're dealing with infertility. Here are a few suggestions.

1. Instead of denying that it is a sad time, talk with a trusted friend, clergy person, or counselor about your emotions.

2. Plan a romantic getaway on Mother's Day or Father's Day.

3. Try going Christmas shopping early when the malls aren't as filled with children.

4. You do have the option of declining a holiday with family if you know it is just going to be too painful this year. Try a new tradition of going skiing or flying to a warm place.

5. As a couple, choose which holiday events to attend. Choose how long you will stay, or choose to stay as long as you are comfortable.

6. You may decline a baby shower invitation without an apology or explanation; just send your gift. You may want to purchase a gift certificate; the new parents can choose what they need, and you won't have to go through the painful experience of shopping in the baby department.

7. Volunteer at hospitals, nursing homes, homeless shelters, and churches during the holidays, for they are often in need of help. Senior citizens who have relatives living far away from home would appreciate a call from you. Contact the visitation person at your parish or congregation to find out who would appreciate a call.

8. If you are asked to be a baptismal sponsor or "godparent" and accept, make sure the child's parents know what you are experiencing, so that they will understand that it may be difficult for you at some points.

Suggested Reading on Infertility

There are several resources you can use in locating these titles: your local library (and inter-library loan system), bookstores, your bereavement minister's personal library, your church library, and local support groups' lending libraries.

Remember, if a book doesn't seem to make sense right now, try reading it again later.

Keep in mind that the fertility treatments described in some books may be outdated. As you try to inform yourself about the technical, medical details of fertility treatment, you should consult the most current books available (as well as your doctor).

Adopting After Infertility. P. Johnston. Perspectives Press, 1995.

Between Strangers. L. Andrews. Harper & Row, 1989.

The Couple's Guide to Fertility. G. Berger, M. Goldstein, and M. Fuerst. Doubleday, 1995.

Crossing the Moon: A Journey Through Infertility. P. Alden. Hungry Mind Press, 1996.

Dear God: Why Can't We Have a Baby? J. Van Regenmorter, S. Van Regenmorter, and J. McIlhany. Baker, 1986.

Dr. Richard Marrs' Fertility Book. R. Marrs, L. F. Bloch, and K. K. Silverman. Delacorte Press, 1997.

Dr. Susan Lark's Fibroid Tumors and Endometriosis Self-Help Book. S. Lark. Celestial Arts, 1995.

The Fertility Sourcebook: Everything You Need to Know. M. S. Rosenthal. Lowell House, 1996.

Getting Pregnant. M. Frisch and G. Rapoport. The Body Press, 1987.

Getting Pregnant and Staying Pregnant: Overcoming Infertility and Managing Your High-Risk Pregnancy. D. Raab. Hunter House, 1991.

Getting Pregnant When You Thought You Couldn't. H. Rosenberg and Y. Epstein. Warner, 1993.

Give Us a Child: Coping with the Personal Crisis of Infertility. L. Stephenson. Harper and Row, 1987.

Healing the Infertile Family. G. Becker. Harper & Row, 1990.

High-Tech Conception: A Comprehensive Handbook for Consumers. B. Kearney. Bantam, 1998.

How Can I Help? A Handbook for Practical Suggestions for Family or Friends of Couples Going Through Infertility. D. Clapp and M. Bombardieri. Fertility Counseling Associates, 1991.

How to Be a Successful Fertility Patient. P. Robin. William Morrow, 1993.

In Pursuit of Fertility. R. Franklin and D. Brockman. Henry Holt, Inc., 1995.

In Search of Motherhood: A True Story of Two Women Who Triumph over Infertility. B. Schulgold and L. Sipiora. Dell, 1992.

In Search of Parenthood: Coping with Infertility and High-Tech Conception. J. Lasker. Beacon Press, 1987.

Infertility: A Guide for the Childless Couple. B. Mennings. Prentice-Hall, 1988.

Infertility: Women Speak out About Their Experiences with Reproductive Medicine. R. Arditti, ed. Pandora, 1989.

The Infertility Book: A Comprehensive Medical and Emotional Guide. C. Harkness. Celestial Arts, 1992.

Longing for a Child. B. Reed. Augsburg Fortress, 1994.

Not Yet Pregnant: Infertile Couples in Contemporary America. A. Greil. Rutgers University Press, 1991.

Sometimes I Hurt: Reflections on the Book of Job. M. Tengom. Concordia, 1986.

Surviving Infertility: A Compassionate Guide Through the Emotional Crisis of Infertility. L. Salzer. HarperPerennial, 1991.

Wanting Another Child: Coping with Secondary Infertility. H. Simons. Lexington Books, 1995.

What You Can Do About Infertility. P. Novotny. Dell, 1991.

"When the Dream Child Dies." B. Spring. *Christianity Today*, 1987, 31, 27-31.

Without Child: A Compassionate Look at Infertility. M. Stout. Zondervan, 1985.

A Woman's Book of Life: The Biology, Psychology, and Spirituality of the Feminine Life Cycle. J. Borysenko. Riverhead, 1996.

You may also want to be aware of the following:

Tapestry Books
P.O. Box 359
Ringoes, NJ 08551
1-800-765-2367
(Offers a catalogue filled with books on infertility, pregnancy loss, and adoption.)

Perspectives Press
P.O. Box 90318
Indianapolis, IN 46290-0318
317-872-3055
(This press publishes only books on infertility, adoption, and related issues.)

# Support Groups and Organizations Dealing With Infertility

*It is one of the most beautiful compensations of this life
that no man can seriously help another
without helping himself.*

RALPH WALDO EMERSON

Check your local Catholic Charities, Lutheran Social Services, United Way, local infertility clinics, or these national organizations to find your nearest support group.

American Fertility Society
2140 11th Ave. S., Suite 200
Birmingham, AL 35205
1-205-933-8494
(An organization for health professionals specializing in infertility. They provide a monthly journal, referrals, and information.)

The Endometriosis Association
International Headquarters Office
8585 N. 76th Place
Milwaukee, WI 53223
1-414-355-2200 or 1-800-992-3636 in US
1-800-426-2363 in Canada
(Extensive resource for women with endometriosis. Literature, newsletters, video, support group information, and crisis line.)

Infertility Awareness Association of Canada (IAAC)
1785 Alta Vista Dr., Suite 104
Ottawa, Ontario KlG3Y6
613-738-0159 (FAX)
(Charitable organization for Canadians experiencing infertility. It offers support, referrals, and education.)

Resolve, Inc.
1310 Broadway
Somerville, MA 02144-1731
617-623-1156
617-623-0744 Helpline (day)
(A national self-help organization for infertile couples. Helpline is staffed during regular business hours Monday through Friday. A very good resource!)

Stepping Stones
Dr. & Mrs. John Van Regenmorter
1804 South Emerson
Denver, CO 80210
(They have been featured on radio's "Focus on the Family" series and publish a newsletter. They minister by telephone and mail.)

Hannah's Prayer Ministries
P.O. Box 5016
Auburn, CA 95604-5016
E-mail: hannahs@quiknet.com
(Christian-based nonprofit organization that publishes a quarterly newsletter and offers chat rooms, resources, pen pals through E-mail, prayer support connections, and handbooks helpful in organizing a local chapter.)

National Infertility Network Exchange (NINE)
P.O. Box 204
East Meadow, NJ 11554
1-516-794-5772
1-516-794-0008 (FAX)
(Peer support for individuals and couples experiencing infertility. Education, referral, advocacy, newsletters, and speaker's bureau.)

Suggested Reading on Adoption and Childless Living

There are several resources you can use in locating these titles: your local library (and inter-library loan system), bookstores, your bereavement minister's personal library, your church library, and local support groups' lending libraries,

Remember, if a book doesn't seem to make sense right now, try reading it again later.

Adoption

Adopt the Baby You Want. M. Sullivan and S. Shultz. Simon and Schuster, 1990.

Adopting After Infertility. P. Johnston. Perspectives Press, 1995.

Adopting the Older Child. C. Jewett. Harvard Common Press, 1978.

Adoption: A Handful of Hope. S. Arms. Celestial Arts, 1990.

The Adoption Directory. E. Paul, ed. Gale Research, 1989.

The Adoption Resource Book. L. Gilman. Harper Perennial, 1992.

The Adoption Triangle. A. Sorosky, A. Barran, and R. Pannor. Corona, 1989.

The Art of Adoption. L. Burger. W.W. Norton, 1981.

Beating the Adoption Game. C. Morton. Harcourt Brace Jovanovich, 1988.

Children of Open Adoption. K. Silber and P. Dorner. Corona, 1989.

Dear Birthmother: Thank You for Our Baby. K. Silber and P. Speedlin. Corona, 1983.

Lifeline: The Action Guide to Adoption Search. V. Klunder. Caradium, 1991.

Making Sense of Adoption. L. Melina. Harper and Row, 1989.

The Open Adoption Book: A Guide to Adoption Without Tears. B. Rappaport. Macmillan, 1992.

The Private Adoption Handbook: The Complete Step-by-Step Guide to Independently Adopting a Baby. S. Michelman, M. Schneider, and A. van der Meer. Dell, 1989.

There Are Babies to Adopt: A Resource Guide for Prospective Parents. C. Ademec. Pinnacle, 1990.

Well-Functioning Families for Adoptive and Foster Children. J. Cohen and A. Westhues. University of Toronto Press, 1990.

Childless Living

Childless by Choice. M. Faux. Anchor Press, 1984.

Childless Is Not Less. V. Love. Bethany House, 1984.

Marriage Without Children. D. Burgwyn. Harper and Row, 1992.

Sweet Grapes: How to Stop Being Infertile and Start Living Again. J. Carter and M. Carter. Perspectives Press, 1989.

You may also want to be aware of the following:

Tapestry Books
P.O. Box 359
Ringoes, NJ 08551
1-800-765-2367
(Offers a catalogue filled with books on infertility, pregnancy loss, and adoption.)

Perspectives Press
P.O. Box 90318
Indianapolis, IN 46290-0318
317-872-3055
(Publishes only books on infertility, pregnancy loss, and adoption.)

Support Groups and Organizations Dealing With Adoption and Childless Living

---

*It is one of the most beautiful compensations of this life
that no man can seriously help another
without helping himself.*

RALPH WALDO EMERSON

Check your local Catholic Charities, Lutheran Social Services, United Way, local infertility clinics, or these national organizations to find your nearest support group.

Adoption

Adoptive Families of America, Inc.
3333 Highway 100 N.
Minneapolis, MN 55422
1-612-535-4829
(This is a support-group organization providing information and referrals for international and special needs adoption. AFA also publishes a magazine for adoptive families.)

American Academy of Adoption Attorneys
P.O. Box 33053
Washington, DC 20033-0053
1-202-331-1955
(Provides referrals to attorneys specializing in adoption.)

National Adoption Information Clearinghouse
1400 Eye St. NW, Suite 1275
Washington, DC 20005
1-202-408-0950 (FAX)
(Provides speakers' bureau, a database for books and articles, referrals, and a directory of adoption agencies.)

National Committee for Adoption, Inc. (NCFA)
1930 17th St., NW
Washington, DC 20009-6207
1-202-328-1200
1-202-463-7563 (Helpline)
(Offers information and referrals and promotes adoption as a positive family-building alternative.)

Childless Living

Child-Free Network
7777 Sunrise Blvd., Suite 1800
Citrus Heights, CA 95661
1-916-773-7178
(Offers newsletters and information on starting groups for couples who, by chance or choice, remain childless.)

No Kidding
Box 27001
Vancouver, BC V5R 6A8
Canada
1-604-538-7736 (24 hours)
1-604-538-7736 (FAX)
(Offers newsletters and information on starting groups for married or single people who don't have children.)

Death of a Child

Setting Up a Program of Bereavement Care for Those Grieving the Death of a Child

There are a number of different situations which can be grouped under the category "death of a child": miscarriage, abortion, stillbirth, or death of an infant, toddler, or older child.

Miscarriage and Stillbirth

When a couple first finds out that a baby is on the way, the emotions of happiness and fear are much like a roller-coaster ride. The woman's body prepares for the baby, causing changes in her breasts, morning sickness, fatigue, etc. In 15-20% of all pregnancies, however, a miscarriage will interrupt this process and end the life of the fetus. (Note: the word "fetus" is used only for medical clarification. In dealing with the families, "baby" is usually the most appropriate word.)

This type of death is not always brought to the attention of the bereavement ministers. But if you happen to hear about it, bereavement care can be very helpful to those who are open to it.

A miscarriage can involve many of the stages of childbirth, including the opening of the cervix and contractions of the uterus. Miscarriage can happen slowly or all at once. Miscarriages usually occur between the 7th to the 14th week of gestation in 15 to 20% of all pregnancies.

After the miscarriage, it takes several weeks for the body to return to normal. Breasts remain tender and milk may even come in, uterine cramping may continue for days, and bleeding and spotting can continue for a week or more.

How this death is interpreted depends on the couple. One study found that 75% of women experienced significant grief after a miscarriage *(When a Baby Dies,* Limbo and Wheeler, 1986).

Whether the pregnancy was planned or not, acknowledging the loss, either verbally or in writing, can offer a sense of comfort.

If a fetus is born dead after twenty weeks, it is considered a stillbirth. The experience of a stillbirth has many similarities to that of miscarriage or abortion, but it is even more likely in stillbirth that parents will be confronted physically with the reality of the baby.

At the Hospital

If you are able to be at the hospital at the time of stillbirth, you may want to act as an advocate for the parents by suggesting that the following procedures be considered:

1. Allow the parents the option of holding the baby.

2. Collect important keepsakes such as

    a. a lock of hair

    b. a set of footprints

    c. a baby hat and booties

    d. a picture of the baby with and without clothing

    e. a blanket the baby touched

    f. the baby's plastic arm and leg band

    g. a life-size silhouette of the baby

3. Have a funeral or memorial service to publicly acknowledge the death of this baby. This gives the parents a chance to express their grief outside of themselves and allows others to embrace and care for them. A funeral would be best delayed if the birth involved physical trauma for the mother. Not having a funeral is one decision parents often regret.

Initial Contact

Immediately after the miscarriage or stillbirth, send out a personalized "Grieving the Death of a Fetus" letter (page 181), using personal pronouns if you know the sex of the fetus.

After your letter has been received, you should call to set up an initial visit to the grieving parents. The following materials are designed to be given at your initial visit:

Physical Symptoms of Grieving	(page 29)
Exercise and Nutrition	(page 32)

At the time of your initial visit, you should also offer "A Ritual for Saying Good-bye," indicating that you would be glad to lead that ritual or that the grieving parents may use the material privately. Let them know that you will send a few more letters over the next few months and that you will call again in another six months, if they wouldn't mind.

Monthly Messages

In addition, the following Monthly Messages should be used during the first several months of bereavement (see pages 19-21 for instructions on incorporating these messages into personalized letters or otherwise including them in bereavement care):

The Grieving Process	(page 38)	2 weeks after loss
Common Myths About Grief	(page 39)	
You and Your Emotions	(page 40)	1 month after loss
Enough Faith?	(page 41)	2 months after loss
I Know There's Life After Death, Right?	(page 44)	3 months after loss
A Special Note	(page 49)	4 months after loss
The Journey Continues	(page 50)	5 months after loss

Plan to visit again at six months. Also plan a one-year visit, to the day if possible, on the anniversary of the loss of the baby. Anniversary dates are very important and many people feel isolated and alone because no one else remembers their loss.

Abortion

Abortion, according to Kenneth Doka, is a disenfranchised grief; in most cases, the griever is given no opportunity to talk about the death or express grief. It is a silent burden.

Of course, an abortion significantly compounds the grieving process. As bereavement ministers, it is extremely important not to judge the mother, but to accept her and help her move through the grieving process. As with other types of grieving, grieving after abortion will continue into the future; those mourning may flash back to the abortion or find themselves calculating how old their child would be and wondering what he or she might look like. Issues may arise especially for women who have additional children or have difficulty getting pregnant later in life.

Offering bereavement care for those grieving an abortion can be an especially delicate matter. As you will see in the following section, we suggest that this bereavement care be done entirely through personal visitation, rather than letter-writing. The sacrament of reconciliation (confession and absolution) can be very important for those wrestling with guilt after an abortion.

Initial Contact

Bring the following materials at your initial visit:

Suggested Reading After a Major Loss	(page 34)
Suggested Reading and Support Groups for Those Grieving an Abortion	(page 187)

At your initial visit, discuss the possibility of meeting again in a few weeks. If the grieving person is willing, you may want to continue to meet monthly for the next several months. As symptoms of grieving manifest themselves, offer the following resources:

Physical Symptoms of Grieving	(page 29)
Exercise and Nutrition	(page 30)
Getting to Sleep	(page 32)

When dealing with miscarriage or abortion, consider use of "A Ritual for Saying Good-bye," if those grieving seem open to such a ceremony. (See pages 282-283.)

Death of a Child

Parents whose children die face difficult and complex grief. Below are a few of the most important issues.

1. Grieving hopes, dreams, and expectations: first steps, birthday parties, graduation, etc.

2. Grieving the lost part of the parent seen in the child, e.g., the child's athletic ability like that of the father, the child's artistic quality like that of the mother.

3. Believing that they had not taken care of the child by protecting her or him. You can help parents deal with guilt by encouraging them to take the following steps:

   a. Recognize legitimate guilt if in fact their act did cause serious harm to the child. This can be dealt with through the sacrament of reconciliation (confession and absolution) and counseling.

   b. Focus on the positive things they did, felt, and thought.

   c. Deal with irrational beliefs and expectations:

      "I must be perfect in everything I do."

      "My child's needs should always come before my own."

      "I must always feel love for my child."

   d. When they are ready, help the parents actualize their altruistic feelings by focusing on what they have learned through this death and in turn share it with others.

4. Feeling helpless and abandoned when avoided by other parents.

5. Expecting her or his marital partner to grieve the same way. There are a few reminders that may be helpful to the couple:

   a. They will grieve differently and will become different people because of the death.

   b. Their different grieving cycles—including disinterest, depression, avoidance, and various degrees of wanting to be touched or not—will affect their sexual intimacy.

   c. Encourage them to express their feelings. Avoiding talking about the dead child or avoiding anything that reminds them of the child can be very damaging.

6. Using the remaining child or children as "replacements" for the child who died. Trying to replace the child who died can be damaging and might not allow for the remaining children's identities to emerge.

(Taken from *Grief, Dying, and Death*, by Therese Rando, Research Press Company, 1984.)

If the death occurs when the child is a teenager, normal ambivalence that the relationship held may add to the parents' difficulty in grieving. Numbers 3a - 3c above may be helpful in resolving guilt or anger and amending the relationship despite the physical death of their child.

Initial Contact

Immediately after the death, send out a personalized "Grieving the Death of a Child" letter (page 188). Individualize this letter as appropriate, using the child's name and appropriate descriptions.

After your letter has been received, you should call to set up an initial visit with the grieving parents. The following materials are designed to be given to them at your initial visit:

Physical Symptoms of Grieving	(page 29)
Exercise and Nutrition	(page 30)
Getting to Sleep	(page 32)

Monthly Messages

In addition, the following Monthly Messages should be sent during the first year of bereavement (see pages 19-21 for instructions on incorporating these messages into personalized letters or otherwise including them in bereavement care):

The Grieving Process	(page 38)	2 weeks after loss
Common Myths About Grief	(page 39)	1 month after loss
You and Your Emotions	(page 40)	2 months after loss
Enough Faith?	(page 41)	
Working With Your Grieving	(page 42)	3 months after loss
Returning to "Normal"	(page 43)	4 months after loss
I Know There's Life After Death, Right?	(page 44)	5 months after loss
Support Groups	(page 45)	6 months after loss
Dealing With Criticism	(page 45)	7 months after loss
More About Exercise and Nutrition	(page 46)	8 months after loss
How Will I Know I'm Feeling Better?	(page 113)	9 months after loss
A Special Note	(page 49)	10 months after loss
Getting Involved Again	(page 49)	11 months after loss
The Journey Continues	(page 50)	one year after loss

Also remember to send Special Day Messages on the child's birthday, the anniversary of the death, Christmas, etc.

Ongoing Visitation

See suggestions for visitation on page 21. For those grieving the loss of a baby, you may want to discuss "Common Responses to the Loss of a Baby" (See pages 196-198) at your second or third visit. This can be a helpful tool in allowing parents to express the grief that they are feeling.

It is a helpful communication tool to open up discussion about the death with the couple. You may also suggest "A Ritual for Saying Good-bye." (See pages 282-283.)

Common Questioning

In any of the above cases, there are questions that a grieving family often brings to the clergy:

1. What did I do that God wanted to punish me?
2. Why didn't I die instead?
3. Was this part of God's plan?
4. Did my baby die because it was God's will?

Let families know that God is with them in their pain and is holding and caring for the child. You don't have to defend God. Just be present.

Celebrate the child's life, no matter how short it was. Don't be afraid to talk about the child and call her or him by name.

Grieving the Death of a Fetus

(A personalized letter with this material should be sent immediately after a miscarriage or stillbirth.)

What a difficult time this must be. (I know how much you wanted this baby. I know the difficulties and trials you went through to conceive a child.) Know that we are praying for you.

You may not find as much support as you need because others don't know about your loss or because they don't understand its significance. Take care of yourself and acknowledge this death as important, even if others don't. Even though it hurts, allow yourself the time to feel the sadness, loneliness, emptiness, and questioning "why."

If you feel that it would be helpful, I have a "Ritual for Saying Good-bye" that could be beneficial for both of you. It would allow you to say good-bye and grieve all the dreams you had for this child.

I will be calling in a few days to see if you would like to talk or use the ritual at that time; I can also leave the ritual for your private use.

Your Readied Room Was Waiting

Your readied room was waiting

but its walls you'd never see.

Jesus, too, had prepared a room for you,

one we've yet to see.

And waited with his angels

for us to say good-bye.

So you could celebrate in perfect peace

above our earthly sky.

(Taken from "To Dearest Colin," by Mary Kate Cavanaugh, Easthampton, Massachusetts. Colin died the day after his birth of heart failure.)

Suggested Reading for Those Grieving a Miscarriage or Stillbirth

There are several resources you can use in locating these titles: your local library (and inter-library loan system), bookstores, your bereavement minister's personal library, your church library, and local support groups' lending libraries.

Remember, if a book doesn't seem to make sense right now, try reading it again later.

Always Pecious in Our Memory: Reflections after Miscarriage, Stilbirth, or Neonatal Death. K. J. Ingram. ACTA, 1997.

Empty Arms: Coping with Miscarriage, Stillbirth, and Infant Death. S. Ilse. Wintergreen, 1990.

Empty Arms: Emotional Support for Those Who Have Suffered Miscarriage or Stillbirth. P. Vredevelt. Questor, 1994.

Ended Beginnings: Healing Childbearing Losses. C. Panuthos and C. Romeo. Greenwood, 1984.

Free to Grieve: Coping with the Trauma of Miscarriage. M. Rank. Bethany House, 1985.

Grieving Grandparents. Centering Resource.

In This Very Hour: Devotions in Your Time of Need: Loss of an Unborn Child. C. Butler. Broadman, 1994.

Life Line: A Journal for Parents Grieving a Miscarriage, Stillbirth or Other Early Infant Death. J. Reid. 1994.

Loss and Bereavement in Childbearing. R. Mander. Blackwell Sci., 1994.

Miscarriage. Centering Resource.

Miscarriage: A Shattered Dream. S. Ilse and L. Burns. Wintergreen, 1990.

Miscarriage: For Parents Experiencing Fetal Death. J. Johnson and M. Johnson. Centering Corporation, 1980.

Motherhood and Mourning: Perinatal Death. L. G. Peppers and R. J. Knapp. Greenwood, 1980.

Ocasa Sin Aurora. Centering Resource. (for Spanish-speaking parents)

"The Pastoral Dynamics of Miscarriage." W. Wassner. *Pastoral Psychology*, 1991, 40(2), 113-121.

Precious Lives, Painful Choices: A Prenatal Decision Making Guide. S. Ilse. Wintergreen, 1993.

Silent Sorrow: Pregnancy Loss: Guidance & Support for You and Your Family. I. Kohn and Moffitt. Dell, 1993.

Still to Be Born. Centering Resource.

Surviving Pregnancy Loss. R. Friedman and B. Gradstein. Little, 1982.

When Pregnancy Fails. Families Coping with Miscarriage, Stillbirth, and Infant Death. S. Borg and J. Lasker. Bantam, 1989.

Centering Corporation
1531 North Saddle Creek Rd.
Omaha, NE 68104
402-553-1200
402-553-0507 (FAX)

"Marked Forever"
Seraphim Communications, Inc.
1568 Eustis St.
St. Paul, MN 55108
1-800-733-3413
(A video about parents' bereavement after the death of their four-month-old baby to SIDS.)

Support Groups for Those Grieving a Miscarriage or Stillbirth

*It is one of the most beautiful compensations of this life
that no man can seriously help another
without helping himself.*

RALPH WALDO EMERSON

AMEND
Maureen Connelly
4324 Berrywick Terrace
St. Louis, MO 63128
1-314-487-7582
(One-on-one counseling for parents experiencing a neonatal death.)

CLIMB, Inc.
P.O. Box 1064
Palmer, AK 99645
1-907-746-6123
(Newsletters, information, and phone support for parents who have experienced multiple loss.)

The Compassionate Friends, Inc. (TCF)
National Headquarters
P.O. Box 3696
Oak Brook, IL 60522-3696
1-630-990-0010
1-630-990-0246 (FAX)
(Chapters offer "telephone friends," monthly support groups, speaker's bureau, newsletter, and conferences.)

The Compassionate Friends of Canada
685 William Avenue
Winnipeg, Manitoba R3E 0Z2

HOPING
Sparrow Hospital
1215 East Michigan Avenue.
Lansing, MI 48909
1-517-483-3873
1-517-351-1404 (FAX)
(Trained staff support and parents who have suffered a similar loss of miscarriage or stillbirth. They also offer a speaker's bureau, newsletter, training material, and workshops.)

Pregnancy & Infant Loss Center
1421 E. Wayzata Blvd., #30
Wayzata, MN 55391
1-612-473-9372
(Literature, support-group information, training, and parent outreach programs.)

Bereavement Services/R.T.S.
Gunderson Lutheran Medical Center
1910 South Avenue
LaCrosse, WI 54601
1-608-791-4747
1-800-362-9567, ext. 4747
1-608-791-5137 (FAX)
(This is an international support program that provides training, seminars, and support materials for those who have lost a baby through miscarriage, ectopic pregnancy, stillbirth, or newborn death.)

SHARE (Source of Help in Airing and Resolving Experiences)
c/o St. Joseph's Health Center
300 - 1st Capital Dr.
St. Charles, MO 63301-2893
1-314-947-6164
1-314-947-7486 FAX
(A national self-help group for parents who are grieving a miscarriage, stillbirth, ectopic pregnancy, or early infant death.)

UNITE Grief Support
c/o Jeanes Hospital
7600 Central Avenue
Philadelphia, PA 19111-2499
1-215-728-3777
1-215-728-2082 (recording)
(Newsletters, conferences, phone help for parents grieving miscarriage, stillbirth, or infant death.)

Suggested Reading and Support Groups for Those Grieving an Abortion

Suggested Reading

Abortions and Healing: A Cry to Be Whole. M. Mannion, Sleed and Ward, 1986.

After Abortion: Stories of Healing. P. King. Liguori.

No One Told Me I Could Cry: A Teen's Guide to Hope and Healing After Abortion. C. Nykiel, 1997.

Support Groups

Abortion Survivors Anonymous
P.O. Box 1533
Alpine, CA 91903
1-619-445-1247 (Sarah)
1-619-578-9079 (Mary)
(Offers a 12-step manual for women recovering from abortion.)

Abortion Survivors Anonymous
P.O. Box 1533
Alpine, CA 91903
1-619-445-1247 (Sarah)
1-619-578-9079 (Mary)
(Offers a 12-step manual for women recovering from abortion.)

Open Arms
Patti Goodoien
P.O. Box 1056
Columbia, MO 65205
1-314-449-7672
(Newsletters, information, and referral for Christian post-abortion emotional support.)

Project Rachel
National Office of Post-Abortion Reconciliation and Healing
3501 South Lake Drive
Milwaukee, WI 53207
1-800-5-WECARE (1-800-593-2273)
(Project Rachel does not provide hotline counseling, but they can give confidential support, information, and referral following an abortion.)

Grieving the Death of a Child

(A personalized letter with this material should be sent immediately after the death of a child.)

What a painful time this must be for you. Please know that we are praying for you.

I'm sure you've asked, "Why me?" "Why now?" I have no words to answer your questions or take away your pain, but I do know that God hears your cries. I believe that he has reached out to receive the spirit of your child and has drawn *(her/him)* close to him.

There are no words that can replace *(name of child)* or take away the terrible pain and struggle you must feel, the awkwardness of planning *(her/his)* funeral, the remembrance of a body so full of life and vitality.

By this time you may not have had the energy to wash *(name)*'s clothes that lay dirty at the bottom of the laundry basket or make *(her/his)* bed. The *(toys, sports equipment, etc.,* may lay right where *(she/he)* dropped it. But there will be time when it feels right to put these things away.

You may find yourself wandering around the house, unable to cook, having never-ending thoughts about *(name)*, and being very tired. These sensations will lessen, and later you will find relief in thinking of something else.

You may feel as though God has left you, but know that nothing can separate you from the love of Christ Jesus.

> *We were buried therefore with him by baptism into death,*
> *so that as Christ was raised from the dead by the glory*
> *of the Father, we too might walk in newness of life.*
> *For if we have been united with him in a death like his,*
> *we shall certainly be united with him in a resurrection like his.*
>
> ROMANS 6:4-5

You may find it helpful to read the words of Jeremiah in the third chapter of Lamentations.

I would like to come and visit with you. I will be calling within the next two weeks. Know that we are praying for you.

> *The Lord is the everlasting God,*
> *the Creator of the ends of the earth.*
> *He does not faint or grow weary,*
> *His understanding is unreachable.*
> *He gives power to the faint,*

and to him who has no might
He increases strength.
Even youths shall faint and be weary,
and young men shall fall exhausted;
but they who wait for the Lord shall renew their strength,
they shall mount up with wings like eagles,
they shall run and not be weary,
they shall walk and not faint.

———————

ISAIAH 40:27-31

The eternal God is your dwelling place,
and underneath are the everlasting arms.

———————

DEUTERONOMY 33:27

Who will separate us from the love of Christ?
Will hardship, or distress, or persecution, or famine,
or nakedness, or peril, or sword?
In all these things we are more than conquerors through him who loved us.
For I am convinced that neither death, nor life, nor angels,
nor rulers, nor things present, nor things to come, nor powers,
nor height, nor depth, nor anything else in all creation,
will be able to separate us from the love of God in Christ Jesus our Lord.

———————

ROMANS 8:31-35, 37-39

Suggested Reading After the Death of an Infant

There are several resources you can use in locating these titles: your local library (and inter-library loan system), your church library, bookstores, your bereavement minister's personal library, local support groups' lending libraries, and funeral homes.

Remember, if a book doesn't seem to make sense right now, try reading it again later.

All Babies. M. Connelly. Centering Corporation, 1993.

Andrew, You Died Too Young: A Family Experience of Grieving and Living Again. C. Chilstrom. Augsburg Fortress, 1993.

The Bereaved Parent. H. Schiff. Viking Penguin, 1978.

Children Die, Too. Centering Resource.

Children Die, Too. J. Johnson and M. Johnson. Centering Corporation, 1992.

Children's Grief. Centering Resource.

Daddy: NINU. J. Johnson and M. Johnson. Centering Corporation, 1988.

Dear Parents. Centering Resource.

Dear Parents. . . . Letters To Bereaved Parents. Centering Resource, 1988.

Difficult Decisions. Centering Resource.

Empty Arms: Coping After Miscarriage, Stillbirth, and Infant Death, or Neonatal Death. S. Ilse. Wintergreen, 1982.

Empty Arms: Emotional Support for Those who have Suffering Miscarriage or Stillbirth. P. Vredevelt. Questar, 1984.

Empty Cradle, Broken Heart: Surviving the Death of Your Baby. D. L. Davis. Fulcrum, 1991.

Fathers Grieve, Too. Centering Resource, 1983.

For Bereaved Grandparents. M. Gerner. Centering Corporation, 1990.

For Better or Worse. Centering Resource.

For Those Who Live. Centering Resource.

Given In Love: For Mothers Releasing a Baby for Adoption. M. Connelly. Centering Corporation, 1989.

Go Gently. Centering Resource.

God Is A Birdwatcher. Centering Resource.

Gone But Not Lost: Grieving the Death of a Child. D. Wiersbe. Baker, 1992.

Goodbye My Child. S. Wheeler and M. Pike. Centering Corporation, 1992.

Grieving Grandparents. Centering Resource.

Healing a Father's Grief. W. Schatz. 1984.

How to Go On Living After the Death of a Baby. L. G. Peppers and R. J. Knapp. Peachtree Publishers, 1985.

How to go on Living When Someone You Love Dies. T. Rando. Bantam, 1991.

How to Survive the Loss of a Child: Filling the Emptiness & Rebuilding Your Life. C. Sanders. Prima Publishers, 1992.

Letters of Hope: Living after the Loss of your Child. T. Griffin. Cedarbrook Press, 1991.

Life Line: A Journal for Parents Grieving a Miscarriage, Stillbirth or Other Early Infant Death. J. Reid. 1994.

Little Footprints: A Special Baby's Memory Book. D. Ferguson. Centering Corporation, 1989.

Lori . . . where are you?: A Mother's Experience of Grief and Loss. E. Visitacion. 1993.

Maternal Bereavement. L. Edelstein. Praeger, 1984.

Misty: Our Momentary Child. C. G. Page. Crossway, 1987.

Newborn Death. J. Johnson and M. Johnson. Centering Corporation, 1992.

Ocasa Sin Aurora. Centering Resource.

On Children and Death. E. Kubler-Ross. MacMillan, 1993.

Our Children Live Forever In Our Hearts. Centering Resource.

Recovering from the Loss of a Child. K. Donnelly. Berkeley, 1994.

Sibling Grief. Centering Resource.

Silver Linings Training System: A Child-Parent Bereavement Program. E. Costa and G. Zambelli. Center for Hospice Care, 1995.

So Will I Comfort You. J. Kander. Marehouse, 1992.

Stillborn: The Invisible Death. J. DeFrain. Free Publishing, 1986.

Sudden Infant Death: Enduring the Loss. DeFrain, Ernst, Jakub, and Taylor. Free Press, 1991.

Thin Ice: A Story of Multiple Death. D. Buthman. Centering Corporation, 1990.

This Time It's Me: For Teens Who Have Just Found Out They're Pregnant. E. Visitacion, M. Vondra, and L. Vondra. Centering Corporation, 1985.

A Time to Decide: A Time to Heal. Centering Resource.

When A Baby Dies: A Handbook for Healing & Helping. R. Limbo and S. Wheeler. Harsand Press, 1986.

When a Baby Dies. The Compassionate Friends.

"When a Child Dies: The Impact of Being a Christian." P. Mabe and M. Dawes. *Journal of Psychology and Theology,* 1991, 19(4), 334-343.

When Hello Means Goodbye. Centering Resource.

When Pregnancy Fails: Families Coping with Miscarriage, Stillbirth, and Infant Death. S. Borg and J. Lasker. Bantam, 1989.

Suggested Reading After the Death of a Child

There are several resources you can use in locating these titles: your local library (and inter-library loan system), your church library, bookstores, your bereavement minister's personal library, local support groups' lending libraries, and funeral homes.

Remember, if a book doesn't seem to make sense now, try reading it again later.

Acute Grief: Loss of an Adult Child. O. Margolis. Greenwood, 1988.

After the Death of a Child: Living with loss through the years. A. Finkbeiner. Free Press, 1996.

The Bereaved Parent. H. Schiff. Viking Penguin, 1978.

A Child Dies: A Portrait of Family Grief. P. Gemma and J. Arnold. Charles, 1994.

Concerning Death: A Practical Guide for the Living. E. Grollman, ed. Beacon, 1974.

Dear Parents . . . Letters to Bereaved Parents. Centering Resource, 1988.

Death and the College Student. Centering Resource, 1972.

Don't Take My Grief Away: What to Do When You Lose a Loved One. D. Manning. Harper San Francisco, 1984.

Five Cries of Grief: One Family's Journey to Healing after the Tragic Death of a Son. M. Strommen and I. Strommen. Augsburg Fortress, 1996.

For Bereaved Grandparents. M. Gerner. Centering Corporation, 1990.

Give Sorrow Words: A Father's Passage Through Grief. T. Crider. Algonquin, 1996.

Healing a Father's Grief. W. Schatz. 1984.

How to go on Living When Someone You Love Dies. T. Rando. Bantam, 1991.

Lament for a Son. N. Wolterstorff. Eerdmans, 1987.

Little Ones to Him Belong: Surviving the Death of a Child. R. Hipps. Smyth & Helwys, 1996.

Meditations for Bereaved Parents. J. Osgood. Gilgal, 1983.

Ocasa Sin Aurora. Centering Resource.

On Wings of Mourning. C. Rowley and W. Rowley. Word, 1984.

Rebecca: A Father's Journey from Grief to Gratitude. R. Jonas. Crossroad, 1996.

Recovering from the Loss of a Child. K. Donnolley. Berkeley, 1994.

Standing Beside You: A Book for Bereaved Parents. L. Mawrer. LK Maurer, 1996.

Surviving the Death of a Child. J. Munday and F. Wohlenhaus-Munday. Westminster John Knox, 1995.

When a Child Dies. C. Pregent. Ave Maria Press, 1992.

When Death Touches Your Life. M. Thompson. Walker & Company, 1988.

When the Unthinkable Happens: A Father's Journey Through Grief. T. Crouthamel. Keystone, 1995.

Who Lives Happily Every After? For Families Whose Child Has Died Violently. S. Turnbull. Centering Corporation, 1990.

Why Are the Casseroles Always Tuna?: A Loving Look at the Lighter Side of Grief. D. Sims. Big A and Company, 1992.

Centering Corporation
1531 North Saddle Creek Rd.
Omaha, NE 68104
402-553-1200
402-553-0507 FAX

Support Groups for Those Grieving the Death of a Child

*It is one of the most beautiful compensations of this life
that no man can seriously help another
without helping himself.*

RALPH WALDO EMERSON

The Compassionate Friends, Inc. (TCF)
National Headquarters
P.O. Box 3696
Oak Brook, IL 60522-3696
1-630-990-0010
1-630-990-0246 (FAX)
(Chapters offer "telephone friends," monthly support groups, speaker's bureau, newsletter, and conferences.)

HOPING - Sparrow Hospital
1215 East Michigan Avenue
Lansing, MI 48909
1-517-483-3873
1-517-351-1404 (FAX)
(Trained staff support and parents who have suffered a similar loss of miscarriage or still birth. They also offer a speaker's bureau, newsletter, training material, and workshops.)

National Sudden Infant Death Syndrome Foundation
Suite 104
8200 Professional Place
Landover, MD 20785
1-301-459-3388 (Maryland)
1-800-221-5105 (Outside Maryland)
(This group offers services and education to families who have lost a child to SIDS.)

Mothers Against Drunk Drivers (M.A.D.D.)
669 Airport Freeway, Suite 310
Hurst, TX 76053
1-817-268-6233
1-800-438-MADD (Victim Hotline)
(M.A.D.D. is a national organization that supports victims, families, and friends in the aftermath of a drunk driving offense.)

The Candlelighters Childhood Cancer Foundation
1901 Pennsylvania Ave., NW, Suite 1001
Washington, DC 20006
(This is an international peer-support network of parents whose children have or have had cancer.)

Common Responses to the Loss of a Baby

The loss of a baby creates tremendous grief, touching all areas of life. Perhaps you'll recognize some of the following responses as your own.

Women

- I feel so empty, emptier than I've ever felt before.

- I wonder if my husband feels bad about our baby. His grief doesn't seem as great as mine.

- I think about the baby all the time; it's like I can't get it out of my mind.

- My breasts ache to nurse the baby. Sometimes I feel a letdown of milk.

- I have experienced unpleasant physical symptoms such as aching arms, fast heartbeat, tiredness, butterflies in my stomach, nervousness, or other symptoms.

- Nobody understands me anymore. I feel all alone.

- My husband and I talk and talk, but never get anything resolved.

- I keep thinking "What did I do to cause this? I must have done something."

- We didn't really want to be pregnant. Did I somehow wish my baby's death?

- I sometimes feel like I'll never feel "normal" again.

- My moods change so fast; I feel like I can't keep up with it.

- I'm so afraid that I'll forget the baby.

- I find that I can't concentrate; I'm forgetful and just can't seem to keep it together.

- I hate having sex. How can we be doing that when our baby has died?

- Since the loss, my husband and I have sex more often. Is that normal?

- I find myself wanting to be protected and taken care of more than ever before.

- I don't like the physical changes I've experienced since I was pregnant.

- I find myself obsessed with getting pregnant again.

- I'm so afraid of getting pregnant. I don't think I could go through this again.

- I'm pregnant again, but I'm afraid to tell anyone. I can't stand the pain of having to tell them something happened.

- I'm jealous of pregnant women and women with babies. I see them everywhere.

- I don't feel attractive anymore. I'm afraid my husband will lose interest in me.

- I've been sick a lot since the baby died. Does that have anything to do with grief?

- Our friends/brother/sister had a baby at the same time we did. How can I stand watching that child grow up?

- My husband seems to be moving ahead more rapidly than I am; he's involved in work and seems back to normal.

- We're both back at work, but I still seem to be doing most of the work at home. It isn't fair.

- I find myself having scary daydreams about my partner or surviving children being killed in an accident.

- My dreams frighten me; they're so real. I dream about _____.

- Sometimes I get so angry at the baby for doing this to me.

Men

- I feel like so much weight is one my shoulders; everyone looks to me to be strong.

- I'm afraid I'll make my wife feel worse if I show my emotions, so I keep them to myself.

- All she does is cry. I'm tired of seeing her sad.

- I'm just not as interested in sex.

- I'd like to have sex more often, but my wife isn't interested.

- I find myself wishing we could be normal again. Will that ever be?

- It seems terrible, but sometimes I resent my wife since we lost the baby. She gets all the attention.

- My wife seems to have withdrawn love from me and dwells on the baby's death.

- My wife seems to need more than I can give her.

- My wife and I are more distant since we lost the baby. We don't talk about important issues, and we don't seem to have much in common anymore.

- I'm concerned about whether or not we should become pregnant again. What will happen to us if we lose another baby?

- I didn't think we were ready for a baby. Did I somehow wish the baby's death?

- We can't agree on whether/when to get pregnant again, and it's starting to cause a conflict.

- I have experienced unpleasant physical symptoms such as aching arms, fast heartbeat, tiredness, butterflies in my stomach, nervousness, or other symptoms.

- I find that I want to talk and talk about the loss. More than anything else, I need someone to *listen* to me.

- My wife seems to talk to other people more than she talks to me. Why can't she share her feelings with me?

- I hate coming home from work and finding her depressed again. Can't we be happy once in a while?

- Our friends/brother/sister had a baby at the same time we did. How can I stand watching that child grow up?

- I am worried about how we are going to make out financially. There are so many bills to pay.

(Adapted from *When a Baby Dies: A Handbook for Healing and Helping*, by R. Limbo and S. Wheeler, RTS Bereavement Services, 1995.)

Special Support for Grandparents

Setting Up a Program of Bereavement Care for Grieving Grandparents

Grieving grandparents are often the silent sufferers. They hurt twice; once for their child and once for their grandchild.

They may be concerned that what caused a miscarriage was an abnormal gene or chromosome passed down to the child. They may feel that it should have been them that died, not the child. They may be feeling anger at the doctor for not saving the baby or even anger at their own children for not taking better care of their grandchild.

Their best role is to be a supportive listener. Instill in them the importance of letting the parents take the lead in planning the funeral and putting away the toys. Encourage them also, however, to find ways to be involved. It will hurt, but it's the only way to move through their pain.

Initial Contact

Immediately after the death, send out a personalized "Grieving the Death of a Grandchild" letter (page 200), using the child's name and personal pronouns. Rewrite for an older child. After your letter has been received, call to set up an initial visit. At your initial visit, bring copies of the following materials:

Physical Symptoms of Grieving	(page 29)
Exercise and Nutrition	(page 30)
Getting to Sleep	(page 32)
Suggested Reading After a Major Loss	(page 34)
Suggested Reading After the Death of an Infant OR	(page 190)
Suggested Reading After the Death of a Child	(page 192)

Monthly Messages

The following Monthly Messages should be sent (see pages 19-21 for instructions on incorporating these messages into personalized letters or otherwise including them in bereavement care):

The Grieving Process	(page 38)	2 weeks after loss
Grandparents Grieve, Too	(page 201)	1 month after loss

Ongoing Visitation

If the grandparents are willing, try to make at least one or two visits. Further bereavement care will depend on the grandparents' openness and the difficulty they experience in coping with their grief.

These books may be useful resources:

For Bereaved Grandparents. M. Gerner. Centering Corporation, 1990.

Grandma's Tears: Comfort for Grieving Grandparents. J. Kolf. Baker, 1995.

Grieving the Death of a Grandchild

(A personalized letter with this material should be sent immediately after the death of a grandchild.)

What a painful time for you and your family. It's been said that as a grandparent, you hurt twice: once when you see your own child hurting and not being able to do anything about it and twice when you lose your grandchild.

Please know that we are thinking about you and praying for you.

> *Do not be afraid, for I have redeemed you;*
> *I have called you by your name, you are mine.*
> *Should you pass through the sea, I will be there with you;*
> *or through rivers, they will not swallow you up.*
> *Should you walk through fire, you will not be scorched*
> *and the flames will not burn you. . . .*
> *You are precious in my eyes . . . I love you. . . .*
> *Do not be afraid, for I am with you.*
>
> ISAIAH 43:2, 4

Grandparents Grieve, Too

Why can't I join her in the aloneness of her grief? As tight as my arms wrap around her, I can't reach that aloneness.

What can I give her to make her better? A cold, wet cloth will ease the swelling of her crying eyes, but it won't stop the reason for her tears. What treat will bring joy back to her? What prize will bring that happy child smile back? Where are the magic words to give her comfort? What chapter in Dr. Spock tells me how to do this? He has told me everything else I've needed to know.

Where are the answers? I should have them. I'm the mother.

I know that someday she'll find happiness again, that her life will have meaning again. I can hold out hope for her someday, but what about now? this minute? this hour? this day?

I can give her my love and my prayers and my care and my concern. I could give her my life. But even that won't help.

(Taken from *For Bereaved Grandparents*, by Margaret Gerner, Centering Corporation, 1990.)

Death of an Adult Child

Setting Up a Program of Bereavement Care After the Death of an Adult Child

When someone dies, older parents are sometimes ignored in comparison with the deceased person's spouse and children. But the older adult has still lost her or his "baby." It always seems wrong to have child precede a parent in death.

Be aware that unresolved anger or guilt may hinder the resolution of grief after the death of an adult child. Pages 178-179, 3a - 3c offers suggestions for absolution and forgiveness even though the child is dead.

The older parent may have other worries or concerns she or he may not admit, such as who will take care of her or him now as they grow older and who will provide for her or his financial, emotional, and physical support. It is most helpful to recognize and address these concerns directly.

Initial Contact

Immediately after the death, send out a personalized "Grieving the Death of an Adult Child" letter (page 205), using the name of the deceased and appropriate pronouns.

After your letter has been received, you should call to set up an initial visit to the grieving parents. The following materials are designed to be given at your initial visit:

Physical Symptoms of Grieving   (page 29)

Exercise and Nutrition	(page 30)
Getting to Sleep	(page 32)
Suggested Reading After a Major Loss	(page 34)

Monthly Messages

In addition, the following Monthly Messages should be sent during the first few months of bereavement (see pages 19-21 for instructions on incorporating these messages into personalized letters or otherwise including them in bereavement care):

The Grieving Process	(page 38)	2 weeks after loss
Common Myths About Grief	(page 39)	1 month after loss
You and Your Emotions	(page 40)	2 months after loss
Enough Faith?	(page 41)	
Working With Your Grieving	(page 42)	3 months after loss

Depending on the relationship of parent and child, send out some or all of the following Monthly Messages (see pages 19-21 for instructions on incorporating these messages into personalized letters or otherwise including them in bereavement care):

Returning to "Normal"	(page 43)	4 months after loss
I Know There's Life After Death, Right?	(page 44)	5 months after loss
Dealing With Criticism	(page 45)	6 months after loss
How Will I Know I'm Feeling Better?	(page 113)	8 months after loss
A Special Note	(page 49)	10 months after loss
The Journey Continues	(page 50)	one year after loss

Also remember to send Special Day Messages on the child's birthday, the anniversary of the death, Christmas, etc.

Ongoing Visitation

Make an initial visit one to two weeks after the death. Remind the grieving person that reactions to the death of an adult child can vary, but that she or he should take her or his own grieving process seriously.

Further visitation will depend on the nature of the relationship of parent and child. See suggestions for visitation on page 21.

Grieving the Death of an Adult Child

(A personalized letter with this material should be sent immediately after the death.)

No matter how old one gets, it hurts. *(Name)* was still your "baby" even though *(she/he)* was a grown *(woman/man) (with children (and grandchildren))*.

There are no answers to all the questions you may have: "Why not me?" "Why now?" But know that God hears your cries.

Know also that we are thinking and praying for you.

Likewise the Spirit helps us in our weakness;
for we do not know how to pray as we ought,
but the Spirit himself intercedes for us with sighs too deep for words.
And he who searches the hearts of men knows what is the mind of the Spirit, because the
Spirit intercedes for the saints according to the will of God.

ROMANS 8:26-27

Suicide

Setting Up a Program of Bereavement Care for Those Grieving a Suicide

Those grieving a suicide go through the same phases of grief that others do, except more chaotically. There may be shock, numbness, and detachment. They may deny the suicide took place, a protective mechanism that can keep the person from being overwhelmed and allow her or him to get through the funeral or go back to work.

Encourage the grieving persons to use words such as "killed herself/himself" and "suicide." These words are painful, but it helps those grieving to deal with reality and prevents the suicide from becoming a "family secret."

The survivors will need to talk about their anger at the person who died, at themselves, at their spouse, at their remaining children and/or their anger at God. It is important not to take the survivor's anger personally or defend God, but to listen, listen, listen.

Fears may set in that can cause them to lose faith in themselves and their abilities. They may fear what will happen to their spouse or their children, or fear their own vulnerability, become scared over their loss of control, or let small things bother them. They may become afraid of what they will do to themselves when they themselves have suicidal thoughts. Reassure them that these thoughts and fears will grow weaker, and they will have a sense of control once again.

Resentment, shame, blame, and guilt may be intensified. They may feel guilty that they didn't pick up on clues and prevent the suicide, and these extreme feelings of guilt may cause them to engage in self-destructive behaviors. They may question how much of a part they played in the suicide. It is important to tell them that these feelings are very common and to reassure them that one person cannot cause another person to commit suicide. They may need to resolve unfinished business by writing a letter to that person, through prayer, and/or the sacrament of reconciliation (confession and absolution).

Parents may wonder if they were somehow a "bad mother or bad father." Reassure the parents that they did the best they knew at the time. You may even suggest they make a list of "good" or "right" things they did when their guilt surfaces. Within a marriage, men and women grieve differently, and they will need to be encouraged to communicate with one another about their feelings and what is going on in one another's life. Making love may feel awkward—as if it were not appropriate to share something pleasant—but help them see that it is their way of caring and nurturing for each other.

Children of parents who committed suicide may feel they did something to cause the parent to kill herself or himself or feel that they have "inherited" a tendency to commit suicide themselves. Reassure the children that one person cannot cause another person to commit suicide and that suicide is not inherited. Encourage the children to talk about their own fears and thoughts about life and death. Young children need to be told honestly about the death; they will become confused and angry if they hear it from others. In the case of suicide, you may want to consider offering bereavement care to the closest friend(s) of the deceased person as well as her or his family.

Initial Contact

Immediately after the suicide, send out a personalized "Grieving a Suicide" letter (page 209). Individualize this letter as appropriate.

After your letter has been received, you should call to set up an initial visit. The following materials are designed to be given at your initial visit:

Physical Symptoms of Grieving	(page 29)
Exercise and Nutrition	(page 30)
Getting to Sleep	(page 32)
Suggested Reading After a Major Loss	(page 34)
Common Myths About Suicide	(page 211)
Suggested Reading for Those Grieving a Suicide	(page 212)
Support Groups for Those Grieving a Suicide	(page 214)

Monthly Messages

In addition, the following Monthly Messages should be used during the first year of bereavement (see pages 19-21 for instructions on incorporating these messages into personalized letters or otherwise including them in bereavement care):

Ongoing Visitation

Those grieving a suicide often need more frequent and intense bereavement visitation, especially in the first six months after their loss. They need to tell their stories over and over because it is usually hard to talk about with other people. Try to visit every month for six months and then every two months for up to two years after the suicide.

Here are five things to keep in mind as you visit with people grieving suicide:

1. Listen to their anger and their stories over and over again.

2. Bring your love and unprejudiced self.

3. Know the "Common Myths About Suicide" (page 211).

4. Assure the survivors that suicide is not inherited.

5. Help them work toward creating a loving memorial to the deceased person.

(Taken from *Survivors of Suicide*, by Rita Robinson, Newcastle Publications, 1992.)

Grieving a Suicide

(A personalized letter with this material should be sent immediately after the suicide.)

What a very difficult time this must be for you.

You may be asking questions such as "Why now?" "What went wrong?" or "Was it me?" These are often common reactions and feelings of those who are left behind. It is hard to understand what was in the mind of your loved one. It is often hard, too, when the police, coroners, and insurance agents have to ask their questions, which can sometimes produce an air of shame about the death.

Often people are not sure how to react to this type of death and whether they should say anything or not. Unfortunately, society is not ready to deal openly with your type of grieving. You may feel lonely and isolated. But we cannot express how important it is to share your thoughts and feelings with a support group or another interested and supportive person.

God is also here. You may feel angry at God or the church. God will listen. He has watched the struggling of your loved one and feels the pain and the loneliness that that person was experiencing. Hindsight often provides us with 20/20 vision, and you may now look back and see clues and signs of your loved one's suicidal feelings. If you are looking back in this way, please don't blame yourself. You did what you could at the time.

It's important to remember right now:

- You are a good person who has experienced a real tragedy.
- You did the best you could. You are not to blame.
- You have a life worth living—and more loving to do.
- You have other people who need you—and you need them.
- You have a future, and right now you have some rebuilding to do.

(Taken from *Suicide of a Child,.* by Joy and Marvin Johnson, Adina Wrobleski.)

God is watching over you and your struggles. He has not abandoned you. You and your loved one are his children. He has not forsaken either of you. May God's light, love, and peace surround you. We are here to listen, anytime.

Likewise the Spirit helps us in our weakness;
for we do not know how to pray as we ought,
but the Spirit himself intercedes for us with sighs too deep for words.
And he who searches the hearts of men knows what is the mind of the Spirit, because the
Spirit intercedes for the saints according to the will of God.

ROMANS 8:26-27

Common Myths About Suicide

- *Those who commit suicide are insane.*

The word "insane" is a legal term. A person who has committed suicide may not have been thinking rationally, but there is no reason to assume that she or he was insane.

- *Suicide runs in families.*

Diseases like schizophrenia, manic-depression, and possible depression can predispose someone to suicide, but there is no "suicide gene."

- *Suicidal people want nothing more than to die.*

They don't want to die; they want to end their pain.

- *All people who commit suicide leave a note.*

Very few people leave a note (less than one quarter), and when they do, it is usually hard to read and understand, and often isn't the real reason they killed themselves. Edwin Shneidman, noted expert on suicide, says that "In order to commit suicide, one cannot write a meaningful suicide note; conversely, if one could write a meaningful note, one would not have to commit suicide. . . ."

(Taken from *Survivors of Suicide*, by Rita Robinson.)

Suggested Reading for Those Grieving a Suicide

Note: Books for teenagers are marked with *.

There are several resources you can use in locating these titles: your local library (and inter-library loan system), your church library, bookstores, your bereavement minister's personal library, local support groups' lending libraries, and funeral homes.

Remember, if a book doesn't seem to make sense right now, try reading it again later.

After Suicide. J. H. Hewett. The Westminister Press, 1980.

After Suicide: A Ray of Hope. E. Ross. Lynn Publications, 1987.

After Suicide: Help for the Bereaved. S. Clark. Steven Hills Book, 1996.

By Her Own Hand: Memories of a Suicide's Daughter. S. Hammer. Soho Press, 1991.

Coping with Suicide: A Pastoral Aid. G. Green. Twenty-Third, 1992.

Dancing with the Skeleton: Meditations for Suicide Survivors. K. Derrek. Centering Corporation, 1996.

*Dead Serious: A Book for Teenagers about Teenage Suicide. J. Leder. Avon, 1989.

Definition of Suicide. E. Shneidman. John Wiley & Sons, 1986.

The Encyclopedia of Suicide. G. Evans and N. Farberow. News/Facts on File, 1988.

Everything to Live For: A Mother's Story of Her Teenage Son's Suicide. S. White-Bowden. White-Bowden, 1993.

Healing after the Suicide of a Loved One. A. Smolin and J. Guinan. S & S Trade, 1993.

I Can't Get Over It: A Handbook for Trauma Survivors. A. Matsakis. New Harbinger, 1996.

In the Weather of the Heart: A Memoir of a Shattered Marriage and a Reckoning with Recovery. V. Monroe. Doubleday, 1996.

Life After Grief: A Soul Journey After Suicide. J. Clarke. Personal Pathways Press, 1989.

Life After Suicide: A Ray of Hope for Those Left Behind. E. B. Ross. Insight, 1997.

Life After Suicide: A Survivor's Grief Experience. T. Barrett. Prairie House, 1989.

A Message of Hope: For Surviving the Tragedy of Suicide. P. Harness-Overley. Bradley, 1992.

My Son . . . My Son . . . A Guide to Healing After a Death, Loss, or Suicide. I. Bolton. Bolton Press, 1995.

No Time for Good-byes: Coping with Sorrow, Anger and Injustice after a Tragic Death. J. Lord. Bargo, 1991.

The Other Victims of Suicide. S. Craft. Hearthstone, 1991.

Prayers for Bobby: A Mother's Coming to Terms with the Suicide of Her Gay Son. L. Aarons. Harper San Francisco, 1995.

The Savage God: A Study of Suicide. A. Alvarez. Bantam, 1973.

Shudda, Cudda, Wudda: Affirmation to Cope with Self-Doubt. A. Chevalier. Health Communication, , 1996.

Silent Grief: Living in the Wake of Suicide. C. Lukas. Bantam, 1990.

A Special Scar: The Experiences of People Bereaved by Suicide. A. Wertheimer. Routledge, 1991.

Stephen Lives! My Son Stephen: His Life, Suicide and Afterlife. A. Puryear. PB, 1997.

Straight Talk About Teenage Suicide. B. Franel and R. Kranz. Facts on File, 1994.

Suicide. C. H. Stapp. Chelsea, 1996.

Suicide. A. Roy, ed. Williams and Wilkins, 1986.

Suicide: Questions and Answers. A. Wrobleski. Afterwords, 1995.

Suicide Survivors: A Guide for Those Left Behind. A. Wrobleski. Afterwords, 1994.

Suicide and Bereavement. B. Danto. Ayer, 1980.

Suicide and Its Aftermath. E. Dunn, ed. W. W. Norton, 1987.

Suicide in America. H. Hendin. W. W. Norton, 1982.

Suicide of a Child. A. Wrobleski. Centering Corporation, 1993.

Suicide of a Young Man. B. Hayes. Hayes Press, 1994.

Suicide Poems. M. Napoliello. U.S. Marketing.

Suicide Survivor's Handbook: A Guide for the Bereaved and Those Who Wish to Help Them. T. Carlson. Benline, 1995.

*Surviving Suicide: Young People Speak Up. S. Kuklin. Putnam, 1994.

Survivors of Suicide. R. Robinson. Newcastle Publications, 1992.

Words I Never Thought to Speak: Stories of Life in the Wake of Suicide. V. Alexander. Jossey-Bass, 1991.

Booklets available from:
    4124 Grove Street
    Minneapolis, MN 55436-2481

Afterwords: A Newsletter For and About Suicide Survivors (Quarterly newsletter by Adina Wrobleski, cost $5.00 annually. Write the above address.)

Support Groups for Those Grieving a Suicide

*It is one of the most beautiful compensations of this life
that no man can seriously help another
without helping himself.*

RALPH WALDO EMERSON

American Suicide Foundation
1045 Park Ave.
New York, NY 10028
1-212-410-1111
(Offers state-by-state directories for support groups. Ask for a listing of the support groups nearest you, literature about suicide, and the *Surviving Suicide* newsletter.)

Survivors of Suicide (S.O.S.)
1-414-442-4638
(This center provides a directory of nationwide suicide survivors support groups.)

Ray of Hope, Inc.
P.O. Box 2323
Iowa City, IA 52244
1-319-337-9890
(Telephone consultation, counseling, literature, and books for post-suicide bereavement.)

Heart Beat
2015 Devon St.
Colorado Springs, CO 80909
1-719-596-2575
(Information, referrals, and chapter development for those who have lost a loved one through suicide.)

Murder

Setting Up a Program of Bereavement Care for Those Grieving a Murder

Murder is so devastating; it turns the survivor's world upside down and inside out. During the first weeks, those grieving a murder may feel as though they are a robot and cannot feel anything at all. Nothing may seem real. They may feel scared and lonely when people aren't around. Everything may remind them of the person who died; they may even express their desire for just a short reprieve from their obsessive thoughts. They may feel guilty because they were somehow involved in the chain of events preceding the murder or because they were not able to protect their loved one.

They may want to learn every last detail of what happened, going over and over a sheriff's or police report. They may run the incident over and over in their minds. They may have fear that the murderer will try to kill them too—even if that person is dead or incarcerated.

They may be reluctant to go out into public for fear of what other people are saying about them. It may take several months before they feel they can function at work or a year before they can clean out the closet of the one who was murdered. They may have nightmares that haunt them every night, leaving them exhausted more than a year after the death.

They may even have thoughts of death themselves. They may start up old habits like smoking or drinking, thinking that if they do these things they will die sooner to be with the person who died. They may even think of suicide so they can be with the person who died and end their own pain.

If a child was murdered, the parent's marriage may suffer. Eighty percent of marriages in which a child was murdered end in divorce. There are many dynamics which can take place here, including the fact that spouses may grieve the death quite differently.

If young parents lose a child, they may be afraid to have more children for fear that they also might be killed. If there are other children, the remaining children may be overprotected and restricted. If there were no other children, the parents have suddenly lost their basic family unit. This may raise many secondary issues of grieving; they may wonder, for example, about who will take care of them as they grow old.

If you find that those grieving a murder are struggling with obsessive-compulsive behavior, you should consider referring them to a professional grief counselor.

Initial Contact

Immediately after the death, send out a personalized "Grieving a Murder" letter (page 217). Individualize this letter as appropriate.

After your letter has been received, you should call to set up an initial visit to the grieving parents. The following materials are designed to be given at your initial visit:

Physical Symptoms of Grieving	(page 29)
Exercise and Nutrition	(page 30)
Getting to Sleep	(page 32)
Suggested Reading After a Major Loss	(page 34)
Suggested Reading for Those Grieving a Murder	(page 219)
Support Groups and Organizations for Those Grieving a Murder	(page 220)

Monthly Messages

In addition, the following Monthly Messages should be sent during the first year of bereavement (see pages 19-21 for instructions on incorporating these messages into personalized letters or otherwise including them in bereavement care):

The Grieving Process	(page 38)	2 weeks after loss
Common Myths About Grief	(page 39)	1 month after loss
You and Your Emotions	(page 40)	2 months after loss
Enough Faith?	(page 41)	
Working With Your Grieving	(page 42)	3 months after loss
Returning to "Normal"	(page 43)	4 months after loss
I Know There's Life After Death, Right?	(page 44)	5 months after loss
Support Groups	(page 45)	6 months after loss
Dealing With Criticism	(page 45)	7 months after loss

Ongoing Visitation

See suggestions for visitation on page 21. Also, keep in mind the following when ministering to those grieving a murder:

1. Listen, listen, listen.

2. Give hugs or some other type of physical touch that is comfortable for both you and the grieving person.

3. Suggest professional counseling if they are in need of more in-depth consolation than you feel you can offer.

4. Suggest a psychiatrist if nightmares or obsessive thoughts become so disturbing that sleep is lost for days. However, try some relaxation and imagery techniques with the person first if you and that person are comfortable doing so.

5. Pray with the person.

6. Suggest writing a letter to the person who was murdered and asking forgiveness or saying final good-byes.

7. Suggest that the person write a letter to the murderer and express her or his feelings.

Grieving a Murder

(A personalized letter with this material should be send immediately after the murder.)

There are no words to express the anguish you must be feeling right now. It must feel like your world has been shattered by *(name's)* death.

You may feel that you are all alone and that your world has come to an end. You may be feeling dead and empty inside. Or you may be experiencing a lot of anger or feelings of wanting revenge. Nothing may seem real. Everywhere you go and everywhere you look you may be reminded of *(name)*. These obsessive thoughts are quite normal. Such thoughts, when they keep returning, may interrupt your day or your sleep. Right now, they may seem unmanageable at times, but in the upcoming days and months they will lessen. If you are experiencing suicidal thoughts or if the obsessive thoughts become too unmanageable during these days, please call the church or the hotline.

We want you to know that *God is with you*, and more than anyone, he can take your pain and anger. Know that we are thinking about you and I will be calling in a few days to see if you would like to talk.

May you feel our embrace.

> *What then are we to say about these things? If God is for us, who is against us?*
> *He who did not withhold his own son, but gave him up for all of us,*
> *will he not with him give us everything else?*
> *Who will bring any charge against God's elect?*
> *It is God who justifies. Who is to condemn?*
> *It is Christ Jesus, who died, yes, who was raised,*
> *who is at the right hand of God, who indeed intercedes for us.*
> *Who will separate us from the love of Christ?*
> *Will hardship, or distress, or persecution, or famine,*
> *or nakedness, or peril, or sword?*
> *…In all these things we are more conquerors through him who loved us.*
> *For I am convinced that neither death, nor life,*
> *nor angels, nor rulers, nor things present, nor things to come,*
> *nor powers, nor height, nor depth,*
> *nor anything else in all creation,*
> *will be able to separate us from the love of Christ Jesus our Lord.*

—ROMANS 8:31-35, 37-39

Suggested Reading for Those Grieving a Murder

There are several resources you can use in locating these titles: your local library (and inter-library loan system), your church library, bookstores, your bereavement minister's personal library, local support groups' lending libraries, and funeral homes.

Remember, if a book doesn't seem to make sense right now, try reading it again later.

Closer to the Light: Learning from Near Death Experiences of Children. M. Morse. Ivy, 1991.

Crime Victim's Guide to Justice. M. Boland. Sphinx, 1996.

Embraced by the Light. B. Eadie and C. Taylor. Bantam, 1994.

"A Grief Like No Other." The Atlantic Monthly, Vol. 280, no. 3, September 1997.

Homicide: The Victim-Offender Connection. A. Wilson. Anderson, 1992.

Homicide in Families and Other Special Populations. A. Goetting. Springer, 1995.

How We Die. S. Nuland. Knopf, 1994.

I Can't Get Over It: A Handbook for Trauma Survivors. A. Matsakis. New Harbinger, 1996.

Just Us: Homicidal Bereavement. W. Henry-Jenkins. Centering Corporation, 1993.

Mourning into Dancing. W. Wangerin. Zondervan, 1996.

Murder: This Could Never Happen to Me. (A handbook for families of murder victims and people who assist them. Call the Mental Health Association of Tarrant County, Texas, 1-817-335-5405.)

No Time for Goodbyes: Coping with Sorrow, Anger, & Injustice after a Tragic Death. J. Lord. Bargo, 1991.

Shudda, Cudda, Wudda: Affirmation to Cope with Self-Doubt. A. Chevalier. Health Communications, 1996.

The Stalking of Kristin. G. Lardner. NAL-Dutton, 1997.

Those of Us Who Care: Friends of a Victim Describe the Aftermath of Homicide. M. Hansen et al. Rainbow, 1993.

We Are Not Forgotten. J. Martin and P. Romanowski, Berkley, 1992.

What Murder Leaves Behind: The Victim's Family. Magee, Doub, Dobb Mead and Company. Dodd, Mead & Co., 1983.

Who Lives Happily Ever After? For Families Whose Child Has Died Violently. S. Turnbull. Centering Coporation, 1990.

Support Groups and Organizations For Those Grieving a Murder

*It is one of the most beautiful compensations of this life
that no man can seriously help another
without helping himself.*

RALPH WALDO EMERSON

Parents of Murdered Children (POMC)
100 East 8th Street, Room B-41
Cincinnati, Ohio 45202
1-513-721-5683 (Emergencies)
1-513-345-4489 (FAX)
(Self-help group for anyone who has had a loved one murdered. Information about the grieving process and the criminal justice system and newsletter.)

Families of Homicide Victims Program
c/o Victim Services Agency
2 Lafayette Street
New York, NY 10007
1-212-577-7700
(This program provides one-on-one counseling for the surviving spouses of murder victims and gives telephone reassurance to other family members and peer support.)

National Organization for Victim Assistance (NOVA)
1757 Park Rd. NW
Washington, D.C. 20010
1-202-232-6682
1-202-462-2255 FAX
(NOVA is a private, nonprofit organization dedicated to providing national advocacy for victim's rights, help for crime victims, service to local programs, and membership support.)

National Victim Center
307 West 7th Street, Suite 705
Fort Worth, TX 76102
1-817-877-3355
1-817-877-3396 FAX
(The Center is a nonprofit organization that provides information to individuals and organizations concerned about victim's rights and criminal justice issues.)

Concerns of Police Survivors, Inc. (COPS)
c/o Suzier Sawyer
P.O. Box 3199
N. Highway 5
Camdenton, MO 65020
1-314-346-4911
(A nonprofit organization offering support, education, and advocacy for survivors of slain police officers.)

Save Our Sons and Daughters (S.O.S.A.D.)
2441 W. Grand Blvd.
Detroit, MI 48208-1210
1-313-361-5200
(They offer a monthly letter and organize conferences and rallies for survivors of homicide victims.)

Mothers Against Drunk Driving (M.A.D.D.)
511 E. John Carpenter Freeway
Suite 700
Irving, TX 75062
1-214-744-6233
1-800-GET-MADD
1-214-869-2206 (FAX)
(This group encourages citizen participation in legislative reform related to drunk driving and provides public education programs, victim assistance, publications, and conventions.)

The Compassionate Friends, Inc.
National Headquarters
P.O. Box 3696
Oak Brook, IL. 60522-2696
1-630-990-0010
1-630-990-0246 (FAX)
(Chapters offer "telephone friends," monthly support groups, speakers bureau, newsletter, and conferences.)

Committee to Halt Useless College Killings (C.H.U.C.K.)
P.O. Box 188
Sayville, NY 11782
1-516-567-1130
(Information, referral, advocacy, and phone support for families who have lost a child through hazing or alcohol in a college group, sorority, or fraternity.)

Traumatic Events

Setting Up a Program of Bereavement Care After a Traumatic Event

The experiences described in this section are unexpected, horrible, and often devastating. They are events against which victims are defenseless. Large-scale disasters create this experience for large numbers of people, often including loss of life and irreparable property damage.

The phases of grieving after such traumatic events are similar to the phases of grieving after someone has died. In some of these catastrophes, people may have seen family members, neighbors, friends, and even strangers die before their eyes. They may have tried to rescue them but were unable to do so. Traumas, ranging from technological disasters to war, to sexual and physical abuse, are chronic grief issues. The grief can be resolved, but it is sometimes years before help is sought.

At this point, there is little research in the area of bereavement due to these traumatic events, especially in the areas of technological disaster, natural disaster, and terrorism. More information should be forthcoming about these issues in the years to come.

You will probably find that as they deal with a severe trauma, many people will regress back to previous ways of coping. They may start smoking again, drinking, or taking drugs. Even though regression is natural to the grieving process, alcohol and drugs can inhibit progress through the grief cycle and prevent the bereaved from doing the difficult work required. Try to work with them early on, especially if you are knowledgeable of past behaviors.

Each kind of trauma creates unique pain and unique challenges. Remember that individuals can respond differently; there isn't a "wrong" way to grieve. There are some situations, however, that require intervention. Alcohol, drug abuse, and violence are not appropriate; individuals who become involved in these behaviors should be referred for professional help. There are also behaviors or attitudes which are normal but must eventually be left behind. Attitudes such as self-blame, guilt, blaming others, extreme anger, etc., are part of the normal process of grieving, but they need to be addressed so that those grieving are able to resolve them. Remember: These attitudes, thoughts, feelings, and behaviors are *normal* responses to *abnormal* situations.

Natural Catastrophes

Natural catastrophes are earthquakes, floods, fires, volcanic eruptions, tornadoes, hurricanes, and the like. Earthquakes, in particular, create fear and, later, shock because there is little advance warning and predictability is still poor.

Fear and trust appear to be the biggest issues after a natural catastrophe. "Will this happen again?" "If I can't trust the very ground I stand on, how can I trust myself and others?" Anxiety becomes high, for example, when it starts to rain after a flood.

Self-blame is another issue after a natural catastrophe. "I shouldn't have left the cat alone." "We should have known better than to buy a house in the flood plain." "I shouldn't have gone out to the mall that day. My brother was left alone, and he died in the tornado. Why should I still be alive?" The bereaved need someone to look at things rationally and to assure them that there was no way of knowing what was going to happen. Comfort them; cry with them. They need to talk and talk and talk. Blaming themselves or others for a long period of time will be detrimental to the grieving process, and they need to be assisted through the process.

Technological Disasters

Technological disasters are disasters that are created by human technologies gone awry: nuclear plant and toxic waste disposal accidents, airplane crashes, train derailments, shipping catastrophes, and mining disasters are all examples. Technological disasters can be especially unsettling because they relate to situations in which we thought we "had control." ("Psychological and psychiatric aspects of technological disasters," in *Individual and Community Responses to Trauma and Disaster: The Structure of Human Chaos*. R. Ursano, B. McCaughey, and C. Fullerton, eds. Cambridge University Press, 1995.)

Nuclear plant and toxic waste disposal accidents appear to be the most difficult because of their unpredictability, the possibility (and sometimes uncertainty) of lasting effects, our unfamiliarity with them, and their "invisibility."

As in the explosion at Cherynobl, the disaster may end, but the trauma of living with the aftereffects continues for years. Is the water fit for drinking? What about the soil? Will it affect the children? Will it affect the unborn child? Will it actually go into the genes and maybe even affect the next generation? What about jobs and contamination to houses? What about the increased concern of cancer and leukemia?

After being exposed to a technological disaster, people tend to become more aggressive, feel more fearful, distrust others, and withdraw and isolate themselves. One and a half years after the accident, researchers Green, Lindy, and Grace found that in the area affected by the Three Mile Island accident there were increases in anxiety, obsessive-compulsive thoughts, poor concentration, withdrawal from others, and related physical symptoms (headaches, stomachaches, rashes, etc.). After five years the obsessive-compulsive thoughts were still high, as were poor concentration and an increase in hostility and suspiciousness (B. Green, J. Lindy, and M. Grace, 1994).

There is now a new syndrome being proposed called the Informed of Radioactive Contamination Syndrome (IRCS), which affects those who become aware that they may be affected by radioactive contamination. This syndrome often mimics an obsessive-compulsive disorder, and it is similar to posttraumatic stress disorder (PTSD) except that it is not confined to a single traumatic event but is ongoing and future oriented (B. Green, J. Lindy, and M. Grace, 1994).

Traffic Accidents

Grief following a vehicular accident varies depending on whether the victim is at fault. Even if they aren't at fault, victims of traffic accidents may blame themselves for being at the "wrong" place at the "wrong" time.

After an accident, victims may feel anxious about taking a similar means of transportation, feeling scared that something like this will happen again, and exacerbating their already existing problems. They may also feel great anger at the person who caused the crash and the inconvenience and adaptations they have had to make to their lives.

Personal Attack, War, Terrorism, and Other Crimes

Victims frequently blame themselves, thinking they deserved this in some way, and feel guilty about not being able to avoid the trauma. Even a victim of terrorism may feel they could have somehow averted the incident (e.g., tried to grab the gun away). Those taken hostage may feel that if they had been smart enough, they could have avoided the capture. The victim of rape may think that she shouldn't have been walking in "that" neighborhood. The victim of a mugging may think he shouldn't have carried a wallet that day. Or the victim of a crime may blame herself for not locking the door.

These victims may think they deserved what they got for some earlier sinful behavior. Other people, even family and friends, may blame the victims. Others may now see them as spoiled or unlucky in some way and may not want to associate with them.

Rape victims in particular feel fear, depression, anxiety, sexual disinterest, reduced pleasure in life, and difficulty sleeping. Physically they may experience irritated throats, vaginal infections, skin rashes, and gastrointestinal upsets.

Veterans who come back from war might have had some debriefing before they came home or spoke with a chaplain about their moral and spiritual problems, but usually they need extra help, especially if they were in the midst of fighting and were exposed to atrocities of battle. Even those who weren't in battle but were surrounded by death and destruction such as the body handlers, doctors and nurses, etc., would need grief counseling.

Veterans may have experienced one or more of the following: seeing a buddy shot and not being able to save him; waiting on a hospital ship for months; living in uncertainty as to when the war would begin; being separated from their loved ones; following a leader whose orders were against their morals; and being in an unpopular war where social support was poor, such as the Vietnam War.

They may be feeling "survivor's guilt" because they lived while some friends did not, or self-blame from making mistakes or poor judgments that may have resulted in the death of someone in their own company or one of their allies.

War allows for acts of great courage and heroism. War also allows for all kinds of behaviors that are unacceptable in the civilian world such as abusive violence, killing, etc. In a bloody war, soldiers come face-to-face with their own "shadow" side, including capacity for violence.

If the veteran has lived with combat-related posttraumatic stress disorder (PTSD) for many years, it may have manifested itself in depression, addiction, or intense physical pain. (See the PTSD criteria below to see if there is possible need for a psychiatric evaluation.) Many war veterans have developed this disorder 20, 30, or 40 years after the event. If this is the case, help is still available. Medications might be necessary to control the symptoms before work can begin.

Posttraumatic Stress Disorder

Any of the traumas listed above may lead to posttraumatic stress disorder. PTSD is characterized by the following:

- You have been exposed to a traumatic event involving actual or threatened death or injury, during which you respond with panic, horror, and feelings of helplessness.
- You re-experience the trauma in the form of dreams, flashbacks, intrusive memories, or unrest at being in situations that remind you of the original trauma.
- You show evidence of avoidance behavior—a numbing of emotions and reduced interest in others and the outside world.
- You experience physiological hyperarousal, as evidenced by insomnia, agitation, irritability, or outbursts of rage.
- The symptoms described above persist for at least one month.

- The symptoms described above significantly affect your social or vocational abilities or other important areas of your life.

(Taken from *I Can't Get Over It: A Handbook for Trauma Survivors*, by A. Matsakis, New Harbinger, 1994.)

Initial Contact

Because the situations described here can vary so widely, you will need to decide which materials are appropriate.

You should plan to make a visit to the grieving person as soon as you become aware of the traumatic situation. The following materials may be appropriate at your initial visit:

Physical Symptoms of Grieving	(page 29)
Getting to Sleep	(page 32)
The Grieving Process After a Traumatic Event (include only relevant details and sections)	(page 229)
Keeping Healthy	(pages 232-234)
Suggested Reading After a Traumatic Event	(pages 235-238)
Support Groups for Those Grieving After Natural Disasters, Crime or Other Traumatic Events	(page 239)

Monthly Messages

Use some or all of the following Monthly Messages, depending on the situation (see pages 19-21 for instructions on incorporating these messages into personalized letters or otherwise including them in bereavement care):

The Grieving Process	(page 38)	2 weeks after trauma or initial visit
You and Your Emotions	(page 40)	1 month after trauma or initial visit
Enough Faith?	(page 41)	2 months after trauma or initial visit
Returning to "Normal"	(page 43)	4 months after trauma or initial visit
Support Groups	(page 45)	6 months after trauma or initial visit
More About Exercise and Nutrition	(page 46)	8 months after trauma or initial visit

Ongoing Visitation

At your initial visit, talk with the grieving person(s) about visiting again in a month or so. After that, you may want to establish a pattern of visiting every three to six months for the next year or two. If there was a traumatic event affecting large numbers of people, starting a support group at your church may be an effective means of reaching larger numbers (if your church is still standing!). (See "How to Start a Bereavement Support Group," pages 309-312.) If you sense that trauma survivors are experiencing ongoing anxiety, you may want to make available "Coping With Anxiety and Panic" (page 255), "Relaxation Resources" (pages 253-254), "Coping With Your Emotions and Managing Stress" (pages 262-263), and "Meditation and Relaxation" (page 265). They may also benefit from "Dealing With Insomnia" (page 250).

If children are present in the home, be sure to address their grief as well (see page 63).

If the parishioner you are working with is a war veteran or if there is a group of war veterans returning from active duty, consider obtaining a copy of the following two resources which suggest ritual as a way of moving from war back into society:

Catharsis in Healing, Ritual, and Drama. J. Scheff. University of California Press, 1979.

"The Therapeutic Use of Ritual and Ceremony in the Treatment of Post-Traumatic Stress Disorder." D. Johnson, S. Feldman, H. Lubin, and S. Southwick. *Journal of Traumatic Stress*, 1995, 8(2), 283-298.

The Grieving Process After a Traumatic Event

God can see into your broken heart, my friend.
He hears the groaning from the depths of your grief.
He can understand what you are experiencing and thinking and feeling.
He knows what you want to say or need to say, but find it impossible to say.
He accepts that helpless feeling as your prayer.

DR. OSWALD HOFFMANN

You have been traumatized. I can't imagine all the thoughts and feelings you must have had at the time it happened, nor the thoughts and feelings you are having right now, but I can tell you a bit about the process of grieving and trauma.

At the time of the trauma you may have felt numb, confused, anxious, and disorganized. You may have experienced shaking and shivering (which are the body's way of expressing emotion) and may have found yourself walking or running aimlessly. You may have also experienced a sense of altruism and a feeling of people helping people. These are all normal reactions in the first stage of grief. This phase doesn't usually last too long, but it does allow you to do whatever needs to be done at the time.

You may find you'll re-experience some of these emotions (when you remember the incident again, when you go back to your home and see the devastation, or when you take the same mode of transportation), or you may have the feeling that it must have all been a dream.

The next phase of grief is called the "honeymoon phase." This usually lasts anywhere from one week to six months after the disaster. Survivors feel the support of others with whom they have made it through a catastrophic event. In the case of community disasters, class boundaries are dissolved and the community is tied together in one common goal. Government and other support agencies are still involved providing help and assistance with clean-up.

The next phase, called the "confrontation or disillusionment phase" is where you end up doing most of your work, and it lasts anywhere from two months to two years or more. Work? Yes, because grieving is work. You may not be doing any heavy labor, but grieving requires a lot of mental work and readjustment. Trauma can also be a wound, and if you use the analogies of work and wounding then you can see the importance of getting extra sleep (even an afternoon nap), good nutrition (to help you heal), and exercise (even a short walk around the block or moving your hands and legs).

Your emotions will run the gamut from days of crying, to anger, to irritability, to anxiousness, to replaying the trauma over and over, to feeling guilty, to feeling shame, to feeling blame, to having startle responses to a particular noise, to trouble concentrating, to depression (don't worry about clinical depression—feeling bad is one of the aspects of grieving), to feeling like you're losing control, to feeling like you're "going crazy," to being fearful of going back to the area where the trauma occurred. Don't worry: these are *normal* responses to an *abnormal* situation! If any of these thoughts and feelings become too uncomfortable for you to bear, please talk with a trusted friend, clergy person, counselor, or psychologist knowledgeable about the grieving process.

Of course, the particular trauma you have endured brings its own unique experience of grief:

Natural Disaster

Grief after a natural disaster may involve grieving your home. Your home was your place of solace where you could be yourself, where your children grew up, or were in the process of growing up. Your home may have been in an established neighborhood where you knew all the residents and had developed deep friendships, but some people may feel they cannot rebuild and you will lose that sense of neighborliness.

Feelings of anger, bitterness, disappointment, and resentment may appear when promises of aid are not met by government and insurance agencies. Communities may resent outsiders coming in to see the damage and even those organizations that are there to help.

Living with other family members until your house can be rebuilt or bought out can pose its own set of problems. And the feeling of group cohesiveness felt initially may dwindle when people start to individually rebuild their homes and businesses.

Your home kept some of your most treasured possessions and keepsakes such as pictures, antiques, or children's memorabilia. Your privacy may have been invaded when personal things were exposed to others. Your sense of security for the future may have been destroyed. These aspects of your home or farm may all be gone, or maybe you've been able to salvage a few things, but the home as you knew it will be changed forever. These experiences can be so painful. But remember that your grief is a normal reaction to an abnormal situation.

———————

(Adapted from the University of Wisconsin Extension Office pamphlet entitled, "Emotional Recovery After A Disaster.")

Technological Disaster

After a technological disaster such as *(describe the disaster which has occurred)*, you may find yourself grieving that your job or your home is no longer a safe place to be. You may grieve that your sense of safety has been violated, and you may worry about the trauma your family and future generations may have to endure. You may be saddened about how your community life has been affected by this and may fear that agencies or companies aren't telling you the truth or giving you all the facts. People may even start to withdraw from you because they perceive you as being contaminated, even though you may not have been close to the disaster. These experiences can be so painful. But remember these are normal reactions to an abnormal situation.

Terrorism/Hostage-Taking/Rape/Personal Attack

When you've been a victim of crime, you may find yourself grieving the loss of feeling that the world is a safe, orderly, manageable, and controllable place. You may mourn the loss of friends who don't understand and even blame you for what happened. You may mourn the image of yourself as an "in-control" kind of person and find yourself weeping, feeling humiliated, ashamed, worthless, and guilty. Know these are normal reactions to an abnormal situation.

War

After a combat experience, you may find yourself unable to integrate your experience "over there" with your life back home. You may be grieving a buddy who died and blaming yourself for not being courageous or assertive enough. You may replay the incident over and over in your mind. Or maybe you followed a leader's orders that were against your morals or mistakenly shot an ally. There are a lot of things that happen in war that are sanctioned and even promoted—killing, violence, etc.—that aren't tolerated at home. It's important to talk about these feelings and thoughts with a trusted friend, counselor, or clergy person.

Transportation Accident

After a *(plane/train/bus/car)* accident, you may find yourself grieving that you couldn't save a fellow passenger or blame yourself for not being courageous or assertive enough. You may replay the incident over and over in your mind, and you may avoid taking that form of transportation again and fear that you will be in another accident. You may feel anger at the pilot or person driving the car, resentment about the inadequacy of the rescue operations, and frustration over the cost of lost work and career opportunities. The accident may have even exacerbated an existing medical condition, and you may have had to sacrifice other activities due to your new limitations caused by the accident.

The last phase of grieving is called the "re-establishment" or "reconstruction" phase. This can last for quite a number of years as people try to reconstruct their lives.

Remember, everyone is different and will go through the process of mourning in varying lengths and in different intensities.

Recovery from grief is not a station you arrive at but a manner of traveling.

DR. IVAN G. MATTERN

Keeping Healthy

It is important that you take good care of yourself, physically and emotionally, as you work through the process of grieving.

1. Eat a diet low in fat and high in complex carbohydrates (grains, cereals, pasta). Cut down or stop smoking and drinking.

2. Get adequate rest and sleep.

3. Walk briskly for at least 30 minutes a day to increase your blood circulation and reduce stress.

4. Pray and meditate daily for at least 20 minutes.

   a. If you're too angry to pray, tell God so. Keep the lines of communication open. Try reading the passages from the Bible where other faithful people were angry at God too. (Psalms 10, 13, 22, 38, 55, 74, 83, 102, & 109)

   b. Try using a mantra (a word or set of words that are repeated over and over) for relaxing meditation. When you start using mantras or verses, don't become discouraged if distracting thoughts come into your mind. There are several ways to deal with distracting thoughts:

      • Keep a piece of paper and a pencil handy to write down what you want to remember.

      • Ask yourself to remember it after your meditation time.

      • Just let the thought go by nonjudgmentally.

      • Bring the disturbing thought before God and ask for guidance.

      • Start with 5 minutes of meditation and work up to 20-30 minutes.

      One variation is to say your mantra to yourself as you breathe in; then, when you blow out, say the word that is the opposite of your mantra. (Example: love—inhale; hate—exhale.) Imagine yourself breathing in the good and breathing out the bad.

      Another variation is to fix an image to your mantra and imagine those images moving in and out of your body. (Example: An image for love might be a warm flame; an image for hate may be a twisted black wire. Flame—inhale; wire—exhale.)

You can make up your own mantra or try one of the following:

- "Light"
- "Love"
- "Courage"
- "Hope"
- "Faith"
- "Peace"
- "Be strong and of good courage; neither fear nor be dismayed; for the Lord your God is with you wherever you go" (Joshua 1:9).
- "God is our hope and strength, a very present help in trouble. . . . Be still then, and know that I am God" (Psalm 46: 1, 10).
- "Lo, I am with you always, to the close of the age" (Matthew 28:20).
- "They that wait upon the Lord shall renew their strength; they shall mount up with wings as eagles, they shall run and not be weary, they shall walk and not faint" (Isaiah 40:31).
- "Come unto me, all you who labor and are heavy-laden, and I will refresh you" (Matthew 11:28).
- "Let not your heart be troubled. You believe in God, believe also in Me" (John 14:1).
- "Let your hope be a joy to you, be patient in trouble, continue steadfastly in prayer" (Romans 12:12).
- "I can do all things through Christ who strengthens me" (Philippians 4:13).
- "Let the peace of God rule in your hearts" (Colossians 3:15).

5. Attend a healing service. God sometimes gives people unexpected healing. But even if you are not healed miraculously, it may help to remind you that God is listening and that God will guide you in the process of healing. Sometimes we just need other people to pray for us and support us when we get too tired to pray for ourselves or when we are questioning our faith.

For where two or three are gathered in my name, there am I in the midst of them.

MATTHEW 18: 20

6. Laugh often. Develop a humor library if you can. Collect books, movies, cartoons, or other paraphernalia that you can watch or read when you're feeling especially down. Even if you can only produce a forced smile and sit upright, it will set the physiology of your body in a positive way to help produce positive emotions. Try it for one to two minutes.

7. Attend a support group. The group will provide a place to talk about your trauma with people who understand.

8. Seek professional counseling if you feel you need it.

9. Recognize that you cannot control events outside you, but you can control your reaction.

10. Make time for your hobbies, volunteer work, sports, artistic endeavors, etc. It's important to find an outlet that will allow you freedom to express your creativity or take your mind off of your grief.

11. Keep a personal journal of your experiences and feelings. Writing them down on paper helps bring them to your conscious mind where you can deal with them more objectively.

12. List five things you are grateful for every day.

13. Read, read, read. The more knowledge you have about the trauma you've undergone, the more confident you will be.

14. Remember the children. They need extra support and reassurance when you're busy with clean-up.

15. Relaxation exercises such as deep breathing and progressive relaxation can offer a sense of peace and calm. In progressive relaxation you begin by tightening your toes, holding them for five seconds, and then releasing the muscles. Work your way up the body, tightening and releasing different muscle groups till you reach your head.

16. Make a "feel-good" box for days when you're especially low. Find the prettiest box you can and fill it with treasured mementos such as: pretty earrings you wear only once in awhile, a special tea or expensive hot cocoa, uplifting sayings or Bible passages, pictures, a wonderful smelling sachet, a beautiful painting on a card, or anything that would make you feel special.

17. Find a "prayer partner" or sponsor who has not gone through your particular trauma but would be sympathetic to your journey. Make a contract with that person for three, six, or twelve months. During that time the person may send you a card, give you a call, go to appointments with you, pray for you, or somehow express her or his concern and care for you. Don't be afraid to ask your friends. They are often looking for ways to help you, and this would give them an opportunity to minister to you.

Suggested Reading After a Traumatic Event

There are several resources you can use in locating these titles: your local library (and inter-library loan system), your church library, bookstores, your bereavement minister's personal library, local support groups' lending libraries, and funeral homes.

Remember, if a book doesn't seem to make sense right now, try reading it again later.

Children and Trauma: A Parent's Guide to Helping Children Heal. C. Monahon. Lexington, 1993.

Daily Thoughts for Those Who Worry Too Much. A. Chevalier. Health Communications, 1996.

The Great International Disaster Book. J. Cornell. Scribner, 1976.

I Can't Get Over It: A Handbook for Trauma Survivors. A. Matsakis. Harbinger, 1996.

Shudda, Cudda, Wudda: Affirmations to Cope with Self-Doubt. A. Chevalier. Health Communications, 1996.

Wright's Complete Disaster Survival Manual. T. Wright. Hampton Roads, 1993.

Floods

Preschool

The Flood That Came to Grandma's House. L. Stallone. Upshur, 1992.

Mushroom in the Rain. M. Ginsburg. Macmillan, 1974.

Silver Pony. L. Ward. Houghton Mifflin, 1973.

Water. C. Vendrell and J. Parramon. Woodbury, 1985.

Kindergarten through third grade

All-of-a-Sudden Susan. E. Coatsworth. Macmillan, 1974.

City Storm. M. Parker. Scholastic, 1990.

Come a Tide. G. Lyon. Orchard, 1990.

Euphonia and the Flood. M. Calhoun. Parent's Magazine Press, 1976.

Hang On, Hester! W. Devlin. Lothrop, Lee and Shepard, 1980.

Fourth through sixth grade

About Disasters. J. Berry. Children's Press, 1990.

The Day It Rained Forever. R. Lee. Little, Brown and Company, 1968.

Flood. B. Knapp. Raintree Steck-Vaughn, 1990.

Floods. A. Erlback. Children's Press, 1994.

Floods. L. Conlon. Rourke, 1993.

Help! Yelled Maxwell. J. Stevenson and E. Stevenson. Greenwillow, 1978.

Hobie Hanson, Greatest Hero of the Mall. J. Gilson. Lothrop, Lee and Shepard, 1989.

The Washout. C. Carrick. Seabury Press, 1978.

Junior high and high School

Angry Waters: Floods and Their Control. R. Fodor. Dodd, Mead, 1980.

Connecticut Low. B. Boehm. Houghton Mifflin, 1980.

Coping with Natural Disasters. C. Arnold. Walker, 1988.

The Day It Rained Forever: A Story of the Johnstown Flood. V. Gross. Viking, 1991.

Disastrous Floods and Tidal Waves. M. Berger. Watts, 1981.

Escape By Deluge. E. Wignell. Holiday House, 1989.

Nature Gone Wild! W. Olesky. Messner, 1982.

No Way Out. I. Ruckman. Crowell, 1988.

Our Violent Earth. National Geographic Society, 1982.

The Terrible Wave: Memorial Edition. M. Dahlstedt. Dahlstedt, 1988.

Earthquakes and Volcanoes

The New Madrid Earthquakes. J. Penick. University of Missouri Press, 1981.

Volcanoes and Earthquakes. J. Erickson. Tab, 1988.

Children

Discovering Earthquakes and Volcanoes. L. Damon. Troll, 1990.

Earthquakes. L. Conlon. Rourke, 1993.

Earthquakes and Volcanoes. D. Lambert. Bookwright Press, 1986.

The Golden Book of Volcanoes, Earthquakes, and Powerful Storms. L. Pringle. Golden Books, 1992.

The Great Shaking: An Account of the Earthquakes of 1811 and 1812 by a Bear Who was a Witness. J. Carson. Orchard, 1994.

I Can Read About Earthquakes and Volcanoes. D. Merrians. Troll, 1996.

Los Angeles Quake, 1994. R. Smith. Abdo and Daughters, 1994.

Mount St. Helens Volcanic Eruption: May 18, 1980. S. Hamilton. Abdo and Daughters, 1988.

San Francisco Earthquake: April 18, 1906. S. Hamilton. Abdo and Daughters, 1988.

Hurricanes and Tornadoes

The Scariest Place on Earth: Eye-to-Eye with Hurricanes. P. Fisher. Random House, 1994.

Children

Hurricane Hugo. S. Hamilton. Abdo and Daughters, 1990.

Hurricanes. A. Erlbach. Children's Press, 1993.

Hurricanes. M. Hooker. Rourke Corporation, 1993.

Hurricanes. S. Lee. F. Watts, 1993.

Hurricanes: Earth's Mightiest Storms. P. Lauber. Scholastic, 1996.

Hurricanes and Tornadoes. N. Barrett. F. Watts, 1989.

Night of the Twisters. I. Ruckman. Crowell, 1984.

Storm Warning: Tornadoes and Hurricanes. J. Kahl. Lerner, 1993.

Tornado! H. Milton. Watts, 1983.

Tornadoes. A. Erlbach. Children's Press, 1994.

Tornadoes. M. Hooker. Rourke, 1993.

Transportation Accidents

No Downlink: A Dramatic Narrative About the Challenger Accident and Our Time. C. Jensen. Farrar, Straus, Giroux, 1996.

Prescription for Disaster. J. Trento. Crown, 1987.

Seven Days to Disaster: The Sinking of the Lusitania. D. Hickey. Putnam, 1982.

Children

The Exxon Valdez. S. Hamilton. Abdo and Daughters, 1990.

Royal Mail Steamship Titanic. S. Hamilton. Abdo and Daughters, 1988.

Space Shuttle Challenger: January 28, 1986. S. Hamilton. Abdo and Daughters, 1988.

The Space Shuttle Disaster. J. McCarter. Bookwright Press, 1988.

The Story of the Challenger Disaster. Z. Kent. Children's Press, 1986.

Technological Disaster

Nuclear Disaster in the Urals. Z. Medvedev. Norton, 1979.

Children

Chernobyl: Nuclear Power Plant Explosion. S. Hamilton. Abdo and Daughters, 1991.

Chernobyl: The Ongoing Story of the World's Deadliest Nuclear Disaster. G. Cheney. New Discovery, 1993.

Nuclear Accident. C. Lampton. Millbrook Press, 1992.

Terrorism and Hostage-Taking

The Aftermath: The Human and Ecological Consequences of Nuclear War. Pantheon, 1983.

Aftermath: The Remnants of War. D. Webster. Pantheon, 1996.

Bound to Forgive: The Pilgrimage to Reconciliation of a Beirut Hostage. L. Jenco. Ave Maria Press, 1995.

Final Warning: Averting Disaster in the New Age of Terrorism. R. Kapperman. Doubleday, 1989.

Hostage Bound, Hostage Free. B. Weir. Westminister Press, 1987.

Hostage: My Nightmare in Beirut. D. Jacobsen. D. I. Fine, 1991.

Inside and Out: Hostage to Iran, Hostage to Myself. R. Queen. Putnam, 1981.

No Hiding Place: The New York Times Inside Report on the Hostage Crisis. R. McFadden. Time Books, 1981.

On Killing: The Psychological Cost of Learning to Kill in War and Society. D. Grossman. Little, Brown, 1995.

The Psychology of War: Comprehending it's Mystique and it's Madness. L. LeShan. Noble Press, 1992.

War: Four Christian Views. R. Clouse. InterVarsity Press, 1981.

High School

Fallen Angels. W. Myers. Scholastic, 1988.

Support Groups for Those Grieving After Natural Disasters, Crime, or Other Traumatic Events

It is one of the most beautiful compensations of this life
that no man can seriously help another
without helping himself.

RALPH WALDO EMERSON

Survivors
c/o Timothy Quinn
S. Santa Fe Ave.
Vista, CA 92083
(Assistance and literature on how to start a group using the 12 steps to support persons who have long-term grief.)

Trauma Survivors Anonymous
2022 15th Ave.
Columbus, GA 31901
1-706-649-6500
(A pastoral institute offering 12 step emotional recovery program guides and training for those interested in leading groups for trauma survivors.)

Military Families Support Network, Inc.
RR 5 Box 427
Dunn, NC 28334
1-910-892-9315
(Newsletters, information, and referrals for veterans and families. Focus on health problems with Persian Gulf veterans.)

Vietnam Veterans of America, Inc.
1224 M St. NW
Washington, DC 20005-5183
1-202-628-2700
(Newspaper and group guidelines to veterans and families of the Vietnam era. Focus on Agent Orange and posttraumatic stress disorder.)

Death of a Pet

Setting Up a Program of Bereavement Care After the Death of a Pet

It may seem silly to have a "Death of a Pet" section, but in some cases pets can be as important as a human family member. As with any other type of death, the experience of grief can vary. For a family who has lived with a pet for years, for a single person who has no companion other than a cat or a dog, or for a handicapped individual who had a trained animal as a companion, the death of a pet can be a major grieving experience. Acknowledging the loss can be a comfort to the individual or the family if they feel odd that they are crying over "just an animal." Remind them that the animal made up a very real "family" that has now changed.

Be especially sensitive to children's grief over the loss of a pet; they may not be as able to express grief and yet feel it keenly.

If those grieving are interested, a "funeral" or "memorial service" may be a helpful way to say good-bye to a pet. As in any other funeral, sharing both joyful and frustrating memories is helpful and shapes a meaningful legacy for the family. If a family has recently gone through another loss, i.e., a death of a grandmother, they may find that mounting grief requires more attention than it would normally.

As soon as you find out about the person's grief over her or his pet, send out a personalized "Grieving the Death of a Pet" letter (page 242), using the animal's name, if known. If you sense ongoing or severe grief, send suggestions for reading (pages 243-244) and information on support groups (page 245).

A follow-up visit with a short prayer may be appropriate depending on the situation one to two weeks after the death.

Grieving the Death of a Pet

(A personalized letter with this material should be sent when you learn of the person's grief over the pet's death.)

When a pet dies, you may feel you've lost one of your best friends. Often people don't understand your sadness, thinking that it's "just a dog or a cat." But to you, that pet was a member of your family. Allow yourself the freedom to grieve the death of your pet as you would a person. A funeral or family ritual may be very appropriate. Memories shared can be some of the best legacies. Your pet entertained, comforted, frustrated, but always loved you.

We want you to know that God loves all creatures great and small and that your pet has a special place in God's care.

Know that we are thinking of you this day.

O Lord, how manifold are your works!
In wisdom you have made them all; the earth is full of your creatures.

PSALM 104:24

Suggested Reading After the Death of a Pet

There are several resources you can use in locating these titles: your local library (and inter-library loan system), bookstores, your bereavement minister's personal library, local support groups' lending libraries, and your church library.

Remember, if a book doesn't seem to make sense right now, try reading it again later.

Coping with Sorrow on the Loss of Your Pet. M. Anderson. Peregrine, 1994.

Coping with the Loss of a Pet: A Gentle Guide for All Who Love a Pet. C. Lemieux. WR Clark, 1989.

Cracker Still Lives Here: A Story of Living, Loving, & Healing. C. Cummings. Rivers Edge, 1995.

Forever Friends: Resolving Grief After the Loss of a Beloved Animal. J. Coleman. JC Tara, 1993.

The Loss of a Pet. W. Sife. Howell, 1993.

Pet Loss: A Thoughtful Guide for Adults & Children. H.A. Nieberg and A. Fischer. Harper Collins, 1996.

Pet Loss and Human Bereavement. W. J. Kay et al. Iowa State University Press, 1984.

Pets and the Elderly. O. Cusak. Haworth Press, 1983.

Pets and the Family. M. Sussman, ed. Haworth Press, 1985.

When Your Pet Dies: Dealing with Your Grief and Helping Your Children Cope. C. Adamec. Berkley, 1996.

Suggested Reading for Children After the Death of a Pet

There are several resources you can use in locating these titles: your local library (and inter-library loan system), bookstores, your bereavement minister's personal library, local support groups' lending libraries, and your church library.

Remember, if a book doesn't seem to make sense right now, try reading it again later.

General

A Special Place for Charles: A Child's Companion through Pet Loss. D. Morehead. Partners in Publishing, 1996.

Bird

The Dead Bird. M. W. Brown. HarperCollins, 1995.

When Violet Died. M. Kantrowitz. Parent's Magazine Press, 1973.

Cat

Goodbye, Mitch. R. Wallace-Brodeur. Whitman, 1995

Mustard. C. Graeber. Macmillan, 1982.

Tenth Good Thing About Barney. J. Viorst. Atheneum, 1971.

When Chester Lost Maybelle. D. Babson. Winstead Press, 1996.

Dog

Accident. C. Carrick. Seabury Press, 1976.

Dog Heaven. C. Rylant. Blue Sky Press, 1995.

Goodbye, Max. H. Keller. Greenwillow, 1987.

Growing Tim. S. Warburg. Houghton Mifflin, 1975.

I'll Always Love You. H. Wilhelm. Crown, 1988.

It Must Hurt a Lot. D. Sanford. Questar, 1985. (grades K-6)

Jim's Dog Muffins. M. Cohen. Greenwillow, 1984.

The Old Dog. C. Zolotow. HarperCollins, 1995.

Remember Rafferty: Pet Loss for Children. J. Johnson. Centering Corporation, 1991.

Toby. M. Wild. Ticknor and Fields, 1994.

Fish

Helen the Fish. V. Kroll. Whitman, 1992.

Support Groups for Those Grieving the Death of a Pet

*It is one of the most beautiful compensations of this life
that no man can seriously help another
without helping himself.*

RALPH WALDO EMERSON

Holistic Animal Consulting Center
29 Lyman Ave.
Staten Island, NY 10305
1-718-720-5548
(This center provides consultation, education, and intervention during the life of the animal and after death.)

Delta Society
P.O. Box 1080
Renton, WA 98057-1080
1-206-226-7357 (day)
(Listing of pet loss resources.)

Miscellaneous Reproducible Handouts

Gone From My Sight

I am standing upon the seashore. A ship at my side spreads her white sails to the morning breeze and starts for the blue ocean. She is an object of beauty and strength. I stand and watch her until at length she hangs like a speck of white cloud just where the sea and sky come to mingle with each other.

Then someone at my side says: "There, she is gone!"

"Gone where?"

Gone from my sight. That is all. She is just as large in mast and hull and spar as she was when she left my side, and she is just as able to bear her load of living freight to her destined port. Her diminished size is in me, not in her.

And just at the moment when someone at my side says: "There, she is gone!" there are other eyes watching her coming, and other voices ready to take up the glad shout: "Here she comes!"

And that is dying.

—Anonymous

A Commitment to Life

Death is a reality that I am coping with today.
While I am feeling like a victim,
    I remind myself that I will survive.
Though grief is normal and I must grieve for my own health's sake,
    I grieve not as one who has no hope.
Though I am familiar with sharing decisions,
    sharing experiences,
    and doing for another as well as myself;
I can be alone without feeling lonely,
I can make decisions for myself, and
I can learn to do for myself all that needs to be done.
More than any other, I know what is best for me.
    I will act on my own advice, as well as others.
    As much as is possible, I elect to be in charge of my life.
I will remember; I cannot help that.
    I do have some control over how long the memories linger.
    I have a choice as to how I deal with my pain.
I give myself permission to live,
    to face reality and change it where I can,
    and accept it where I cannot.
Like any other human being, I need to be close to another, at times.
    The death of one so loved does not change that need.
    I will actively seek closeness with others as the need arises.
I choose to live and expect the best that life has to offer.
    While death is a reality, I will remember that
    neither death nor life shall separate us
    from the love of God. I am not *alone.*
I make my commitment to live life to the fullest,
    with God's help.

—Author Unknown

Dealing With Insomnia

Insomnia refers to a persistent difficulty in falling asleep or staying asleep. It is a symptom, not a cause, of some condition that interferes with one's sleep. Insomnia can result from an interaction of biological, physical, psychological, and environmental factors. More than 70 million Americans habitually cannot achieve continuous sleep at night.

Three Types of Insomnia

- Transient insomnia involves occasional episodes of restless nights due to environmental changes (jet lag, nearby noisy activities) or exciting or anxiety-producing experiences (a fight with the boss, a new romance).

- Short-term insomnia, lasting a few weeks, generally arises from temporary stressful experiences (the death of a loved one, the fear of losing a job, new pressures). Some people have trouble adjusting their sleeping and waking schedules to meet new needs (a change in working hours).

- Chronic insomnia may last an extended time, months or years. Identifying the causes of these more serious sleep problems may require an evaluation by your physician or a specialist.

Causes of Chronic Insomnia

Poor sleep habits, which interrupt or decrease the ability to sleep, keep individuals from obtaining the amount of sleep they need to function.

Psychological problems can also cause chronic insomnia. Having highly ambitious desires or demanding peak performance daily can cause persistent anxiety, which can keep people awake. Many try too hard to sleep. Others may experience severe depression, which can profoundly affect sleep and sleep cycle.

Extended use of medication (tranquilizers, stimulants, steroids, and many other medications) can restrict one's deep restful sleep.

Excessive use of alcohol may act as a sedative for two to three hours and then cause disturbed sleep in the latter half of the night.

Disruptive sleeping and waking schedules (i.e., irregular bedtime and waking time) confuse the body's biological clock. Some insomniacs take naps to combat excessive daytime sleepiness, but this only further confuses the body's clock for sleep.

The natural process of aging and additional health problems diminish deep restful sleep and the amount of nighttime sleep to an average of six hours for the elderly.

Identifying the causes of insomnia may require a visit to your family physician or a sleep specialist, who will take your medical history and review your symptoms. They may ask you to keep a log of your daily activities and your sleep habits in order to provide clues for appropriate treatment.

The need for quality sleep should be taken seriously; lack of sleep can lead to other physical and emotional problems.

(Used with permission from Maryann Kaul, R.N.)

Worry-Reduction Techniques

1. When I find myself worrying, I will divert my attention from the future to the present.

2. The worst is very unlikely to occur; even if it does, I will handle it.

3. Worrying will not make good things happen or prevent bad things from happening.

4. I will try to take one thing and one day at a time.

5. I will do planning, but reduce my worrying.

6. Relaxation will reduce both worrying and anxiety.

7. I will refrain from engaging in unreasonable worry-related safety checking and avoidance behaviors.

8. People and situations do not upset me; I do.

9. I cannot control anyone else's thoughts, feelings, and behaviors.

10. I will face my fears of rejection and criticism.

11. I will recognize and let go of those things that I cannot change.

(Used with permission from Dr. Richard Moser, Psychologist, MeritCare Neuroscience Clinic, Fargo, ND.)

Relaxation Resources

There are several places you can look for these resources: your local library (and interlibrary loan system), your church library, bookstores, music shops, your bereavement minister's personal library, and local support groups' lending libraries.

Music

Canon in D with Ocean. Pachelbel. Invincible Records, 1986.

Deep Breakfast. R. Lynch. Music West Records, 1986.

From Heart to Crown. Rob Whitesides-Woo. Search for Serenity, 1986.

Going Home. Daniel Kobialka. Li-Sem Enterprises, 1990.

The Healer's Touch. Max Highstein. Search for Serenity, 1986.

In Celebration of Life. Yanni. Private Music, Inc., 1991.

Key to Imagination. Yanni. Private Music, Inc., 1986.

Miracles. Rob Whitesides-Woo. Search for Serenity, 1986.

Music by Solitudes. Dan Gibson Productions Ltd., 1989.

No Blue Thing. R. Lynch. Music West Records, 1989.

Out of Silence. Yanni. Private Music, Inc., 1987.

Rainbows. Daniel Kobialka. Li-Sem Enterprises, 1992.

Sky of the Mind. R. Lynch. Music West Records, 1986.

Sojourn. Scott Fitzgerald. Search for Serenity, 1986.

Sweet Dreams and Lullabies. Steven Halpern. 1990.

Touch the Sky. Max Highstein. Search for Serenity, 1987.

When You Wish Upon a Star. Daniel Kobialka. Li-Sem Enterprises, 1991.

Exploring Nature with Music. Environmental Sound and Visual Experiences. Harmony.

    Volume 1-*By Canoe to Loon Lake.*

    Volume 2-*The Sound of the Surf.*

    Volume 3-*Among the Giant Trees of the Wild Pacific Coast.*

    Volume 4-*Niagara Falls.*

    Volume 5-*Dawn on the Desert.*

    Volume 6-*Storm on Wilderness Lake.*

Volume 7-*Night in a Southern Swamp.*

Volume 8-*Sailing to a Hidden Cove.*

Volume 9-*Seascapes.*

Volume 10-*Tradewind Islands.*

Volume 11-*National Parks and Sanctuaries.*

Volume 12-*Listen to the Loons.*

Solitudes Sampler-A sampling of first eleven Volumes.

Suggested Reading

The Call of Silence. B. Hanson. Augsburg, 1980.

EveryBody's Relaxation Guide: Imaginative Ways of Adding Relaxation to Your Life. J. Scanlan. Evergreen Media, 1991.

Guided Grief Imagery. T. A. Droege. Paulist Press, 1987.

Imagery & Relaxation: Awakening the Inner Healer. B. Dossey. Bodymind Systems, 1989.

Learn to Relax: A Fourteen Day Program. J. Curtis. Coulec, 1991.

Listening To Your Inner Voice: Discovering the Truth Within You and Let It Guide Your Way. D. Block. CompCare, 1991.

A Little Book of Relaxation Techniques. D. Colton. Mat Possessions.

Opening To God. C. Stahl. Upper Room, 1977.

Praying Our Goodbyes. J. Rupp. Ave Maria Press, 1988.

The Quiet Mind: Techniques for Transforming Stress. J. Harvey. Himalayan, 1989.

Quiet Moments—Kid's Relaxation: A Guide to the Tape Series for Parents & Teachers. G. Mills. Media Health, 1986.

Relaxation & Meditation Companion: Take a Deep Breath . . . Relax (audio). C. Gaffney. Mind-Body Center, 1996.

Relaxation for Children. J. Richard. Aust. Council Educ. Res., 1995.

The Relaxation Response. H. Benson. Avon, 1976.

Self-Relaxation: Comfort in Times of Tension. H. Christiansen. Juul, 1981.

Setting the Seen: Creative Visualization for Healing. A. Cohen. A. Cohen, 1982.

Six Seconds to True Calm: Thriving Skills for 21st Century Living. R. Siegel. Little Sun, 1996.

Taming Your Dragons: A Collection of Creative Relaxation Activities for Home & School. M. Belknap. Belknap, 1994.

Tots in Tension. R. Liberman and H. Liberman. Tranquil, 1985.

Words That Heal: Affirmations and Meditations for Daily Living. D. Block. CompCare, 1990.

Coping With Anxiety and Panic

1. Remember, feelings of panic are just exaggerations of normal bodily stress reactions.

2. Sensations are neither harmful nor dangerous—just unpleasant. Nothing worse will happen.

3. Anxiety is temporary. Instead of fighting it, relax into it. Just let it be.

4. Focus on facing the fear rather than trying to avoid it or escape from it.

5. Don't add to the panic with frightening thoughts of where panic will lead.

6. Stay in the present. Be aware of what is happening to you rather than concern yourself with how much worse it might get.

7. Wait and give the fear time to pass.

8. Notice that when you stop adding to panic with frightening thoughts, the fear begins to fade.

9. Wait and give the fear time to pass.

10. Look around you. Plan what you will do next as the panic subsides.

11. When you are ready to go on, do so in an easy, relaxed manner. There is no hurry.

12. Think about the progress made so far, despite all the difficulties.

(Used with permission from Dr. Richard Moser, Psychologist, MeritCare Neuroscience Clinic, Fargo, ND.)

Safety Tips When You Live Alone

Living alone can present some unique safety concerns, especially if you are a woman. Safety tips and rape prevention techniques are provided by WOAR (Women Organized Against Rape), Fargo Rape and Abuse Crisis Center, and the Fargo Police Department.

Using the Telephone

1. Be careful of telephone scams. Often we are too trusting and give out too much information over the phone. Remember, if they call and say, "You've won an all-expense-paid vacation to the Bahamas, if you only buy this inexpensive radio for $34.95 and give me your credit card number," tell them, "no." If it is too good to be true, it usually is.

2. Other telephone tips:

   a. Never tell someone you don't know that you're alone.

   b. Never tell them you're going on vacation or when you are leaving.

   c. Never give your credit card numbers over the phone when you have not called them personally.

   d. Never give a female more information. It is reported that men and women give more personal information to a woman caller than a man.

   e. If someone calls and asks you to take a survey, tell the caller you don't have time over the phone but you would be more than happy (if you really are) to fill it out later at your convenience. Ask the caller to mail you a copy.

3. If you receive an obscene phone call, don't talk to the caller; hang up. If he calls back, blow a whistle into the receiver. If he continues to bother you, call the phone company. Try tapping on the mouthpiece and saying, "Operator, this is the call I want you to trace."

4. Refuse to give out any personal information over the telephone. When it is necessary to give your telephone number to agencies, etc., give them your daytime work number. Make sure other employees know not to give out personal information about you over the telephone.

5. Know emergency numbers. Have a telephone extension near your bed.

6. Teach children caution in answering the door or the telephone.

In Hotel Rooms

1. Always stay above the second floor in a hotel.

2. Always use all of the locks on the door.

3. If you are given a room key, avoid allowing others to read the room number. (Thankfully, many room locks are now electronic.)

4. Leave your TV, radio, and a light on when you leave the room.

5. Use the hotel safe if you will be staying more than a few days.

6. Stand next to the panel when getting on an elevator. If you are uncomfortable about the people, don't get on.

7. Avoid the stairwells.

8. Call and check with the office to make sure the maintenance people are authorized to come up to your room instead of assuming that something needs to be fixed in your room.

9. Make a mental plan in your head, asking the question, "What would I do if . . . ?"

10. Ask at the desk to have a security guard escort you to your room.

On the Street

1. Be aware of yourself and your surroundings.

2. Be familiar with your own frequently used routes. Be aware of possible troublesome areas and plan ahead what you might do in case of attack.

3. Vary your routes home, especially at night.

4. Try to walk with other people or take public transportation, especially after dark.

5. If you must walk alone, walk in the middle of the sidewalk, out of reach of people hiding in doorways or parked cars. Stay on well-lighted streets. Try to walk where other people walk, rather than on a deserted street. If there is little traffic, you might want to walk in the middle of the street.

6. If you suspect that you are being followed, look behind you. Cross the street; walk in a different direction; vary the speed of your walk. If a person persists in following you, go into the nearest lighted house or open business and call a friend, a cab, or the police. Don't be afraid to scream or make noise—you may scare away a would-be attacker.

7. If you must walk in an unfamiliar area, get a map and plan your route in advance. Always walk briskly and confidently. Don't look lost or as if your mind is a million miles away. Don't look vulnerable—look strong and aggressive.

8. Wear sensible clothes for walking. Run if necessary. Don't constrict yourself with platform shoes or too many packages.

9. If a car pulls up beside you, stay more than an arm's length away. Don't become involved in a long conversation. If a car continues to follow you, cross the street or turn and go in the opposite direction. If he persists, record his license number and call the police from the nearest open business or home.

10. If you carry a purse, newspaper, or umbrella, keep it tucked under your arm.

11. While waiting for a bus or a light to change, notice how you stand. Try to be balanced, with your feet apart and hands out of your pockets. Be aware of people and cars around you.

12. Wear a whistle wrapped around your wrist and use it when you think you should.

13. If you fear danger, yell "Fire!" or "Call the police!" rather than "Rape!" or "Help!" Go to the nearest lighted place and get in quickly. Break a window instead of ringing the bell. If you run, make it quick and run the whole way.

14. Wear a waist pouch instead of carrying a purse.

While Using Public Transportation

1. While waiting on a subway platform, stay near the attendant's booth. Sit in a well-populated car. Avoid sitting near groups of men. Stay alert.

2. Don't get off at your normal stop if you suspect you are being followed. Ride on to a busy stop and go directly to the change booth. Tell the attendant to call the police.

3. On a bus or trolley, sit near the driver. If someone starts bothering you, make a commotion. Don't just politely move his hand off your body.

When Driving

1. Always check the back seat and floor of your car before getting in.

2. Drive with your doors locked and windows partially rolled up. Don't make it easy for someone to reach in and open your door.

3. Park in well-lighted parking areas near to the building you are visiting. Note where you have parked so you can walk directly to your car. Have your keys ready in your hand so you can get in quickly. If there is a man near your car or two or three others, turn around and go find the security guard to help you to your car.

4. Put your purse and packages on the floor or in the glove compartment, out of easy reach of passersby.

5. When pulled up at a stop light, keep your car in gear. If someone approaches your car while you are stopped, keep your hand on the horn.

6. If you think a car is following you, head toward the nearest police station or business district. Don't drive home; he might follow you. Try to make a mental note of the color and make of his car. If you can see the license plate, try to remember the number. Don't wait around to see it, though. Get away from the car.

7. Don't pull over if the car behind you flashes its lights. If it is the police, they will have a siren and flashing red or blue lights on top of the car.

8. Make sure you have at least a quarter tank of gas whenever you drive.

9. If you stop for gas at night, stay in the car.

10. If all of your keys are on the same chain, separate house keys from car keys when leaving the key with a parking lot attendant. Don't put your name or address on your key chain.

11. Take your keys to lock the car door when leaving.

If You Have Car Trouble or See Another Driver in Trouble

1. If your car breaks down on the highway, pull over to the side of the road. Keep your doors locked, windows up, and stay in the car. Check to make sure no one is around, get out, and raise your hood. Wait for the highway patrol to stop.

2. If a man stops to help you, open the window just a crack. Ask him to stop at the nearest phone and call for assistance. Don't get out of the car or let him try to fix it. Not every man is a rapist, but you can never tell.

3. Road flares should be kept in your glove compartment in the event of car trouble at night. Light one or two, and place them on the ground behind your car.

4. If you spot a disabled vehicle, note the location and stop at the first safe telephone to call the police or highway patrol. If you don't know the number, dial the operator and she or he will connect you. (Cellular phones have now become fairly common and would be an added safety measure if you're traveling alone.)

5. Do not get in a stranger's car to get help. Stay with your car.

Safety at Home

1. There should be lights in all entrances where you live. If you live in an apartment building, make sure all halls are lighted.

2. Make sure all doors have strong 1-1/2" deadbolt locks. A key-in-the-knob lock offers no security at all. Keep your doors locked at all times.

3. Make sure all windows have locks. If you live on the first floor, see about the possibility of having bars installed. The same applies to windows looking out on porch roofs, especially in row houses. If you sleep with windows open, lock them open (a wood block can be used at the top so the window can only be opened so wide). Make sure the opening is too small for a slim body to slide through.

4. All windows should have shades, blinds, or curtains. Keep them shut when you are dressing or if the window is on the ground level.

5. If you live by yourself or with other women, use only first initials on mailboxes and in the phone book. Do not use your first name. Keep your husband's name, if deceased, as the listing.

6. Know your neighbors. Work out a procedure for alerting them in case of an emergency.

7. Always find out who is at your door before opening it. Have a peephole installed, if you do not have one. If the person claims to be a service person, put on your chain lock and ask for his identification through the crack. If you do not have a chain lock, ask him to slide his card under the door. If you suspect the man, call the service company to verify that a service man is supposed to be visiting you. If you're alone and not expecting anyone, answer the door calling, "I'll get it, Bill."

8. When returning home, have your keys ready in your hand. If someone is following you or watching you, don't let them know where you live.

9. If a person comes to your door saying that she or he needs to call a tow truck, etc., offer to make the call. Don't open the door.

10. When you come home from shopping, you may want to lock the door behind you. Watch your alley or garage. And always have your key in your hand ready to use for the car or the house.

11. Avoid using basement laundry rooms alone, especially at night. Make sure you lock your door when you go.

12. "Beware of Dog" signs and large dog bowls can be inexpensive deterrents.

"Legal Weapons" as Protection

1. Do not rely on weapons, as they may be taken from you and used against you. The following weapons are to be used *only to stop an attack with enough time to get away*. Don't worry about winning a fight; worry about getting away.

    a. Lighted cigarette: use on the face.

    b. Plastic lemon filled with ammonia: aim for his eyes. Will induce temporary blindness.

    c. Umbrella: put one hand in the center, the other at the end. Use a jabbing motion toward neck or stomach.

    d. Hatpin: carry in your hand or clothing. Wrap hand around it and scrape face or jab at neck.

    e. Keys: carry in hand with ends sticking out through finger. Use a blow of the fist or scrape across his hand or face.

    f. Hardbound book: hold with both hands and smash edge into side of nose or throat.

2. Search your kitchen and bathroom shelves for other objects that could be used as weapons to allow you time to get away (aerosol sprays, or dirt from the plants).

If You Are Raped

1. Don't be ashamed or embarrassed. Do the following things:

2. Call the police. Give your location, and tell them you were raped.

3. Try to remember as many facts about your attacker as possible: clothes, height, weight, age, skin color, scars, etc. Try to describe his car, where he went, license number, etc.

4. Do not wash or douche before the medical exam—you will destroy important evidence. Do not change your clothing. Bring new clothing if you can.

5. At the hospital, you will have a complete exam, including a pelvic exam. Show the doctor all scratches, bruises, etc.

6. Tell the police exactly what happened. Try not to get flustered. Have a friend or relative accompany you if possible. It does not matter if you knew the rapist. Be honest, and stick to your story.

7. If you do not want to report to the police, see a doctor soon. Make sure you are treated for pregnancy and sexually transmitted diseases.

8. Call the Rape and Abuse Crisis Center—anytime—24 hours a day.

We hope these suggestions are helpful and don't make you overly concerned about your safety, but rather cautious now that you are alone. Practicality, intuition, and prayer can work wonders for your well-being.

(Used with permission of Women Organized Against Rape, 1233 Locust St., Suite 202, Philadelphia, PA 19107.)

Coping With Your Emotions and Managing Stress

Here are some suggestions to help you deal with your grief:

1. Exercising. Try a walk around the block, a game of golf, or whatever exercise you enjoy.

2. Crying.

3. Talking about your feelings with a trusted friend, counselor, or pastor.

4. Writing your thoughts on paper and expressing your feelings to the person who died, to a doctor, to God, etc. Then you may choose to destroy your writing or place it in a secure place.

5. Praying—for the person who died and for yourself in coping with the necessary adjustments in your life.

6. Meditating and relaxing. This can offer you a brief respite from your emotions and obsessive thoughts and allow your body to heal. See your "Grieving Workbook" for ideas.

7. Drawing, dancing, singing, or any other type of creative expression. Make up a song and sing it as loud as you can, or paint or color the emotions inside of you.

8. Watching a funny movie. This can offer a diversion from your grief work for a while, and laughter allows for the release of tension.

9. Thanking God for the support you have received, for friends, for books, etc. An attitude of thankfulness can be difficult at the beginning but will be an important aspect of living later.

10. Reading about grief and loss. See "Suggested Reading After a Major Loss."

11. Listening to music. This can offer relaxation and comfort—it can be a mood-changer.

12. Taking a warm bath.

13. Getting a massage. It helps relax your body and helps your body feel cared for and loved.

14. Eating nutritious meals. Sometimes dinner hours are lonely times—share them with a friend.

15. Walking in nature. This can soothe the soul as you hear the sounds of life and watch the cycle of the seasons.

16. Throwing yourself into a hobby. It helps you take your mind off of your grief work for a while.

17. Caring for a pet. They give back unconditional love.

18. Limiting the amount of alcohol, cigarettes, and drugs (sleeping pills, tranquilizers, etc.) you consume and the amount of time you watch television.

19. Limiting your exposure to pesticides, herbicides, and chemical fertilizers.

20. Limiting the amount of sugar, salt, and caffeine you consume.

21. Getting adequate sleep. If you aren't, please refer to the handout on falling asleep.

22. Drinking six to eight glasses of pure water every day.

23. Keeping up good posture with neck elongated and your head up straight as if there's a hook at the top. Good posture can change your mood and confidence.

24. Wearing a smile, even when you don't feel like it can change your mood. You don't have to fake being happy, but if you're tired of being sad and need a break—try a smile.

Meditation and Relaxation

Meditation can be very helpful in dealing with stress and anxiety. Here is one technique you can use:

Sit quietly in a comfortable chair for two to thirty minutes. (You may want to gradually increase the amount of time you meditate.) Be aware of yourself being held by the chair. Then become aware of your body sending a wave of meditation to the muscles from the top of your head to the tips of your toes.

You may want to begin with a brief reading from scripture, a devotion, or simply saying the name "Jesus" or "Christ" a few times as you sit quietly. See yourself sitting next to Jesus.

Next, take two to three deep breaths, focusing on your breathing. When you focus on your breathing, you are reminding yourself of the rhythm of life. Life is holding on and life is letting go. Breathing in and breathing out. It is the breath of God that gave you life.

Allow yourself to be held and supported by God. As you sit in quietness, listen for the still, small voice of God. After your quiet time, simply say "thank you."

You may find this uncomfortable at first, but try it two or three times and see if it doesn't become more comfortable for you as a helpful tool in managing stress in your life.

The Steps:

1. Sit comfortably and feel a wave of relaxation through your body.
2. Scripture, other reading, or calling on the name of Jesus Christ.
3. Two or three deep breaths, focusing on your breathing.
4. Sit quietly and listen.
5. Say "thank you."

Suggested Reading on Issues Related to Aging Parents

There are several resources you can use in locating these titles: your local library (and inter-library loan system), your church library, bookstores, your bereavement minister's personal library, and local support groups' lending libraries.

Remember, if a book doesn't seem to make sense right now, try reading it again later.

The Big Squeeze: Balancing the Needs of Aging Parents, Dependent Children & You. B. Shapairo. Mills Sanderson, 1991.

Can Mom Live Alone? Practical Advice on Helping Aging Parents Stay in Their Own Home. V. Carlin. Free Press, 1991.

Caring for Aging Parents: Straight Answers That Help You Serve Their Needs Without Ignoring Your Own. R. Johnson. Concordia, 1995.

Caring for Your Aging Parents. B. Deane. NavPress, 1989.

Daughters Caring for Elderly Parents: The Relationship Between Stress & Choice. M. Berg-Weger. Garland, 1996.

If I Live To Be One Hundred: A Creative Solution for Older People. V. Carlin and R. Mansberg. Princeton Book Company, 1989.

Lost Touch: Preparing for a Parent's Death. M. Becker. New Harbinger, 1992.

Parent Care Survival Guide: Helping Your Folks Through the Not-So-Golden Years. E. Pritikin and T. Reece. Barron, 1993.

Seven Steps to Effective Parent Care: A Planning & Action Guide for Adult Children with Aging Parents. D. Cohen and C. Eisdorfer. Putnam, 1993.

Should Mom Live With Us? And Is Happiness Possible If She Does. V. Carlin and V. Greenberg. Free Press, 1992.

Trading Places: Caring for Elderly Parents. H. Holstege. CRC, 1996.

When Love Gets Tough: The Nursing Home Decision. D. Manning. Harper San Francisco, 1990.

Where Can Mom Live? A Family Guide to Living Arrangements for Elderly Parents. V. Carlin and R. Mansberg. Free Press, 1987.

Support Groups for Those Caring for the Chronically Ill or Aging

*It is one of the most beautiful compensations of this life
that no man can seriously help another
without helping himself.*

RALPH WALDO EMERSON

CAPS (Children of Aging Parents)
1609 Woodbourne Rd. #302A
Levittown, PA 19057
1-215-945-6900
1-215-945-8720 (FAX)
(Newsletters, information, support, and referral for caregivers of the elderly.)

Well Spouse Foundation
P.O. Box 801
New York, NY 10023
1-800-838-0879
1-212-644-1241
(Newsletters and support group setup for those living with partners who are chronically ill.)

DEBUT (Daughters of Elderly Bridging the Unknown Together)
Area 10 Agency Aging
2129 Youth Ave.
Bloomington, IN 47401
(Phone network and weekly meetings for daughters struggling with aging parents.)

Suggested Reading Related to Ongoing Illness

There are several resources you can use in locating these titles: your local library (and inter-library loan system), your church library, bookstores, your bereavement minister's personal library, and local support groups' lending libraries.

Remember, if a book doesn't seem to make sense right now, try reading it again later.

After You Say Goodbye: When Someone You Love Dies of AIDS. P. Froman. Chronicle, 1992.

AIDS: Intervening with Hidden Grievers. B. Dane and S. Miller. Greenwood, 1992.

AIDS: The Ultimate Challenge. E. Kubler-Ross. Macmillan, 1993.

AIDS & the New Orphans: Coping with Death. B. Dane and C. Levine, eds. Greenwood, 1994.

Anatomy of an Illness as Perceived by the Patient. N. Cousins. Bantam, 1981.

The Art of Dying. P. Weenolsen. St. Martin, 1996.

At Life's End: Words of Comfort & Hope. D. Deffner. Concordia, 1995.

A Caring Response to an AIDS-Related Death. National Funeral Director's Association.

Choices: For People Who Have a Terminal Illness, Their Families, and Their Caregivers. H. Von Bummel. NC Press, 1987.

Coping with Childhood Cancer: Where Do We Go From Here? D. Adams and E. Deveau. Kinbridge, 1984.

Final Passages: Positive Choices for the Dying and Their Loved Ones. J. Ahronheim and D. Weber. S & S Trade, 1992.

Grief and AIDS. L. Sherr. Wiley, 1995.

Healing the Dying. M. Olson. Delmar, 1996.

How to Live Between Office Visits: A Guide to Life, Love, & Health. B. Siegel. Wheeler, 1993.

I Don't Know What to Say: How to Help and Support Someone Who is Dying. R. Buckman. Key Porter, 1988.

Just Hold Me While I Cry. B. Stasey. Elysian Hills, 1993.

Letting Go: Morrie's Reflections on Living While Dying. M. Schwartz. Walker, 1996.

Living With Loss: Experiencing Bereavement with Special Attention to HIV/AIDS. L. Kavor. Chi Rho, 1991.

Loss and Anticipatory Grief. T. A. Rando, ed. Lexington, 1986.

Love, Medicine and Miracles. B. Siegel. Harper & Row, 1986.

No Time for Nonsense: Self-Help for the Seriously Ill. R. Jevne and A. Levitan. Lura Media, 1989.

On Death and Dying. E. Kubler-Ross. MacMillan, 1993.

Running with the Angels: The Gifts of AIDS. B. Stasey. Elysian Hills, 1994.

Sacred Dying. B. Kaufman and S. Kaufman. Epic Century, 1996.

Start the Conversation: The Book About Death You Were Hoping to Find. G. Stone. Warner, 1996.

The True Work of Dying: A Practical & Compassionate Guide to Easing the Dying Process. J. Bernard and M. Schneider. Avon, 1996.

We Are Not Alone: Learning to Live with Chronic Illness. S. Pitzelle. Workman, 1986.

When Someone Is Dying: The Words You Both Need. M. Hall, ed. Writeside, 1988.

Support Groups for Those Dealing With Terminal Illness

Center for Attitudinal Healing
19 Main Street
Tiburon, CA 94920
1-415-435-5022
(A center dedicated to the power of positive thinking and love to overcome stress and illness, through support and education services.)

Exceptional Cancer Patients (ECaP)
1302 Chapel Street
New Haven, CT 06511
1-203-865-8392
(A nonprofit organization, founded by Bernie Siegel, M.D., that provides clinical services for people facing chronic or catastrophic illness, educational programs, training, consulting, information, and referral services.)

Make Today Count
P.O. Box 222
Osage Beach, MO 65065
(A national support group for persons with a life-threatening illness and their families.)

National Association for People with AIDS
1413 K St. NW #7
Washington, DC 20005-3405
1-202-898-0414 (day)
(A nonprofit organization providing education and technical assistance to local People With AIDS (PWA) groups.)

Reflection #1

"Likewise the Spirit helps us in our weakness; for we do not know how to pray as we ought, but the Spirit himself intercedes for us with sighs too deep for words"

ROMANS 8:26

Late at night when the world is fast asleep, I'm awake thinking about . . .

_____

_____

_____

_____

_____

_____

_____

_____

_____

_____

_____

Prayer:

Dear God,
I am hurting so much. Please help me and my family survive
the death of my loved one. Amen.

Additional thoughts:

_____

_____

_____

_____

Reflection #2

*I am worn out from groaning;
all night long I flood my bed with weeping and drench my couch with tears. My eyes
grow weak with sorrow; they fail because of all my foes.*

PSALM 6:6-7

What I wish I hadn't said was . . .

_____

_____

_____

_____

What I wish I would have said was . . .

_____

_____

_____

_____

_____

Prayer:

Dear God,
I miss my loved one so much. I wish I could have had more time with her or him.
Please take care of my loved one and let her or him know how much I love and miss her
or him. Amen.

Additional thoughts:

_____

_____

_____

_____

Reflection #3

I have told you these things, so that in me you may have peace.
In this world you will have trouble.
But take heart! I have overcome the world.

JOHN 16:33

What I wish I would have done was . . .

_____

_____

_____

_____

What I wish I would not have done was . . .

_____

_____

_____

_____

Prayer:

Dear God,
I do not know exactly how to act or feel. I am angry, guilty, sad, confused,
and hurt inside. Please help me to sort out some of my feelings. Amen.

Additional Thoughts:

_____

_____

_____

_____

Reflection #4

Be strong and courageous;
Do not be terrified; do not be discouraged,
for the Lord your God will be with you wherever you go.

JOSHUA 1:9

There are a few things I can't stand to do since you died . . .

_____

_____

_____

_____

_____

_____

Prayer:

Dear God,
I miss my loved one so much. Help me to remember everything I can about her or him. She or he means so much to me. Amen.

Additional thoughts:

_____

_____

_____

_____

_____

_____

_____

Reflection #5

*Come to me, all you who are weary and burdened,
and I will give you rest.*

MATTHEW 11:28

When you died I thought I couldn't go on. I had to because . . .

_____

_____

_____

_____

_____

_____

_____

_____

Prayer:

Dear God,
Every day there are things that remind me of my loved one. Help me to
cope with the reminders in a positive way. Help me to be the best person
I can be inside. Amen.

Additional thoughts:

_____

_____

_____

_____

_____

Reflection #6

Jesus said to her,
"I am the resurrection and the life;
he who believes in me, though he die, yet shall he live,
and whoever lives and believes in me shall never die.
Do you believe this?"

JOHN 11:25

There are questions I would like to ask you . . .

_____

_____

_____

_____

This is how I think you would answer . . .

_____

_____

_____

_____

Prayer:

Dear God,
There are so many unanswered questions that I have. It is about six
months after my loved one's death, and I am still confused. Help me to find
answers to my questions or to deal with the fact that there are no answers. Amen.

Additional thoughts:

_____

_____

_____

Reflection #7

*The hour is coming, indeed it has come, when you will be scattered,
each one to his home, and you will leave me alone.
Yet I am not alone because the Father is with me.*

JOHN 16:32

I first began feeling hope about living when . . .

_____

_____

_____

_____

_____

_____

_____

_____

Prayer:

Dear God,
I feel so lonely at times. Help me to remember I am never alone with you by my
side. Amen.

Additional thoughts:

_____

_____

_____

_____

_____

_____

Reflection #8

Though he stumble, he will not fall,
for the LORD upholds him with his hand.

PSALM 37:24

The biggest challenge I continue to face is . . .

_____

_____

_____

_____

_____

_____

_____

_____

Prayer:

Dear God,
Thank you for helping me survive this far. I know I have a long way to go, but with
your help I will continue to survive. Amen.

Additional thoughts:

_____

_____

_____

_____

_____

_____

Reflection #9

Blessed be the God and Father of our Lord Jesus Christ,
the Father of mercies and the God of all consolation,
who consoles us in all our affliction,
so that we may be able to console those who are in any affliction
with the consolation with which we ourselves are consoled by God.

2 CORINTHIANS 1:3-4

The qualities I miss most about you are . . .

_____

_____

_____

_____

_____

_____

_____

Prayer:

Dear God,
Thank you for giving me memories. They are so helpful through this difficult time.
Amen.

Additional thoughts:

_____

_____

_____

_____

_____

Reflection #10

Love bears all things,
believes all things,
hopes all things,
endures all things.
Love never ends. . . .

I CORINTHIANS 13:7-8

What I will miss most about our relationship is . . .

_____

_____

_____

_____

_____

_____

_____

Prayer:

Dear God,
It seems everyone wants me to "get over" my loved one's death.
Help me to remember to give myself time. Grieving takes time.
I love my loved one so much. Amen.

Additional thoughts:

_____

_____

_____

_____

_____

Reflection #11

We know that in everything God works for good
with those who love him,
who are called according to his purpose.

PSALM 116:8-9

Your death has changed me by . . .

_____

_____

_____

_____

_____

_____

_____

Prayer:

Dear God,
It has been almost a year since my loved one died.
She/he will always be missed and loved.
My loved one's memory will always be remembered and cherished.
I have changed, and I am stronger.
Thank you for giving me strength. Amen.

Additional thoughts:

_____

_____

_____

_____

_____

Reflection #12

For you, O Lord, have delivered my soul from death,
my eyes from tears, my feet from stumbling,
that I may walk before the Lord in the land of the living.

PSALM 116:8-9

The ways you continue to live on in me are . . .

_____

_____

_____

_____

_____

_____

Prayer:

Dear God,
As the one-year anniversary of my loss comes closer,
many feelings and emotions are brought up.
Help me get through this time
so I can look forward to a wonderful future full of memories. Amen.

Additional thoughts:

_____

_____

_____

_____

_____

A Ritual for Saying Good-bye

(A service for children who were not conceived, who were miscarried or stillborn, or who died in infancy)

Before you begin your service and in the privacy of your own home, name your child or your "dream" child. Draw a picture of what your child would look like or write down what features the child would have had: the sex of the child, the hair color, eye color, what she or he might have gone on to do and be, etc. Write down what you hoped you could have given to the child, sharing your thoughts and dreams for her or him. Tell the child about the difficult experience you have had and how sad you are that you couldn't have shared your life with her or him. Imagine what you would have been like as parents.

Next, as a couple share how this will change your life together: what old dreams you need to let go and what new dreams you are now free to dream.

Then invite friends and family who would be sympathetic in holding a remembrance service, inviting a clergyperson for help if you wish. The service can be as formal or informal as you like. Some parts of the service you may want to include are:

- The naming of the child and her or his uniqueness before God

- Sharing your pictures and/or descriptions of the child

- Sharing your struggles

- Words of comfort from the Bible

    Appropriate passages would include:

    Deuteronomy 33:27a

    Isaiah 40:27-31

    Isaiah 65:17-18, 20a

    Jeremiah 31:15

    Psalm 139:1-15

    1 John 3:1-2

    Luke 18:15-17

    Romans 8:26-7

- Hymns

  Appropriate hymns might include:

  "Amazing Grace"

  "Children of the Heavenly Father"

  "Have No Fear, Little Flock"

  "It Is Well With My Soul"

- Prayers of comfort for the parents and for all who mourn

- Acknowledgment of the losses other than the child, possibly including the loss of

  feeling what it would be like to be pregnant

  being called "mommy" or "daddy"

  the experience of parenting

  being able to breast-feed

  being able to share family rituals or pass them down

  having grandchildren

- A spoken "letting-go" of the past dream and the sharing of new dreams

- Blessings on the new life you are now pursuing together

Part IV

RESOURCES FOR BEREAVEMENT MINISTERS

When to Refer Someone for Professional Counseling

It is difficult to know exactly when to refer someone for professional counseling. Everyone is different in how they handle their grieving and how long their grieving lasts. As a general rule, you should be concerned if you find people consistently involved in behavior that threatens their ability to take care of themselves or their dependents. You should also be sensitive to your own sense that the situation has become "too much" for you.

Expressions of anger or depression in the form of violence or self-destructive behaviors would clearly be a red flag calling for more intensive intervention. Other behaviors may not be as extreme, but their persistence does endanger the grieving person or her or his dependents. Pay attention to the length of time that the behavior persists. If someone doesn't have the energy to wash the dishes, that is not a problem. But if you see the same dishes in the sink for two weeks, you should have concern. Your first response might be to offer help with the dishes, but this is a situation you should monitor carefully.

Suicidal tendencies are another area to pay attention to. Grieving people may say something like, "I wish this would end," as a way to express despair, rather than to indicate suicidal intent. Such a comment, however, might prompt you to do more in-depth assessment by asking if there is any past history of mental disturbance or serious depression, if they are thinking of hurting themselves, and if they have any specific thoughts about how they might do so. If you perceive the threat of suicide to be a serious one, you should make a specific plan to get them to professional counseling. Ask them to contract with you that they will not hurt themselves until they see a counselor (and perhaps try to stay with them), and then look immediately for a counselor who can see them. Make an appointment as soon as possible. If you must wait for more than a day or two, make a long-term plan, including having members of the bereavement team or other church members visit at least once a day.

Teenagers or children who display suicidal thinking or behaviors such as constant sadness, extreme withdrawal from family and friends, severe anger or listlessness, alcohol or drug use, loss of pleasure in previously enjoyable activities, disregard for personal appearance, or extreme listlessness or insomnia should also receive close attention.

You should also be concerned if you sense denial concerning the death or loss. People in denial may deny that the death even happened, leave home furnishings and physical objects exactly as they were at the time of death, or deny the importance of death by saying things like, "We weren't close anyway." They may also withdraw significantly, refusing to develop the skills they need to carry on with life.

It is probably wise to find two or more counselors to whom you might be able to refer, so that when the situation arises, you will be able to contact them quickly. They may also be able to help discern whether professional intervention is necessary in cases when you are unsure.

(Adapted from *Grief Counseling and Grief Therapy*, by J. William Worden, Springer Publishing Company, 1982.)

Dealing With Caregiver Burnout

If bereavement ministers forget to care for themselves, they may fall prey to burnout.

In his book *Death and Grief: A Guide for Clergy*, Alan Wofelt says those suffering from caregiver burnout typically find themselves more irritable and short-tempered. They may also experience headaches, backaches, long-lasting colds, or other physical complaints. It is important not to overlook these symptoms, but rather to recognize them as a sign that something is wrong.

Those most vulnerable to burnout feel that they are indispensable and that no one else can do the job they can. Yet, they are often unable to accomplish much because they can't focus on the present. This lack of concentration may have them feeling depressed where lethargy, difficulty sleeping, loss of appetite, and changes in their mood may take place. They may even wonder if the people even appreciate their services and think there's no point in getting involved.

If any of these symptoms sounds familiar to you, you may need to pull back, get in touch with your feelings, and talk with a trusted friend for support and guidance. (Refer to pages 262-263 for more stress busters.)

Dr. Richard Blue, a licensed psychologist specializing in stress management and worker burnout, recommends the following ten steps to prevent burnout:

1. Watch for negative thinking. It can distort your thinking and decrease your job satisfaction.

2. Dispute your negative thinking. Give yourself credit for the things you do right.

3. Practice assertiveness. Speak up in a tactful and diplomatic way.

4. Release your anger in a manner that is not damaging to you or anyone else such as exercising or a hobby.

5. Talk about your frustrations with someone who will listen.

6. Maintain your sense of humor.

7. Participate in a regular exercise program.

8. Develop outside interests.

9. Learn to "let go." Use positive self-talk.

10. Practice relaxation techniques.

(Adapted from Hospice of the RRV Newsletter, April 1994.)

Come to me, all you that are weary and are carrying heavy burdens,
and I will give you rest. Take my yoke upon you, and learn from me;
for I am gentle and humble in heart, and you will find rest for your souls.
For my yoke is easy, and my burden light.

MATTHEW 11:28-30

Support Resources for Bereavement Ministers

Centering Corporation
1531 North Saddle Creek Rd.
Omaha, NE 68104
1-402-553-1200
1-402-553-0507 (FAX)

Concern for Dying
250 West 57th Street
New York, NY 10028
1-212-246-6962

National Self-Help Clearinghouse
Room 620N
Graduate School and University Center
City University of New York
33 West 42nd Street
New York, NY 10036
1-212-840-1259
(A clearinghouse on peer support groups of all kinds across the nation.)

Association for Death Education and Counseling
638 Prospect Ave.
Hartford, CT 06105-4298
(This organization promotes death education and counseling through materials, programs, conferences, and professional networking and resource referral.)

The Elizabeth Kubler-Ross Center
South Route 616
Head Waters, VA 24442
(A center for the promotion of unconditional love and enrichment of life for all people. The center provides clinical and educational services and audio-visual materials.)

Center for Loss & Life Transition
3735 Broken Bow Road
Fort Collins, CO 80526
1-303-226-6051 (FAX)
(The center provides training, workshops, and bereavement publications.)

National Catholic Ministry to the Bereaved
606 Middle Ave.
Elyria, OH 44035
1-440-323-6262
(An organization that provides training, bereavement start-up material, and a newsletter.)

Bereavement and Loss Center of New York
170 East 83rd Street
New York, NY 10028
1-212-879-5655

Grief Education Institute
1780 S. Bellaire Street
Denver, CO 80222

Integra: The Association for Integrative and Transformative Grief
P.O. Box 6013
East Lansing, MI 48826

Thanos Institute
P.O. Box 1928
Buffalo, NY 14231-1928
1-716-636-0383
1-800-742-8257
(An institute that provides education and material to schools, funeral homes, and others who work in bereavement.)

Helpful Toll-Free Numbers

These numbers can change. Call your local Community Resources or Hotline for updates.

AARP (American Association of Retired Persons)	1-800-468-2100
Abortion Hotline National	1-800-772-9100
Access to Respite Care & Help (ARCH)	1-800-473-1727
Adoption Center/National	1-800-862-3678
Aid for Hearing Impaired	1-800-521-5247
AIDS Hotline	1-800-472-2180
AIDS Hotline National (CDC)	1-800-342-2437
Alcoholism and Drugs, National Council on	1-800-622-2255
Alliance for the Mentally Ill (National)	1-800-950-6264
Allergy and Immunology	1-800-822-2762
Alzheimer's National Office	1-800-272-3900
American Kidney Foundation	1-800-638-8299
American Parkinson's Disease Association	1-800-223-2732
Asthma and Allergy Foundation of America	1-800-727-8462
Auto Safety Hotline	1-800-424-9393
Back Pain Hotline	1-800-955-7848
Better Hearing Institute	1-800-327-9355
Blind, American Council on the	1-800-424-8666
Blind, American Foundation for the	1-800-232-5463
Blind and Visually Handicapped, National Library for	1-800-424-9100
Blindness Prevention National Society	1-800-331-2020
Boys Town National Hotline	1-800-448-3000
Brain Injury Association	1-800-444-6443
Breast Cancer Support Program	1-800-221-2141
Cancer Information Service	1-800-422-6237
Cancer Response System	1-800-342-4535
Candlelighters—Childhood Cancer Information	1-800-366-2223
Cerebral Palsy Association	1-800-872-5827
Center for Child Disabilities, National	1-800-999-5599
Child Abuse Hotline	1-800-422-4453
Child Help USA—Child Abuse Information	1-800-422-4453
Childfind of America, Inc.	1-800-426-5678
Childhood Cancer Information	1-800-366-2223
Childhood and Youth with Disabilities, Info. Center	1-800-999-5599
Childreach	1-800-556-7918
Children's Craniofacial Association	1-800-535-3643
Children's Hospice International	1-800-242-4453
Cleft Palate Foundation	1-800-242-5338
Cocaine Hotline	1-800-262-2463
Consumer Products Safety Commission, U.S.	1-800-638-2772
Consumer Products Safety Commission, U.S. (TDD)	1-800-638-8270
Cornelia DeLange Syndrome	1-800-753-2357
Council of Citizens with Low Vision	1-800-733-2258
Covenant House (Crisis Line for Kids)	1-800-999-9999
Crohns and Colitis Foundation of America	1-800-343-3637
Cystic Fibrosis Foundation	1-800-344-4823
Deaf, Captioned Films for	1-800-237-6213

Deaf, Crisis Center for (TDD only)	1-800-446-9876
Depression After Delivery, Inc.	1-800-944-4773
Depressive Association, Manic	1-800-826-3632
Diabetes Foundation, American	1-800-232-3472
Diabetes Foundation, Juvenile	1-800-223-1138
Donor Cards (Organ Donors)	1-800-247-4273
Down Syndrome National Congress	1-800-232-6372
Down Syndrome Society	1-800-221-4602
Drug Abuse Hotline & Referral Service	1-800-662-4357
Dyslexia Society, Orton	1-800-222-3123
Education and Training People with Disabilities	1-800-544-3284
Education of Young Children, National Association	1-800-424-2460
Endometriosis Association	1-800-992-3636
Energy Inquiry and Referral Service	1-800-523-2929
Environmental Protection Agency	1-800-535-0202
Epilepsy Information Line	1-800-332-1000
Epilepsy Foundation of America	1-800-332-1000
Eyecare Project for Seniors	1-800-222-3937
Fraud Information Center, National	1-800-876-7060
Gambling/National Council on Problem	1-800-522-4700
Guide Dog Foundation for the Blind	1-800-548-4337
Handicapped Hotline Library of Congress	1-800-424-8567
Health Information Clearinghouse	1-800-336-4797
Head Home/National Runaway Hotline	1-800-448-4663
Hearing Aid Helpline	1-800-521-5247
Hearing Helpline	1-800-327-9355
Hemophilia Foundation	1-800-424-2634
Hotline, Covenant House Nineline	
(Directory of Hotlines and Crisis Intervention Centers)	1-800-999-9999
Hospice Education Institute	1-800-331-1620
Hospice Organization/National	1-800-658-8898
Huntington's Disease Society of America	1-800-345-4372
Job Accommodation Network	1-800-526-7234
Job Opportunities for the Blind	1-800-638-7518
Just Say No International	1-800-258-2766
Juvenile Diabetes International Foundation	1-800-533-2873
Kidney Foundation National	1-800-622-9010
La Leche League, International	1-800-525-3243
Leprosy Missions, American	1-800-543-3131
Library of Medicine	1-800-638-8480
Liver, American Foundation	1-800-223-0179
Lou Gehrig's Disease International	1-800-782-4747
Lung Line	1-800-222-5864
Lupus Foundation Information Line	1-800-558-0121
MADD (Mothers Against Drunk Driving)	1-800-438-6233
Major Appliance Consumer Action Panel	1-800-621-0477
Medic Alert Foundation International	1-800-344-3226
Medicare Hotline	1-800-638-6833
Missing and Exploited Children, National Center for	1-800-843-5678
Myasthenia Gravis Foundation	1-800-541-5454

National Association of Working Women	1-800-522-0925
National Captioning Institute	1-800-533-9673
National Down's Syndrome Congress	1-800-232-6372
National Down's Syndrome Society	1-800-221-4602
National Empowerment Center	1-800-POWER-2-1
National Health Information Center	1-800-336-4797
National Organization for Rare Disorders	1-800-999-6673
National Parkinson's Foundation	1-800-327-4545
National Senior Service Corp Hotline	1-800-424-8867
National Center for Stuttering	1-800-221-2483
Neurofibromatosis Foundation	1-800-323-7938
Nutrition Hotline (American Dietetic Association)	1-800-366-1655
Organ Donations	1-800-528-2971
Orton Dyslexia Society	1-800-222-3123
Parents Without Partners International	1-800-637-7974
Peace Corps	1-800-424-8580
PMS Access	1-800-222-4767
Post-Partum Support International	1-800-944-4473
Prevent Blindness America	1-800-331-2020
Rare Disorders National Organization	1-800-999-6673
Rehabilitation Information Center, National	1-800-346-2742
Reye's Syndrome Foundation, National	1-800-233-7393
Runaway Switchboard, National	1-800-621-4000
Sexually Transmitted Disease Hotline	1-800-227-8922
Short Stature Foundation Helpline	1-800-243-9273
Shriner's Hospital	1-800-237-5055
SIDS (Sudden Infant Death Syndrome) Alliance	1-800-221-7437
Small Business Administration, National	1-800-827-5722
Social Security Claimants Representatives	1-800-772-1213
Spasmodic Torticollis Association	1-800-487-8385
Speech Language Hearing Association, America	1-800-638-8255
Spina Bifida Association of America	1-800-621-3141
Spinal Cord Injury Association	1-800-962-9629
STD (Sexually Transmitted Diseases) Hotline	1-800-227-8922
Stuttering Foundation of America	1-800-992-9392
Stuttering, National Center for	1-800-221-2483
Sudden Infant Death Syndrome	1-800-221-7437
TOPS (Take Off Pounds Sensibly) Club, Inc.	1-800-932-8677
Tough Love International, Inc.	1-800-333-1069
Tourette Syndrome Association	1-800-237-0717
Tuberous Sclerosis Association, National	1-800-225-6872
Unicef	1-800-252-5437
United Cerebral Palsy	1-800-872-5827
United Leukodystrophy Foundation	1-800-728-5483
United Ostomy Association	1-800-826-0826
US Consumer Product Safety Division	1-800-638-2772
VD (Veneral Disease) National Hotline	1-800-227-8922
Vietnam Veterans of America	1-800-424-7275
VOICES In Action, Inc.	1-800-786-4238
Women's Health America	1-800-222-4767

(Information provided by HOTLINE, a program of Community Resources, Inc., Fargo, ND.)

Suggested Reading For Bereavement Ministers

There are several resources you can use in locating these titles: your local library (and inter-library loan system), your church library, bookstores, local support groups' lending libraries, hospices, and funeral homes.

* The asterisk indicates that these books are good beginning resources to start your own bereavement library.

Aarvy Aardvark Finds Hope: A Read-Aloud Story for People of All Ages. D. O'Toole. Compassion, 1989.

After a Child Dies: Counseling Bereaved Families. S. Johnson. Springer, 1987.

*The Art of Condolence. L. Zunin and H. Zunin. HarperCollins, 1991.

Attachment and Loss: Loss, Sadness and Depression (Vol. III). J. Bowlby. Basic, 1980.

Bereavement: Counseling the Grieving Throughout the Life Cycle. D. Crenshaw. Crossroad, 1995.

Bereavement Ministry: A Leader's Resource Manual. H. Young. Twenty-Third Publications, 1997.

Beyond Sympathy: What to Say and Do for Someone Suffering an Injury, Illness, or Loss. J. H. Lord. Pathfinder, 1989.

*Children Mourning. K. Doka, ed. Hospice Foundation of America, 1995.

Clergy Response to Suicidal Persons and Their Family Members: An Interfaith Resource Book for Clergy and Congregations. D. Clark, ed. Explorations Press, 1993.

*Comforting Those Who Grieve: A Guide for Helping Others. D. Manning. Harper and Row, 1987.

Coping with Suicide: A Pastoral Aid. G. Green. Twenty-Third, 1992.

Counseling the Childless Couple. W. Bassett. Books Demand.

The Courage to Care: Helping the Aging, Grieving, and Dying. J. Watson. Baker, 1992.

Creating Meaningful Funeral Ceremonies: A Guide for Caregives. A. Wolfelt. Companion Company, 1994.

*Death and Grief: A Guide for Clergy. A. Wolfelt. Accelerated Development, 1980.

Death and Spirituality. K. Doka and J. Morgan, eds. Baywood, 1993.

*Disfranchised Grief: Recognizing Hidden Sorrow. K. Doka, ed. Lexington, 1989.

Don't Take My Grief Away. D. Manning. HarperCollins, 1979.

Dying and the Bereaved Teenager. J. Morgan. Charles, 1990.

Dying, Grieving, Faith, and Family: A Pastoral Care Approach. G. Bowman. Haworth, 1997.

Embraced by the Light. B. Eadie. Gold Leaf Press, 1992.

Finding My Way: Healing and Transformation Through Loss & Grief. J. Schneider. Seasons, 1984.

Finding the Right Words. Offering Care and Comfort When You Don't Know What to Say. W. Bockelman. Augsburg Fortress, 1989.

The First Year of Bereavement. I. O. Glick, R. S. Weisee, and C. M. Parkey. John Wiley and Sons, 1974.

Getting Through Grief: Caregiving by Congregations. R. Sunderland. Abingdon, 1993.

God Understands. E. Roels. The Bible League, 1993.

Good Grief. G. Westberg. Fortress Press, 1962.

Grief and Growth: Pastoral Resources for Emotional and Spiritual Growth. R. S. Sullender. Paulist Press, 1985.

Grief and Mourning in Cross-Cultural Perspective. P. Rosenblatt. HRAFP, 1976.

Grief Counseling and Grief Therapy. J.W. Worden. Springer, 1982.

Grief, Dying, and Death. T. Rando. Research Press Company, 1984.

Grief Ministry: Helping Others Mourn. D. Williams and J. Sturzl. Resource, 1992.

Grief Ministry Facilitator's Guide. J. Sturzl and D. Williams. Resource, 1992.

Grief, Transition, and Loss: A Pastor's Practical Guide. W. Oates. Fortress, 1997.

The Grieving Child. H. Fitzgerald. Simon and Schuster, 1992.

Growing Through Grief: A K-12 Curriculum to Help Young People Through All Kinds of Loss. D. Toole. Mountain Rainbow, 1989.

Guided Grief Imagery: A Resource for Grief Ministry and Death Education. T. Droege. Paulist Press, 1987.

Handbook of Adolescent Death & Bereavement. C. Corr and D. Balk. Springer, 1996.

Healing the Bereaved Child: Grief Gardening, Growth Through Grief & Other Touchstones for Caregivers. A. Wolfelt. Companion, 1996.

Health and Fitness Excellence: The Scientific Action Plan. R. Cooper. Houghton Mifflin Company, 1989.

Heart of the Mind. C. Andreas and S. Andreas. Real People Press, 1989.

Helping People Through Grief. D. Kuenning. Bethany House, 1987.

Helping the Bereaved: Therapeutic Interventions for Children, Adolescents, and Adults. A. Cook and D. Workin. Basic, 1992.

Horrific Trauma: A Pastoral Response to the Post-Traumatic Stress Disorder. N. Sinclair. Hawthorn, 1993.

How Can I Help When Someone Dies: What Do I Say After, "I'm Sorry?" D. Moore. 1992.

How to Bring Help and Hope to the Grieving. V. Parachin. Ed. Ministries, 1992.

I Don't Know How To Help Them: A Book for Friends & Families of Bereaved Parents. L. Maurer. LK Maurer, 1996.

I Know Just How You Feel. E. Linn. The Publisher's Mark, 1986.

I Never Know What to Say: How to Help Your Family and Friends Cope with Tragedy. N. Donnelly and Herrman. Ballantine, 1990.

I Want to Help But How? How to Help Grieving People. E. Bailey. CSS, 1993.

Journey to the Other Side. D. Wheeler. Ace, 1977.

Life After Life. R. Moody. Bantam, 1975.

Life Is Goodbye Life Is Hello: Grieving Well Through All Kinds of Loss. A. Bozarth-Campbell. CompCare, 1982.

Making Sense Out of Sorrow: A Journey of Faith. F. McCurley and A. Weitzman. 1995.

Making Sense Out of Suffering. P. Kreeft. Servant, 1986.

The Ministry of Consolation: A Parish Guide for Comforting the Bereaved. T. Curley. Alba, 1993.

Ministry to the Bereaved. L. Updike. Herald House, 1986.

Our Greatest Gift. H. Nouwen. Harper San Francisco, 1994.

Overcoming Grief and Trauma. M. Lawrenz and D. Green. Baker, 1995.

Pastoral Care and Counseling in Grief & Separation. W. Oats. Augsburg Fortress, 1976.

The Pastoral Care of Depression: A Guidebook. B. Gilbert. Haworth, 1997.

Praying Our Goodbyes. J. Rupp. Ave Maria Press, 1988.

Premonitions, Visitations, and Dreams of the Bereaved. E. Linn. Pub. Mark., 1991.

Preparing for Grief. D. Childers. D. Childers, 1994.

Reflections on Life After Life. R. Moody. Bantam, 1977.

Resources for Ministry in Death & Dying. R. Branch and L. Platt. Broadman, 1988.

Responding to Grief: A Complete Resource Guide. R. Gilbert. The Spirit of Health!, 1997.

Self-Talk, Imagery, and Prayer in Counseling. N. Wright. Word, 1995.

Spiritual, Ethical, and Pastoral Aspects of Death and Bereavement. G. Cox and R. Fundis, ed. Baywood, 1992.

Stress, Loss, and Grief. J. Schneider. Aspen Systems Corporation, 1984.

Survival Handbook for Widows. R. J. Loewinsohn. American Association of Retired Persons, 1984.

Surviving When Someone You Love Was Murdered: A Professional's Guide to Group Grief Therapy for Families and Friends of Murder Victims. L. Redmond. Psychological Consultants, 1989.

To Comfort the Bereaved: A Guide for Mourners and Those Who Visit Them. A. Levine. Aronson, 1994.

Treatment of Complicated Mourning. T. A. Rando. Research Press, 1991.

Understanding Mourning: A Guide for Those Who Grieve. G. Davidson. Augsburg, 1984.

Walking with Those Who Hurt. Joyce Rupp. Ave Maria Press, 1989. (cassette tape set)

A Way of the Cross for the Bereaved. T. Curley. Alba, 1996.

When Faith Is Tested: Pastoral Responses to Suffering and Tragic Death. J. Zurheide. Fortress, 1997.

When Going to Pieces Holds You Together. W. Miller. Augsburg, 1976.

Where Is God in My Suffering? Biblical Responses to Seven Searching Questions. D. Simundson. Augsburg, 1983.

Without You: Poems for Those Who Grieve. J. Mueller. Leaflet Ministry from Augsburg Fortress.

Witness From Beyond. R. Taylor. Hawthorn, 1975.

Wounded Healer. H. Nouwen. Image, 1990.

Journal articles:

"Bereavement, Ministerial Attitudes, and the Future of Church-Sponsored Bereavement Support Groups." F. Sklar and K. Huneke. *Omega*, 1987-88, 18(2), 89-101.

"Job's Agony: A Biblical Evocation of Bereavement and Grief." H. van Praag. *Judaism*, 1988, 37, 173-187.

Also look under "Support Resources" (pages 289-290).

> The Centering Corporation
> 1531 North Saddle Creek Road
> Omaha, Nebraska 68104-5064
> 1-402-553-1200
> 1-402-553-0507 (FAX)
> (A bereavement catalog and resources.)

Contact your local funeral director to see if they have the following books for free, or contact the companies yourself and order a bulk shipment to have on hand:

> Medic Publishing Company
> P.O. Box 89
> Remond, WA 98073-0089
> 1-206-881-2883
> > *Healing Grief.* Amy Jensen.
> > *Sibling Grief.* Marcia Scherago.

> Thanos Institute
> P.O. Box 1928
> Buffalo, NY 14231-1928
> 1-716-636-0383
> 1-800-742-8257
> > *Jolie & The Funeral* (a children's book)
> > & others

> Batesville Management Services
> P.O. Drawer 90
> Batesville, IN 47006
> 1-800-622-8373
> > *A Scrapbook of Memories,* by Dr. E. Grollman (for children)
> > "Talking about Death with Children" (a videotape for elementary age children)
> > "Understanding Grief: Kids Helping Kids" (a videotape for adolescents age 9-14)
> > "Talking with Young Children about Death"(a brochure for adults)

"A New Road to Grief Recovery" (six session video available through Augsburg Fortress)

Learning Resource Center
National Funeral Directors Association
11121 West Oklahoma Avenue
Milwaukee, WI 53227-4096
1-414-541-2500

Care Note Resources
Abbey Press
St. Meinrad, IN 47577
(Multiple grieving titles for leaflet ministry.)

"Grief Helper Program"
Aid Association for Lutherans
4321 North Ballard Road
Appleton, WI 54919-0001
(Provides helpful information on making condolence calls and offers an excellent special needs checklist.)

Grief Recovery
Chaplain Larry Yeagley
Adventist Life Seminars
Rt. 1, Box 248
Crystal Springs, MS 39059
1-601-892-5559

Center for Loss and Life Transition
3735 Broken Bow Road
Fort Collins, CO 80526
    Videotape: *A Teen's View of Grief*
    Brochures about children:
        Helping Infants & Toddlers When Someone They Love Dies
        Helping the Bereaved Sibling Heal
        Helping the Grieving Child at School
        Helping Children with Funerals
        & others

Appendix A

Helpful Forms for Setting Up Your
Bereavement Program

Could You Help With Our Bereavement Ministry?

Our bereavement ministry team coordinates efforts to care for those who are working through grief following a death or other important loss. Often, those who are grieving need not only counseling, but practical, everyday help.

If you are interested in being a part of our outreach to the grieving, please take a moment to fill out this form. Check any of the following items with which you could help, and return this form by placing it in the offering plate or bringing it to the church office.

_____ Bringing meals to the home

_____ Bringing groceries to the home

_____ Coming to the home in order to help with laundry, cleaning, preparing meals, etc.

_____ Coming to the home to help with house maintenance such as yard work

_____ Child care

_____ Transportation to and from appointments, shopping, etc.

_____ Help with personal care

_____ Help with financial planning and decision-making

_____ Help in searching for and finding a job

_____ Other:_____

_____ I am interested in joining the bereavement ministry team.

Basic Information

Name: _____

Nature of bereavement (e.g, death of wife):_____

Name of deceased:_____

Address: _____

Phone: (H)_____ (W)_____

Next of kin/Contact person: _____

Address: _____

Phone: (H)_____ (W)_____

Special Days:

    Date of Death/Loss   _____   Other significant dates:

    Birthday of deceased   _____   _____

    Birthday of spouse   _____   _____

    Wedding anniversary   _____   _____

Special Needs/Concerns/Circumstances:

_____

_____

_____

_____

_____

Bereavement Surveys

#1

Living alone provides unique challenges. The people of _(church name)_ want to help you to meet those challenges. Please check off any items that would be helpful for you. Mail this card to the church office _(address)_ or phone us at _(phone number)_ . We will contact you promptly.

___Someone to talk to regularly

___Transportation to church, shopping, appointments, etc.

___Meals or food preparation

___House repairs

___Lawn care/snow removal

___Car maintenance

___Financial advice

___Other

Information on:

___Local support groups

___Volunteering opportunities

___Relaxation techniques

___Sleep problems

___Diet and nutrition

___Other

Name_____

Address_____

Phone number_____

#2

You have experienced many changes in the past months. If there is any way that the people of _(church name)_ can help you, we want you to let us know. Please check off any items that apply to you. Mail to this card to the church office _(address)_ or phone us at _(phone number)_ . We will contact you promptly.

___ I would like to speak to

    ___ pastor   ___ parish nurse

    ___ Stephen Minister   ___ professional counselor

___ I want to be more involved in volunteer work.

___ It is hard for me to be involved in church activities.

___ I have financial questions and would like assistance.

___ I need assistance with my home maintenance.

___ I have medical concerns.

___ Other

Name_____

Address_____

Phone number_____

Record of Contacts

Name: _____

Nature of bereavement
(e.g, death of wife):_____

Name of deceased:_____

Address: _____

Phone: (H)_____ (W)_____

Kind of Contact   Date   Notes
(Letter/Visit/Phone)

_____

_____

_____

_____

_____

_____

_____

_____

_____

_____

_____

_____

_____

_____

Appendix B

*How to Start a Bereavement
Support Group*

How to Start a Bereavement Support Group

Self-help or support groups offer encouragement, education, and support to those working through grief. A support group can be a very valuable addition to your total program of bereavement ministry.

First, however, ask yourself whether there is anyone else out there. You may not have to set up your own group; there may be groups running in or near your area that you are not aware of. Contact the national support group listings for your particular type of bereavement support listed in this book. If there aren't any support groups near your area, ask the existing groups about "start-up" packets, examples of their flyers, press releases, or samples of any material they have used.

Second, assess the need for a group. Find out—over the phone or through individual visits—if enough people from your congregation are interested in a bereavement support group and what schedule of meetings they are interested in committing to: would they like to meet weekly for six to ten weeks, or would they prefer a monthly meeting? If you feel that you have enough interest, go ahead with your plans. At one of the early meetings, you may want to discuss opening the group up to those from outside the church.

Third, determine who will organize the group. Clergy are often placed in the role of making referrals or being a group advisor, consultant, or a guest speaker. But clergy can also be instrumental in starting and running a support group, especially if they have experienced a loss in their life. If clergy are not involved in organizing a group, one to two highly energetic or dedicated individuals can take charge. Often gathering a team of group leaders can be beneficial; shared responsibility can help prevent burn-out.

Those placed in charge of the group can then go on to make several additional decisions. . . .

First, choose the format. Will the group meet once a month or once a week? Will you meet for a certain amount of time (e.g., ten weeks) and then re-evaluate, or will you simply plan to meet indefinitely? What day and time will the group meet? (Keeping it consistent is easier to remember, e.g., Thursday at 7:00 p.m. or the first Tuesday of every month at 7:30 p.m.) Will you use a book or workbook as the basis for your discussions, or will you simply encourage sharing? Will you form a group or groups composed of certain members or will the group(s) continue to remain open to newcomers? Will you bring in speakers? Some groups prefer only speakers who have had a mourning experience, some only clergy, some counseling professionals, and others laity. (See the "Speaker Evaluation" sheet on p. 315.) Suggested presentation titles are as follows:

- Coping with the holidays
- Finances
- Companionship
- Family and friends (How your family and friends may react to the death)
- Dealing with denial
- Dealing with anger
- Dealing with depression
- Dealing with guilt
- How do I handle my feelings?
- Spirituality/Dealing with being at church
- How will I know when I am feeling better?
- How to cope with criticism and develop self-esteem
- Taking care of myself (exercise, nutrition, and relaxation)
- Is there life after death?
- Singlehood and freedom
- How does mourning work?
- Can I learn to laugh again?

You may want to try one format and then have the group evaluate it to determine which direction to take from there.

Next, choose the site. If the group is composed only of your own church members, you may simply choose your own church, but if you have determined that you want to open it up for the community, you may need to answer more questions such as the following:

- Is there a church that is more central?
- Could you use their facilities at no charge?
- Is it a crime-free area?
- Is the church handicapped-accessible?

Once you have found a site, you must also choose a specific room. Keep the following questions in mind:

- Is it the right size for your group? (If the room is too large it may feel cold, but if it's too small, there may not be room for growth.)
- Is there air conditioning?
- Are there other meetings going on at the same time? If so, is there enough privacy? Will the noise disturb the group?
- Is there easy access to seating, restrooms, and a sink or kitchen for making coffee and refreshments?
- Is there easy access to projectors and blackboards for speakers?

Next, think about ways to publicize the group. Of course, you will want to place announcements in your church bulletin. If you wish more community involvement, you may want to:

- Send flyers to other congregations.
- Place flyers in libraries, hospitals, hospices, community centers, funeral homes, and post offices.
- Place an announcement in the community calendar section of the local newspaper.
- Talk with a newspaper editor about the group and the issue of bereavement.
- Try local talk shows on radio and television.

Finally, you will need to plan the logistics of the meeting. Refreshments often make people feel welcome. If you decide to serve refreshments, you will need to answer the following questions:

- Who will bring refreshments? (You can try a sign-up sheet for refreshments in the future. See the "Volunteer Sign-up Sheet" on page 314.)
- Who will get napkins, cups, plates, and coffee from other resources? (Check funeral homes, hospitals, and large corporations for donations.)
- Who will make the coffee and set out napkins, plates, cups, condiments (sugar/cream)?

Other important questions to consider include:

- Who will arrive early and set up tables and chairs?
- Who will greet and introduce new members?
- Who will introduce the speaker or run the meeting?
- Who will be handing out name tags and making sure people sign in? If you expect a large number of people (40-50) you may want to mark numbers on the name tags corresponding to the number of groups you want to have so when the large group is divided, people can divide according to the number on their name tag. (For example, if you want to have five groups, label the name tags "1," "2," "3," "4," "5," "1," "2," etc.) A workable group size is usually 8-15 people.
- Who will bring the handouts and/or books to share?
- Who will lead the small group discussions?

The First Meeting

Leaders should arrive early to arrange the surroundings and be relaxed and comfortable to meet others as they come in. Start on time. Suggest that people bring refreshments to their seats, if you choose to serve coffee right away.

Once the group has been established and there is no speaker, you may want to try a "letting-go" exercise. This helps members focus on the group and the topic at hand. This can take the form of deep breathing, poetry, music, a story, a Bible passage, or something humorous.

Introduce yourself and any other leaders and share why and how this group came into being. Discuss any rules at this time (e.g., no smoking inside the building). You may also want to lay down some "ground rules" for discussion, including the cardinal rule that anything said in the support group be kept confidential. Introduce the speaker if you have one.

Find out in a one-minute update from each person how she or he is doing or a question she or he may have.

Discussion may begin by addressing the concerns raised during the one-minute update, or, if a speaker precedes discussion, you may focus on the topic of her or his presentation. You may also use the Monthly Messages included in this book as possible discussion topics.

Keep the language positive by encouraging people to use "I" messages. Example: "I feel jealous when I see other women and men together" This helps keep the feelings on themselves, and it helps identify the feelings. Keep away from "shoulds." (Example: "Well, you shouldn't feel that way.") Instead, try "Have you tried . . . ?" or "This worked for me . . . ." As the time draws near to a close you may want to ask what has been helpful or what those present have learned from that night's meeting.

Finally, end the meeting on time. One and a half to two hours is adequate time to meet. You may try closing with deep breathing, poetry, music, a story, a Bible passage, or something humorous. Allow a few minutes at the end of the meeting for socializing, exchanging phone numbers, etc., and for volunteers to sign up for the next meeting.

Here is a sample schedule:

6:30 p.m.—Set-up and greetings
7:00 p.m.—Announcements and introductions
7:05 p.m.—Speaker
7:30 p.m.—Small group discussions
8:30-9 p.m.—Socializing

Many support groups find the need for more support or group socializing outside the formal meeting time. This can be addressed by the starting of traditions, e.g., holiday dinners, "fall festival" potlucks, etc. Other groups have met to go out dancing, bowling, eating out, etc.

There are natural "ups" and "downs" of enthusiasm and attendance of any group, especially if you run a monthly group. Remember to hang in there and ask for support of other groups or professionals.

You may especially need to provide encouragement to men to attend support group meetings. You may be able to introduce two men to one another and suggest that they attend together.

(Adapted from Patricia L. Beckman's thesis, "Mutual Support Groups: Organizational and Maintenance," Moorhead State University Library.)

Sign-in Sheet

Date_____

Topic:_____

Speaker:_____

Participants

Name   Address   City   Zip Code   Phone

_____

_____

_____

_____

_____

_____

_____

_____

_____

_____

_____

_____

_____

_____

_____

_____

_____

_____

Volunteer Sign-Up

For next session on:_____

	Name	Phone number
Make coffee	_____	_____
Desserts (Also, come 20 minutes early, set out plates, cups, napkins, etc.)	_____ _____ _____	_____ _____ _____
Greeters (Need one or two people)	_____ _____	_____ _____
Set up tables	_____ _____	_____ _____
Take down tables	_____ _____	_____ _____
Introduce speaker	_____	_____
Handouts	_____	_____
Poetry	_____	_____
Sit at sign-in table	_____	_____

Speaker Evaluation

Date_____

Topic_____

Speaker_____

Please answer "yes" or "no" to the following questions to help us select speakers in the future.

1. Did the speaker adequately address your concerns and questions about this topic?

2. Did you feel the speaker had a fair knowledge of the material she/he was presenting?

3. Do you feel the speaker has touched your life?

4. Should we ask this speaker back again?

5. General comments and/or suggestions.

Thank you.

Self-Help Resources

There are several resources you can use in locating these titles: your local library (and inter-library loan system), bookstores, local support groups' lending libraries, hospices, and funeral homes.

Bereavement Support Groups: Leadership Manual, rev. ed. Grief Education Institute, 1988.

"Clergy and Self-Help Groups: Practical and Promising Relationships." E. Madara and B. Peterson. *The Journal of Pastoral Care,* September 1987, Volume 41, No. 3, 213-220.

Comforting Those Who Grieve: A Guide for Helping Others. D. Manning. Harper and Row, 1987.

The Healing Journey: Manual for a Grief Support Group. A. Grant. Vista, 1994.

Helping People to Help Themselves: Self-Help and Prevention. L. Borman, L. Borck, R. Heis, and F. Pasquale, eds. Haworth Press, 1982.

Helping You Helps Me: A Guide Book for Self-Help Groups. K. Hill. Canadian Council on Social Development, 1987.

How to Form Support Groups for Grieving People. Hope For Bereaved.

How to Start and Lead a Bereavement Support Group. A. Wolfelt. Center for Loss & Life Transition, 1993.

Mutual Help Groups: Organization & Development. P. Silverman. SAGE, 1980.

Self-Help Groups for Coping with Crisis. M. Lieberman and L. Borman. Books Demand.

The Self-Help Sourcebook: The Comprehensive Reference of Self-Help Group Resources. American Self-Help Clearinghouse. Covenant Med., 1995.

Starting and Running Support Groups. B. Overbeck and J. Overbeck. TLC Group, 1992.

Index

Afterword

Jan and I have enjoyed working together in the church and in writing this book for the church. We have found the material contained in this book to be very helpful in our ministry as a sort of "toolbox." Our hope and our prayer is that it will encourage and support your ministry to those who are grieving.

As you find ways of incorporating these materials into your ministry, or if you have questions, we would like to hear from you. Please write us at:

David Aaker and Jan Nelson
c/o Ave Maria Press
Notre Dame, IN 46556

In His healing presence,

Pastor David A. Aaker